INTRODUCTION TO TRAVEL AND TOURISM

INTRODUCTION TO TRAVEL AND TOURISM

Lalita Sharma

CENTRUM PRESS
NEW DELHI-110002 (INDIA)

CENTRUM PRESS
H.O.: 4360/4, Ansari Road, Daryaganj,
New Delhi-110002 (India)
Tel: 23278000, 23261597, 23255577, 23286875
B.O.: No. 1015, Ist Main Road, BSK IIIrd Stage,
IIIrd Phase, IIIrd Block, Bangalore-560085 (INDIA)
Tel: 080-41723429
Email: centrumpress@gmail.com
Visit us at: www.centrumpress.com

Introduction to Travel and Tourism

First Edition, 2010

ISBN 978-93-80540-18-4

PRINTED IN INDIA

Printed at **Mehra Offset Press, Delhi**

Contents

Preface

Tourism is one of the most international of industries, with both the public and private sectors increasingly concerned with issues of international competitiveness and benchmarking. This is no less so for domestic tourism where international standards are derived for service delivery and facilities - indeed in destinations, international benchmarks have been used to drive-up the standards and the quality of the domestic industry.

Enormous increases in travel by public, along with incidents of terrorism, accidents, and disease, raise a variety of ethical issues not normally covered in the training of public personnel administrators or in the standard administrative ethics course. Issues of accessibility for individuals with disabilities may be familiar to personnel administrators and students of ethics, but take on vast new dimensions when those individuals travel abroad.

Travel and tourism related issues involved in health, safety, and accessibility may include identification of individual and institutional responsibilities, informed consent, contingency planning, emergency response mechanisms, fairness, and equal treatment. This book provides an overview of trends and issues, explores their dimensions, and identifies relevant strategies to prepare public administrators to deal appropriately with these concerns. The study treats both tourist and educational travel abroad, and considers risks to host societies as well as to travelers.

Author

Chapter 1

Introduction

BASIC DEFINITIONS

The marketability of individual destinations and global tourism is vulnerable to sudden changes in market perceptions. Acts of man or nature can transform the reputation, desirability and marketability of the most popular tourism destinations overnight. The 1991 Gulf War involved a United States-led 30-nation coalition of forces against Iraq. The attacks on New York City and Washington DC on September 11, 2001, in which hijacked Boeing 767 and 757 commercial aircraft were engaged as flying missiles which blew up the World Trade Centre in New York City and part of the Pentagon in Washington DC, massively disrupted global tourism.

The 2001 attacks generated worldwide panic, compromising the security of commercial aircraft and global tourism safety with specific focus on the United States, Europe, Central Asia and the Middle East. Many cases outlined in this study demonstrate that a crisis in one country has a ripple effect on neighbouring destinations.

For the sake of clarification, a destination may be defined as a country, state, region, city or town which is marketed or markets itself as a place for tourists to visit. In most cases referred to in this book, countries will be the primary focus of attention.

For most international travellers, tourism is a discretionary act. Many countries have invested heavily in tourism and have acquired a high level of economic dependence on inbound tourism. Events which compromise the viability of a destination may result in considerable economic disruption to the country, state or region.

For individuals, this situation could result in loss of income, unemployment and poverty. However, few tourists will consider these implications in determining their choice of destination. Their prime concern is to travel to a destination satisfying their own desires with a minimum of complications or threats to their safety and well-being.

Global tourism crises, including those mentioned above, are evidence that destination crisis marketing can no longer be treated as a problem confined to a few specific destinations; it is now a global issue. Since September 11, destination crisis marketing has been moved beyond the cloisters of academia to become a critical economic, political and social priority for many nations to which tourism is a significant industry.

A book dealing with destination crisis requires a contextually appropriate working definition of the term 'crisis'. Bill Faulkner and Roslyn Russell in their discussion of turbulence, chaos and complexity, refer to crisis and disaster. They mention that the common definition of crisis is 'an action or failure to act that interferes with the organisation's ongoing functions and the attainment of its objectives, viability, or survival ... with detrimental effects as perceived by employees, clients or constituents'.

This definition is more appropriate to managerial failure than the crises caused by external factors. Certainly there are no shortages of travel industry crises resulting from mismanagement. However, the crises examined and analysed in this volume have all arisen due to events beyond the direct control of destination authorities. Faulkner and Russell's second definition of a disaster is more applicable to the cases discussed in this book. They define a disaster as a situation in which 'a tourism destination is confronted with sudden, unpredictable, catastrophic changes over which it has little control'.

To modify Faulkner and Russell's definition and relate it to the crises examined in this study the author defines a destination crisis in the following terms: 'A crisis is a situation requiring radical management action in response to events beyond the internal control of the organisation, necessitating urgent adaptation of marketing and operational practices to restore the confidence of employees, associated enterprises and consumers in the viability of the destination.'

The threat of terrorism is understandably a major issue in destination choice. The popularity and desirability of specific destinations is influenced by many factors. These include economic factors such as affordability, special events such as Olympic Games or World Expos and the vagaries of fads and fashions. A wide range of perceptions governs the desirability and appeal of a destination to the potential traveller.

TRAVEL MOTIVATION

A major determinant in a traveller's decision to visit a destination is the perception of safety and security. Specific events or a series of events may undermine these perceptions of a destination. This book will examine five specific event typologies which undermine the safety and security image of tourist destinations and result in a destination crisis.

These are:

- International war or conflict and prolonged manifestations of internal conflict;
- A specific act or acts of terrorism, especially those directed at or affecting tourists;
- A major criminal act or crime wave, especially when tourists are targeted;
- A natural disaster, such as an earthquake, storm or volcano, causing damage to urban areas or the natural environment and consequently impacting on the tourism infrastructure;
- Health concerns related to epidemics and diseases; these may be diseases which impact on humans directly or diseases affecting animals, which limit access to tourist attractions.

These events or circumstances, individually or in

combination, have a negative impact on perceptions of the safety, security or desirability of tourist destinations. Each circumstance poses challenges to tourism authorities and the tourism industry to implement appropriate strategies to restore the image of affected destinations.

Certainly, those factors do not represent the totality of issues which can impact negatively on destination image; however, the core issue in this book involves analysing how a destination and its tourism industry conduct a marketing campaign to restore its image and recover its market from the damage caused by these events. A number of case studies are used to demonstrate that a properly focused marketing campaign plays a major role in restoring a destination's image and consumer perceptions of it. *Restoration marketing* is an integral element in the overall recovery of the destination.

Contingency management is discussed as a major component of tourism destination marketing. The specific contingencies examined—war, terrorism, crime waves, epidemic and natural disasters—have devastating impacts on any community, region, state or nation.

This book focuses on their repercussions on eleven destinations around the world. Any destination is potentially vulnerable to one or more of the above threats to destination safety and market perception; consequently, it is imperative for all destination authorities to prepare and develop contingency plans to respond to varying levels of threats.

CASE STUDIES

Each of the eleven cases will focus on specific events and the responses of the tourism industries and local tourism authorities to them.

The cases include:

- *New York and Global*: The challenge to restore New York and the United States as a tourism destination following the September 11 terrorist attack and the subsequent global ramifications;
- *Egypt*: Restoring confidence after terrorism directed at tourists in 1992–97;

- *Israel*: The marketing response to the conflict generated between Israel and the Palestinian Authority following the breakdown of the peace process since September 2000;
- *Sri Lanka*: Marketing a destination during a civil war;
- *Fiji*: Fiji's response to the coup of 1987 and the George Speight rebellion of 2000;
- *Turkey*: Turkish tourism recovery after the 1999 Izmit earthquake;
- *United Kingdom*: Response to the foot-and-mouth disease outbreak of 2001;
- South africa: Marketing a destination during the post-Apartheid crime wave;
- *Australia*:Tasmania's response to the Port Arthur massacre of 1996;
- *Croatia*: The croatian tourism industry's recovery after the war with Serbia, 1992–96;
- *The Philippines*: Restoring tourism after natural disasters, civil war and political instability during the 1990s.

While each case contains unique characteristics, there are a number of common elements which apply to these case studies. The above events resulted in a significant downturn in tourism numbers to the destination and created a climate of fear and concern about its overall safety and viability. In all cases, a marketing strategy was required to restore confidence in the destination. The duration of these strategies was subject to significant variations.

In the case of war and natural disaster, considerable time was involved in repairing physical damage to the infrastructure of the destination as a prerequisite to starting a marketing campaign.

It is an erroneous assumption that a restoration and recovery marketing campaign can be implemented only when the crisis is deemed to be over. In the case of Britain, Sri Lanka and Israel, marketing of the destinations continued during Britain's foot-and-mouth disease problems of 2001; the political conflict between Israel and the Palestinians since September

2000 (unresolved at the time of writing) and Sri Lanka's long-term civil war are examples of ongoing crises where marketing has been necessary. Some of these marketing strategies may be broadly defined as 'damage control'. Some of these marketing programs have involved an aggressive campaign to lure tourists by either highlighting alternative images to those disseminated by the mass media, or through the method of 'isolation'—that is, promoting parts of the destination unaffected by the existing problem.

In all cases, marketing strategies were implemented to address the specific problems encountered and create public awareness of actions undertaken to redress them. In all case studies, a media and public relations campaign was directed at the travel industry with emphasis on prioritising promotions directed at key source markets. In the majority of cases examined, the restoration of tourism was regarded as a significant element in the overall economic, social and political recovery of the destinations concerned.

The field of destination recovery and restoration is an under-researched discipline within tourism studies and management practice. Yet it is a critically important element of tourism planning. The 'what if' or contingency planning aspect of tourism, especially destination management, has been a long-standing weak link in tourism destination management and marketing. By comparison, international airlines have well-established contingency measures in place in the event of crashes.

However regrettable, aircraft sometimes crash, cruise ships sink and hotels can be destroyed by natural disasters or through the deliberate or accidental actions of human beings. The calmest, most orderly and tranquil locales can quickly descend into chaos through an act of nature, criminality, war or terrorism. A dramatic example of an aberrant, one-off crisis occurred in Tasmania, Australia at the historical site of Port Arthur in April 1996 when (according to the official version) a young man armed with an automatic rifle killed 35 people, many of whom were interstate and overseas tourists.

This event instantly plunged the Tasmanian tourism

industry into crisis and engendered a marketing recovery process which is considered a role model for destination marketing management of a recovery programme following a single-event crisis.

The case studies include countries as diverse as Israel and Sri Lanka, both of which have experienced repeated and prolonged episodes of war and intercommunal acts of terrorism. Although tourists have rarely been specific targets of terrorism in Israel, Israeli tourism authorities and marketers have endured a constant struggle to counter a widely held perception that Israel is a dangerous destination for tourists. Although most political violence has been confined to specific regions, Israel presents an especially interesting marketing case study of perception management.

There are many parallels between the Israeli experience and that of Sri Lanka, where conflict between the government and Tamil separatists has largely been confined to the northeast of the country. Unlike the Israel situation, Tamil terrorists have occasionally targeted tourists within the broader context of their civil war tactics.

Political terrorism in Egypt specifically targeted tourism as a core strategy to undermine the national economy and the political system. Repeated acts of terrorism directed at tourists during the 1990s culminated in the Luxor massacre of November 1997. International tourism is the dominant source of foreign currency income for Egypt, so a slump in inbound tourism directly impacts on the Egyptian economy.

Following episodes of terrorism, the Egyptian government, in association with the Egyptian Tourist Authority, embarked upon an intensive campaign to restore confidence in destination Egypt. The strategy incorporated two significant prongs: the correction of security lapses that made tourists a soft target for terrorism in Egypt; and a major PR and marketing campaign to incentivise tourism and restore international confidence in Egypt as a major destination.

Croatia represents a notable example of a country which sought to integrate tourism within a national recovery strategy following prolonged warfare. Large regions of Croatia were off limits for international tourists during four years of conflict with neighbouring Serbia. In the Croatian case, the restoration of the tourism industry was integrated within a state-driven policy of economic recovery and was a major factor in attracting foreign investment and foreign currency. The signing of the Dayton Agreement in December 1995 was far more effective in restoring traveller confidence in Croatia than any specific marketing campaign.

In 1987 and 2000, Fiji experienced two episodes of political instability, which heavily impacted on its economically vital tourism industry. The 1987 coup, led by Sitiveni Rabuka, which overthrew an elected multiracial government, and George Speight's abortive attempt in 2000 to overthrow and take hostage the elected multiracial government, had a severe impact on the Fijian tourism industry.

During the events and in their immediate *denouement*, the Fijian Ministry of Tourism and its marketing arm, the Fiji Visitors Bureau, mounted carefully planned campaigns in association with airlines and tour operators to restore tourism confidence in Fiji's tourism industry. During both crises, the Australian and New Zealand governments actively discouraged their citizens from visiting Fiji, which impacted heavily upon Fiji's two largest tourism source markets.

The Fijian case highlights the significance of government tourism advisories as a factor in shaping tourism perceptions of specific destinations. Aside from advisories that directly prohibit citizens from visiting a specific country or region, negative advisories about the safety or advisability of visiting a destination influence tour operators, travel insurance providers and travellers in their respective decisions to promote, provide insurance cover or visit a destination.

South African tourism has suffered significant image problems as a result of street crime in South Africa's major cities. However, the South African situation has not stopped tourism growth, with South Africa's tourism marketing authorities managing the impact of crime as a hazard to tourists rather than as a crisis.

There are certain regions of the world which, due to their

climate, geographical and geological locations, are prone to specific forms of natural disasters. The tropics are in the path of hurricanes, typhoons and cyclones; parts of Turkey are vulnerable to earthquakes; San Francisco and Los Angeles in the United States, Tokyo and Kobe in Japan and Wellington in New Zealand are built on top of geological time bombs on the major fault lines of the earth's crust; and Naples in Italy is one of many cities in the world located in close proximity to active or potentially active volcanoes.

Most technologically advanced countries and regions have well-established contingency plans for responding to natural disasters. However, many less-developed countries are under-prepared for major natural disasters and cannot cope, especially if the occurrence is located far from major urban and regional centres. There are also cases where the scale of a natural disaster is so vast that it is beyond established emergency contingencies.

Intentionally, or unintentionally, media coverage often magnifies the extent of the impact of destruction within the actual disaster zone and turns it into a national problem. Two case studies dealing with the problem of marketing destinations in the wake of a natural disaster are examined here. The exceptional tourism recovery achieved by Turkey following the 1999 Izmit earthquake was an outstanding example of combining international sympathy for the plight of the victims with an effective PR campaign.

This strategy clearly communicated the distinction between the damage wrought within the earthquake zone and Turkey's tourism infrastructure, which remained largely intact and unaffected by the disaster.

The Philippines has been beset by three types of crisis: terrorism, political instability and natural disaster. The 1991 eruption of Mt Pinatubo demonstrated that the Philippine government was able to effectively employ disaster-management methods to ensure the orderly evacuation of thousands of people prior to the eruption. The Philippine tourist authorities also managed this natural cataclysmina manner which minimised the disruption to tourism growth during the period 1991–97, incorporating the Mt Pinatubo experience into the formulation of the country's tourism master plan.

Epidemic and disease are among the least researched areas of tourism crisis management. Yet this subject has for many years been an issue affecting the decisions of tourists to either visit or avoid specific destinations. Outbreaks of typhoid, cholera and other infectious diseases have always been a factor determining inoculation policy and entrance requirements for most countries in the world.

The recent outbreak of the HIV virus has had a major impact on tourist participation in what is loosely described as the 'sex tourism' industry. The high incidence of HIV in Africa and Southeast Asia has had a significant impact on social policy in these countries and also influenced the nature of tourism attractions in them. The case study examined in this book does not, however, relate to human epidemics.

The blanket media coverage accompanying the outbreak of foot-and mouth disease in the United Kingdom during the first half of 2001 impacted severely on the British agricultural sector and inflicted significant harm on the British tourism industry.

The closure of farms and rural regions severely damaged the rural sector of Britain's tourism infrastructure, a sector which had been assiduously marketed for many years. The intensity and extent of media coverage generated an image of Britain as a country ravaged by this disease and severely compromised its overall image as a tourism destination.

The British Tourist Authority's approach to the foot-and-mouth epidemic crisis is particularly interesting, as it is one of the world's first cases in which the Internet played a major role in the management of destination marketing during and after a tourism crisis.

THE MEDIA AND DESTINATION CRISIS

A significant element in this study is an examination of the role of the international media in both publicising the actual crisis and in reporting (and in some cases ignoring) recovery and restoration programs. Globalisation of the media and their enhanced ability to report events as they occur give rise to a mixture of benefits and problems for tourist authorities. The international media appear to have a penchant for focusing upon a number of key elements which determine the newsworthiness of an issue. Favoured items tend to be defined under the following categories:

- Crime;
- Crisis;
- Conflict;
- Conquest;
- Corruption;
- Catharsis;
- Cataclysm;
- Rescue;
- Scandal;
- Triumph over adversity.

Any content analysis study of media news reporting will ascertain that these elements dominate lead stories in print and electronic media. They tend to focus on what is broadly described as 'bad news'.

The ingredient of magnification—the degree to which any of the above elements is exaggerated—determines whether the publication, television, radio programme or website is deemed to be 'responsible' or sensationalistic. Issues such as editorial and political bias, in addition to accessibility of sources, will have a large bearing on the frequency, extent and nature of coverage.

Democratic countries committed to the broad concept of freedom of the press are open to uncontrolled reportage of variable accuracy. A crisis has a higher probability of being subject to media coverage than the recovery and restoration stages. The role of effective public relations management is critical for tourist authorities in democratic countries to ensure that recovery and restoration efforts are reported at all, let alone in proportion to the coverage of the actual crisis.

Non-democratic countries impose far more control over media coverage; consequently, reporting of the crisis and the recovery process is often stage-managed by governments. Media relations remains one of the most critical elements in crisis management.

The supervision of media coverage of both the crisis and the crisis management process is a core issue for tourism authorities and tour operators. The establishment and maintenance of effective media relations is a critical function of destination tourist authorities. Media relations extend beyond developing a network of contacts with local media and usually require the development of global contacts.

The November 1997 Luxor massacre, Israeli-Palestinian political violence and the 2001 foot-and-mouth disease crisis in the United Kingdom were all subject to worldwide attention and scrutiny. When foreign tourists are victims or are indirectly affected by a particular crisis, they are often subject to media attention in their home country. Conversely, the international pervasiveness of American, British and German global news networks such as CNN, BBC and Deutsche Welle meant that many local issues in those countries become globally disseminated.

It is arguable that an incident on the scale of the New York/Washington DC attacks of September 11, 2001 would have attracted extensive coverage had they occurred in any large city elsewhere in the world. However, their occurrence in the United States and the targeting of the military and financial symbols of American power and prestige guaranteed blanket worldwide media coverage.

The instantaneous nature of news reporting, especially via the electronic media, requires that tourist authorities immediately implement their contingency plan, deploy their crisis management team and initiate communication with the media. Failure to prepare for a crisis scenario places the tourist authority consistently on the defensive when responding to reporters' questions at media press conferences. Tourist authorities must exercise maximum control during interviews and initiate the agenda of the media's coverage of the crisis.

Once a strong cooperative relationship is developed with the relevant media, it is also likely that the media will seek to cover the tourist authorities' management of the actual crisis and post-crisis developments. The Tasmanian government's sensitive and effective media management of the Port Arthur massacre, coupled with an effective post-crisis tourism marketing programme, resulted in Tasmania experiencing a relatively rapid tourism recovery following the Port Arthur massacre in 1996.

The Egyptian Ministry of Tourism, the Fiji Visitors Bureau, the Turkish Ministry of Tourism and the British Tourist Authority all include examples of effective media management of specific recent crises which impacted on their respective tourist industries followed by relatively swift recoveries.

ALLIANCES BETWEEN TOURISM AUTHORITIES AND THE PRIVATE SECTOR

An integral part of effective marketing management of crises and their restoration phases is for tourist authorities to establish and maintain effective alliances with those private and government organisations sharing common vested interests. Airlines, hoteliers, resorts, museums, attractions and wholesale tour operators all depend on the successful selling and marketing of destinations which form all or part of their programs.

In times of crisis, the effectiveness of these working relationships is often put to the test. It is a common element of a post-crisis recovery process for one or all of these organisations to engage in intensive marketing programs featuring temporary discounts or incentives as tactics in the recovery strategy. Tourist authorities and national carriers often subsidise blitz-marketing campaigns by the private sector. A tourist crisis in one destination often has regional implications. Cooperative marketing programs can potentially benefit neighbouring destinations.

Many of the case studies in this work demonstrate the significance of public-private sector alliances in managing marketing campaigns during the crisis period and in the recovery and restoration phases. One of the most important elements of this alliance is between national tourism authorities and flag carrier airlines. In many countries, the airline industry is privatised and some countries, including Britain, the United States and Australia, have more than one major international/domestic carrier.

Nevertheless, in times of crisis either the flag carrier or the major carriers will band together to market the destination out of crisis. EgyptAir played a major role in Egypt's market recovery following the Luxor massacre in 1997. In the United States, Delta Airlines was one of a number of US carriers which encouraged travellers to visit New York City after the September 11 attack, through its offer to supply thousands of free tickets to Americans travelling to New York.

Airlines play a vital role in facilitating the travel of media and travel industry professionals making familiarisation visits. During a crisis period, the importance of familiarisation trips is greatly magnified. The travel industry is vital to any successful *push marketing* (directed at retailers) campaigns. Airlines traditionally work with tourist authorities in carrying travel journalists.

The media are central to a successful *pull marketing* campaign (marketing directed at consumers). The Fiji Visitors Bureau provides a model of a highly effective alliance with the national carrier Air Pacific and major resorts in hosting large delegations of travel agents and travel writers after the 2000 coup. This book focuses on restoration and recovery of destinations in the field of tourism marketing. The author readily acknowledges that the repair of infrastructure, rebuilding, medical rehabilitation and financing are all necessary elements of the recovery process and constitute a field of study in their own right.

Many people readily dismiss marketing as the equivalent of 'spin doctoring'—that is, adopting a selective approach to the truth. A successful recovery and restoration programme should be conducted ethically. Consumers and travel professionals demand a truthful assessment of a crisis situation; failure by destination authorities to deliver may provide short-term gains, but in the longer term false reporting of a situation is easily exposed, calling into question the veracity of the tourist authority and reflecting negatively on the destination.

The British Tourist Authority (BTA)'s handling of the foot-and-mouth disease problem is an example in which open and honest management of marketing information has resulted in 'short-term pain for long-term gain'. During the foot-and-mouth crisis, the BTA's website informed travellers of event cancellations and the closure of parks, reserves, attractions, regions and accommodation. The website was frequently updated.

While this information was clearly harmful to those places or events affected, the BTA information enabled travel agents and travellers to plan their visit to Britain in real time. As the epidemic waned, demand for travel to Britain quickly recovered and the BTA won the respect of many consumers and travel industry professionals for its reliable information.

It is often assumed that a crisis or complaint is something to dread. In fact, much good can come from a crisis. At its most base, the scene of a battle, crime or natural disaster often becomes a tourist attraction. In many parts of the world, scenes of natural disaster, battlefields and crime scenes have become tourist attractions.

For example, the Alma Tunnel in Paris where Princess Diana died in 1997 became a focal point for tourists. The management of a crisis will (for unintended reasons) sometimes push a little-known destination into public prominence. Prior to Lebanon's civil wars and foreign invasions in the period 1975–95, many visitors regarded Beirut as the 'Paris of the Middle East'. Beirut has now undergone a gradual transformation, restoring its former ambience. The Croatian city of Dubrovnik suffered severe damage during the Croatian-Serbian war of 1991–95, but has since been fully restored and is once more Croatia's leading tourist attraction.

Lessons learned from a crisis should be incorporated into the day-to-day marketing of a destination. All case studies focus on the work of national/state or regional tourism authorities in the direction or coordination of crisis management. In many cases, the national, state or regional authorities work in conjunction with the private sector. In some instances, major operators and, in others, consultancy firms are contracted to provide independent management and marketing advice. There are specific cases in which the private sector plays a pre-eminent role in the restoration and recovery process.

The United States is the most prominent example of this. Centralisation of decision-making and public relations is a common element in the more successful cases studies. Uniformity in the marketing approach does not necessarily apply to all source markets. The distance from the destination, together with demographic, sociological and political factors, will often determine the most effective marketing strategy applicable to each source market.

Professional marketers and marketing analysts are familiar with the concept of a SWOT analysis: Strengths; Weaknesses; Opportunities; Threats.

A SWOT analysis forms an integral part of each of the case studies examined. These crises have been managed with varying degrees of success. It is hoped that the reader may find some value in the concepts analysed and that the case studies will provide insightful illustrations of successful and unsuccessful applications of crisis management. Although the focus of this book is tourist destinations, these concepts have universal applications in the field of business and commerce.

While destination marketing during and following crises is a relatively new field of inquiry, a number of researchers have already made significant contributions in this discipline. Abraham Pizam and Yoel Mansfield are among the leaders in research relating to crime, war and terrorism. In 1998, the World Tourism Organization published a *Handbook of Disaster Reduction in Tourism Areas,* which focused primarily on the management of destinations which had suffered from natural disasters.

Anthony Concil, the Tokyo-based IATA (International Air Transport Association) Manager, Corporate Communications, has produced kits on marketing management for airlines following crashes and other incidents which might harm the airline's image. Globally, IATA's Communications division assists airlines in managing crises. Unlike airlines, much of the tourism and hospitality industry has belatedly realised that crisis management is a core rather than a peripheral aspect of its business.

This work seeks to add an extra dimension to the existing literature by analysing case studies of the major uncontrollable external factors which constitute a destination crisis. It also seeks to examine the marketing recovery and restoration of a destination, both during and following these crises. Academics including Bill Faulkner, Yoel Mansfield, Abraham Pizam, Linda K. Richter, Christian Nielsen and Michael Hall have been among pioneers of this field. They would all readily acknowledge that there is much research still to be done in this discipline.

The author wrote this book in the midst of Israel's long running destination crisis and the international crisis which arose from the New York and Washington DC attacks of September 11, 2001. The subject matter in this book presented a daily professional challenge and was far from a matter of theoretical research. The issues examined here apply to any reader involved as a teacher, student or practitioner of marketing tourism. The work is of universal relevance to all fields of marketing.

Chapter 2

Restoration of Destinations

The crises highlighted in this book were caused by external factors impacting negatively on the appeal and marketability of the destinations concerned. All were beyond the direct managerial control of destination authorities. The principal causes of crises covered here—war, terrorism, political/social unrest, crime waves, epidemics and natural disasters—fit the definition of a crisis as described in the opening chapter. There is no doubt that many other factors deter tourists from travelling to a destination.

These include airline crashes, fatal accidents on tours, industrial relations breakdowns, chronically poor service and tourism infrastructure standards, business failures (especially of airlines, coach or tour companies, such as Pan Am in the United States, Laker Air in the United Kingdom or Ansett in Australia) which render some destinations isolated or under-serviced. The above examples represent the plurality of factors, which impact negatively on the marketability of a destination. Crises resulting from management failures, although relevant to destination crisis management, are not covered in this book.

The management of a destination crisis is greatly influenced by its duration. Most crises—especially one-off events such as the 1999 Turkish earthquake, an isolated terrorist or a criminal attack on tourists such as the 1996 Port Arthur massacre in Tasmania or the Luxor massacre in Egypt in 1997 —can be dealt with in two main stages: stage 1, involving the consolidation management of the actual crisis; and stage 2, the implementation of a postcrisis recovery programme and strategy.

However, longer-term crises such as the 'low-medium intensity political violence' experienced by Israel, the Philippines and Sri Lanka, can place destination authorities in a position where they are unable to indefinitely suspend destination promotion during the crisis and are forced to implement an in-crisis marketing strategy. In such cases, destination authorities are ready to implement a contingency plan to fully restore their markets after the crisis is deemed to be over.

Specific such cases in this book, including Fiji's coups of 1987 and 2000, sporadic terrorist attacks against tourists in Egypt in the early 1990s and the 2001 foot-and-mouth problems in Britain, required a twin-track crisis-management policy. In these cases an incrisis and a post-crisis marketing plan worked in tandem. The uncertainty of the crisis's duration necessitated a parallel approach.The Philippines is a particularly challenging case because the country's tourism authorities have been obliged to maintain tourism marketing in the face of several external crisis types: simultaneous terrorism, natural disaster, crime and epidemics.

The September 11 attacks against the World Trade Centre in New York City and the Pentagon in Washington DC expanded from being a terrorist threat to the American tourist industry to a global tourism crisis. This particular event took the concept of crisis management in tourism far beyond issues of destination marketing to challenging the marketability of international air travel. Clearly, as the scale and complexity of a crisis escalates, more processes are required to manage its restoration and recovery.

THE DESTCON SCALE

ASSESSING THE SEVERITY OF A DESTINATION CRISIS

Global armed forces have rated the status of military readiness in times of threat to a nation's security on a five-point scale known as defence readiness conditions, DEFCON. The scale ascends from DEFCON 5: Normal peacetime readiness to DEFCON 1: Maximum force readiness. A comparable scale is relevant to identifying the status of a destination condition termed DESTCON. In general terms, these are descriptions of DESTCONs:

- *Destcon* 5: Normal marketing conditions;
- *Destcon* 4: Normal, increased intelligence and strengthened marketing measures;
- *Destcon* 3: Increase in marketing readiness, above normal readiness;
- *Destcon* 2: Further increase in marketing readiness, less than maximum readiness;
- *Destcon* 1: Maximum crisis marketing readiness.

The following expands on destination conditions:

- *Destcon* 5: Minimal perceived threat to the marketability of the destination.
- *Destcon* 4: Isolated problems within the destination: crime, low-level political disturbances, which may require avoidance of specific areas but have minimal impact on the overall marketability of the destination. South Africa is the prime example discussed in this study.
- *Destcon* 3: There are major problems within identifiable regions in the destination which are well-publicised and present a credible threat to tourists in the seareas. Threats include ama jorcrime event/s, out breaks of terrorism, a localised natural disaster or an epidemic. Major problems in a neighbouring destination may impact on the marketability of the principal destination. Cases examined matching this situation include Turkey, Fiji and Port Arthur. In most cases, these are one-off highly publicised localised crises which often deter tourists from visiting the entire destination.
- *Destcon* 2: A crisis of this magnitude places large parts of the country at or under imminent threat of war or destruction from natural disaster. This stage includes widespread terrorism, natural disaster, disease or widespread disorder in which the safety of tourists

is under measurable threat. Consequently, governments of source markets caution heightened levels of concern or insist on complete avoidance. Case studies analysed here which have reached this level include Croatia, Israel, the Philippines, Egypt and Sri Lanka. The problems experienced in these situations frequently have a negative impact on the marketability of neighbouring destinations.

- *Destcon* 1: A crisis of this magnitude not only threatens the marketability of one destination but also has widespread global or regional repercussions on tourism. In most instances, this involves a major act of war or terrorism, which draws in many nations. The attacks on New York City and Washington DC on September 11, 2001 and their global repercussions most closely correspond to this level of crisis.

There are some instances in which a crisis situation exists according to the definitions outlined above. By muting the response, little attention is drawn to the situation as a *crisis*. South Africa's tourism authorities cannot be accused of ignoring the serious crime rate in the country; however, they treat it more as an avoidable tourist hazard than as a crisis, thus diffusing crime as a threat to the viability and appeal of the destination.

Several countries have managed to treat endemic social and political problems in a similar manner. In the case studies examined here, low-level Tamil terrorism in Sri Lanka and multiple problems in the Philippines did not impinge on tourism growth during certain periods. However, when those problems crossed the invisible line from *background hazard* to crisis, tourism numbers often plummeted.

The level of media exposure influences the distinction between a tourist hazard, a crisis and even the DESTCON rating. The international media intensively cover the United States, Britain and Israel. Consequently, aberrant events are subject to intensive coverage and widespread dissemination. Terrorist attacks in Israel are routinely reported and disseminated in the international media. Conversely, there is relatively little international media attention given to terrorism in Sri Lanka unless it occurs in or near the capital, Colombo, or impacts directly on tourists and foreign nationals. Coverage is subject to the media's access to a conflict or crisis zone. Few international journalists are able to encounter terrorist groups in the Philippines, but journalists have almost unrestricted access to the flashpoints of the Israeli-Palestinian conflict.

The extent of media access relates to the political system and the openness of the society. A factor contributing to the success of Egypt's tourism recovery after the 1997 Luxor massacre was the tight controls imposed by the Egyptian government and its tourism authority on media coverage and reporting. Conversely, there was far more discussion about the foot-and-mouth crisis in the United Kingdom. Whilst the British Tourist Authority was able to present an internally consistent media message during the foot-and-mouth crisis, other groups and organisations in Britain freely expressed contrary views. This was visibly evident in relation to defining suggested no-go areas for tourists.

A major factor determining the shifting status of a problem from a background hazard to a crisis impacting on international tourism is the international political impact of the issue. When terrorism in Turkey, Sri Lanka or the Philippines is restricted to an isolated localised crisis far away from major cities and tourist centres, it is largely ignored internationally. However, when terrorist attacks target foreign tourists or tourist infrastructure, then the matter becomes an international incident.

If a government from a destination's strategically important source market issues a negative travel advisory, it can seriously harm inbound tourism and may attain destination crisis magnitude. During Fiji's abortive coup of 2000, travel advisories of the British, Australian and New Zealand governments calling on their citizens to defer travel to Fiji proved an effective political weapon when wielded by the governments of three of tourism-dependent Fiji's principal source markets.

The third factor which influences the management of a

crisis affecting tourists is the degree to which the events are aberrant to the social norms of that society. The 1996 Port Arthur massacre in Tasmania was an incident so completely contrary to the late twentieth century Tasmanian social context that it constituted a tourism crisis. By comparison, a suicide bombing in Israel—which may have resulted in a similar number of casualties and is equally horrific—will not by itself trigger a tourism crisis for Israel, due to the fact that such events (especially since September 2000) have occurred on numerous occasions and reinforce the stereotype of Israel as a risky destination for tourists.

The preceding discussion provides a context for the destination crisis management and restoration steps outlined below. Each situation is very different, and there is no universal response to a crisis nor a contingency plan applying to every destination crisis. Each situation requires specific variations on the approaches outlined. It is hoped that the steps outlined below clearly explain the process of destination crisis marketing.

They seek to take into account the various external crises impacting on tourist destinations and provide a logical series of management processes towards a restoration and recovery programme. Events which trigger a crisis are often aberrant, destructive and traumatic in the short term.

Effective crisis contingency planning results in long-term benefits for destination authorities and the tourism industry. Detailed planning leads to improved infrastructure, security management, service, and more innovative and effective marketing programs. Highly trained and coordinated management and staff are required to implement crisis prevention policies. Well-prepared destination authorities will quickly move from crisis to recovery mode.

STEPS TO MARKETING MANAGEMENT OF A DESTINATION CRISIS

- Identify the event/problem as either a crisis or a hazard.
- Establish a crisis management team and define roles.

- Promote the destination during and after the crisis.
- Monitor recovery and analyse the crisis experience.

STEP 1: IDENTIFY THE EVENT/PROBLEM AS EITHER A CRISIS OR A HAZARD

The destination authority needs to ask the following questions:

- Will this event/problem be widely and negatively publicised in key source markets?
- Does it have the potential to threaten the safety or well-being of tourists?
- Were tourists directly affected?
- Have foreign governments altered or threatened negative travel advisories as a result of the event/problem?
- Have insurance companies deleted or limited coverage to the destination?
- Are airlines, shipping, rail or coach operators and tour operators considering withdrawing or limiting services and products to the destination?
- Are travel agents in source markets reducing bookings to the destination?
- Are the destination representatives overseas or interstate reporting a substantial growth of negative inquiries from the public and the travel industry? Is there substantial growth in cancellations and a reduction in forward bookings?
- Are media groups hosted by the destination grossly delaying publication, broadcast or screening of material about the destination with or without explanation?
- Is there a statistically significant (seasonally adjusted) drop in arrivals and hotel occupancy levels?
- Is there pressure within the tourism infrastructure to reduce employment levels?
- Is there a local sense of political urgency regarding the prospects of the tourism industry?
- Are tourism receipts significantly (seasonally adjusted) reduced?

If the answer to at least three of the above questions is 'yes', then the destination authorities should treat the situation as a crisis. This is not an absolute and definitive identification of a crisis; rather, the above questions constitute a representative list of key indicators.If the answer is 'yes' to less than three of the questions, the situation should be treated as a hazard and the best means to manage hazards is with honesty and discretion. South Africa has a serious crime rate, acknowledged even in its own tourism promotional literature.

While South African tourism authorities advise prospective travellers on how to minimise their exposure to crime, the warnings are given in conjunction with a broader range of travel advice. It is a matter rarely discussed in tourism promotion or advertising and, although subject to occasional media coverage, it is normally referred to within a broader context of destination coverage.

Some foreign governments mention crime in South Africa in their advisories, but it is not regarded as a reason to avoid or defer travel. Hazard management is not a question of evading a problem, but placing it within an appropriate perspective.

STEP 2: ESTABLISH A CRISIS MANAGEMENT TEAM

There are a number of elements involved in managing a destination crisis. At the management level (subject to the size of the organisation), there may be a requirement for several teams to manage the crisis. The overall responsibility for crisis management in any destination authority rests with the chief executive officer (CEO) or an appointed crisis manger, who will normally establish global guidelines.

In the cases of destination authorities with representatives either within the country or in overseas source markets, there may be regional or national factors which require variations from the head office approach.

The major elements, especially from a marketing perspective, include:

- Media and public relations;
- Relations with the travel industry in source markets;

- Operations and situation assessment and dissemination focusing on internal national/international staff and the industry within the destination;
- Destination response coordination with the local tourism and hospitality industry;
- Liaison with local/regional and national government authorities;
- Implementation of alliances with tour operators, airlines, shipping lines and/or land transport providers which service the destination.

Each team requires a single key spokesperson or point of contact, plus backup contact (where possible). In dealing with outside organisations, every effort has to be made to follow a consistent line.

Even the most democratic organisations may internally debate the organisational position adopted during the crisis, but once determined it is important that recipients of the message perceive it to be from a united organisation. Having established the crisis management team, it is important to determine the key roles of these teams.

MEDIA AND PUBLIC RELATIONS

In the heat of a crisis it is a natural emotional inclination of destination authorities to treat the media as adversaries. A crisis is a media staple followed closely by corruption and official dishonesty. It is essential to be as honest and open with the media as circumstances permit. This does not imply that it is appropriate to be untruthful, but in circumstances where national or tourist security may be compromised, it is appropriate to be selective about what is revealed to the media. The media representatives of key source markets will primarily be concerned about the impact of a destination crisis on people from their home audience.

Typically, if 50 tourists are killed in a terrorist attack in the Middle East, the *New York Times* will focus on victims from New York City, the United States and then other countries in that order. Managing media coverage requires preparation to deal with the frequently localised concerns of media outlets. There are several common questions with which media managers should be familiar:

- What is being done to assist victims?
- What is the extent of the damage/casualties?
- What is being done to reduce, minimise or eliminate future risks?
- What can the government/destination authorities do to guarantee safety?
- Why did this event occur in the first place?
- Who is to blame?
- How long will the crisis last?

Destination authorities are rarely able to answer all of these questions, but it is important not to be perceived as evasive, glib or unhelpful. If the media contact cannot answer certain questions, then that person should direct the media to people or authorities who are qualified to do so. In an interview or press conference situation, it is a paramount requirement to control the interview and in some circumstances a prepared statement may be more useful than fielding questions. In crisis situations, tourism authorities work in conjunction with other government departments.

Tourism authorities should have specific answers to the first four questions listed above. In the twentyfirst century, it is increasingly essential to have the information readily available on a website and also in a format in which visual images and text can be rapidly communicated by email.

The website has begun to replace the printed press kit as a preferred tool of media communication and public relations, especially for instant news reports. In cases such as questions relating to blame and the original cause of a crisis, it may be more appropriate for authorities unrelated to tourism to deal with these issues. In virtually all crises discussed here, it is crucial to have a principal media spokesperson and contact point. The content should then be transmitted to the destination's interstate or overseas representatives and emulated as closely as possible.

In anticipating key questions, it is essential to maintain a series of simple bullet points. The electronic media are especially harsh on verbosity and the mastery of '30-second grabs' is a major responsibility for media managers. Press releases should be concise and limited to one page. Wherever possible, anticipate questions and be ready with answers. Preparedness to provide the media with relevant information makes a reporter's life easier and in most cases will engender an atmosphere conducive to cooperation between the destination authority and the media. Cooperation is then likely to extend to media coverage of the restoration and recovery process.

It is always worthwhile for the media to view both the crisis and the restoration and recovery process at first hand. A fine line can be drawn between familiarisation visits being perceived as an honest inspection or a staged PR exercise. Interviews with tourists from the source markets, local officials and local tourist and hospitality industry professionals should be included. The key message destination authorities seek to communicate is that, while a crisis has occurred, positive steps are being taken to return to normality.

At all stages, it is important to recognise the critical role the media play in shaping public attitudes to tourism destinations. Reporters should be treated with due respect and courtesy. Destination authorities should control the parameters of discourse with media professionals, thus ensuring that the media have as much access to information as possible.

The duration of a crisis is a key issue for media management. In most cases, the crisis is a short-term affair involving a brief consolidation phase followed by a recovery phase. In a short-term crisis, destination authorities can readily prepare the media for a recovery phase. When a crisis extends into months, media management becomes an entirely different proposition.

A common crisis management practice is to isolate the problem area from the rest of the destination and point to the distinction between a 'trouble spot' and the remainder of the destination. In extreme cases such as Croatia's fouryear war with the Yugoslav Federation (1992–1996) and Israel's conflict with the Palestinian Authority since September 2000, isolation strategies are more difficult to employ. Although violence may predominate in specific areas, random and unpredictable outbreaks can occur anywhere. In such instances, the issue of secure forms of tourism to these destinations needs to be stressed.

There are instances where destination authorities adopt an approach in which they publicly refuse to acknowledge that a crisis situation exists and enter a phase of denial. This approach undermines the credibility of the destination authority for the media, but it sometimes works for the consumer market.

RELATIONS WITH THE TRAVEL INDUSTRY IN SOURCE MARKETS

Successful marketing of tourism requires maintaining a balance between pull marketing (appealing direct to consumers) and push marketing (appealing to those who sell travel in a manner that will encourage them to sell a specific destination). Travel professionals, in common with the public are influenced in their perceptions of destinations by media coverage and this can result in travel consultants advising their clients on the merits of a destination based on their media-sourced impressions.

Destination authorities frequently need to treat the travel industry in a similar fashion to the media. A high priority is to assist industry professionals to be more aware of the situation in destinations than their consumers. While informative and updated websites, industry updates and seminars are all valuable aids to communicating the situation in a destination in crisis, there is nothing more powerful than personal experience.

Destination authorities should seek to identify those members of the travel industry in their source markets who are well respected by their colleagues and invite them to visit and inspect the destination, circumstances permitting. An independent testimonial carries far more *gravitas* than the spokesperson of a destination authority.

The Turkish Ministry of Tourism achieved a remarkable and rapid recovery of tourism following the 1999 earthquake. A factor enhancing this recovery was the policy of hosting large groups of travel industry professionals from most major source markets to witness the devastation of the earthquake and the fact that most tourist attractions were untouched. The Turks adopted a similar programme with the media, and the message that Turkey was safe for tourists to visit was quickly disseminated in both the pull and push dimensions of the tourism market. Travel retailers and wholesalers who are confident and knowledgable about a destination are able to allay consumer concerns and sell the destination.

It is also valuable in a crisis for destination authority representatives to maintain regular briefings with the local travel industry to keep them up to date with the crisis and the recovery and restorative measures undertaken. Involving industry colleagues recently returned from the destination in providing testimonials is a most valuable enhancement during these briefings.

OPERATIONS AND SITUATION ASSESSMENTS WITH INTERNAL STAFF BRIEFINGS

There are occasions during which destination authorities effectively disseminate information about a crisis to the market, but in so doing ignore the people closest to the crisis—their own staff. The effective management of a crisis is enhanced when staff and representatives of the destination authority are fully appraised of the operational and marketing implications of their own crisis management.

They need to be aware of the line adopted in dealing with the media, foreign governments and the tourism industry. Internal communications and effective internal briefing are vital elements of successful crisis management. Staff must be fully briefed on the situation and on the roles of their closest colleagues, enabling them to alternate between roles when necessary.

It is a common practice for destination authorities to outsource consultancy services to assist in crisis management.

Most countries examined utilised such services. This does not suggest that the destination authorities lack the internal expertise to fulfil this role, but rather it is prudent to obtain the expertise available from dispassionate professional outsiders able to draw on their company's experience in managing international tourism and other business crises. Expert consultants provide independent assessments of the extent to which the destination authority is managing the various facets of its crisis and recovery programs, free from the internal culture and politics of the organisation.

There is great value in many crisis situations for overseas or interstate representatives of the destination authority meeting together in the destination to exchange ideas and personally experience the impact of the crisis, recovery and restoration programme. As discussed earlier, the most detailed and vivid written or audio-visual briefings are no substitute for first-hand experience. External representatives are also able to apply the marketing approach most relevant to their specific marketing environment.

In the United States, which abolished centralised national government tourism marketing authorities in 1996, the challenge of marketing destination USA after the New York City and Washington DC attacks of September 11 was largely in the hands of the private sector and was coordinated by the Travel Industry Association.

The US case was an exception to the general rule of destination crisis management coordinated by centralised government controlled destination authorities. Despite September 11, destination marketing of the United States remains the most pluralistic in the world. Consequently, maintaining a coordinated approach is a major challenge in establishing common terms of reference when marketing the United States globally.

DESTINATION RESPONSE COORDINATION WITH THE LOCAL TOURISM INDUSTRY

A key measure of successful destination crisis management is the degree to which the various elements of the destination's tourism industry cooperate to manage the crisis and the subsequent recovery process.

This involves accommodation and transportation providers, tour operators, resorts and attractions, restaurants and food outlets, as well as regional and local tourist authorities. During a crisis there may be a requirement to transport and accommodate tourists from a crisis zone to a 'safe' zone at short notice and in a manner that minimises cost and inconvenience to the tourists. During the recovery phase, it is a common practice to offer reduced-price holidays or value-added special offers as incentives for tourists to return to a destination or former crisis zone.

Destination authorities may need to subsidise these incentives. In the case of Fiji, the Fijian tourism industry formed an umbrella association called TAG (Tourism Action Group) to coordinate marketing and pricing policies of hotels, attractions, resorts, airlines and car rental firms during the recovery phases following the coups of 1987 and 2000. The Fijian case was an example of highly centralised and coordinated action on the part of both the government and the private sector of the tourism industry, to stimulate a value-added and price-driven recovery.

A less centralised, but nevertheless high, level of coordination existed within the British tourism industry during its recovery following the footand-mouth crisis in 2001. Following September 11, New York City's tourist authority was able to elicit massive support from airlines, hotels and attractions to encourage tourists to return to New York. However, the recovery process for the US tourism industry has varied throughout the country. While the Tourism Industry Association of America and Visit USA organisations have marketed destination USA energetically throughout key source markets overall, private sector coordination has been uneven.

Israel has experienced a long-term tourism crisis since September 2000. The Israel Ministry of Tourism closely coordinated marketing activities with the national carrier El Al Airlines. Conversely, Israeli hotels have adopted varying approaches to tourism pricing. Some have increased prices to compensate for lack of patronage, while others have reduced prices to attract patronage. The lack of consistency confuses consumers and travel professionals alike.

After the November 1997 Luxor massacre, the Egyptian Tourist Authority, EgyptAir, the local tourism and hospitality industry conducted a professionally coordinated campaign to stimulate recovery.

A crisis does not require the inhibition of private sector competition within the tourism industry. Although cooperation must be increased, a recovery phase tends to be more rapid and successful if the destination authorities and the tourism industry are seen to be working in concert rather than at crosspurposes. Fiji, Egypt, Turkey, Croatia and Tasmania exemplified highly coordinated and very rapid post-crisis recovery phases.

LIAISON WITH LOCAL AND REGIONAL TOURISM AUTHORITIES AND FOREIGN GOVERNMENTS

In most cases, a tourism crisis will affect an entire country. However, the epicentre of the crisis will be the most gravely affected. The Port Arthur massacre in the Australian state of Tasmania had a minimal impact on tourism to Australia as a country and a limited impact on Tasmania, but the tragedy's impact on the Port Arthur region was quite profound.

At the opposite end of the scale, the attacks on New York City and Washington DC impacted heavily on the two cities, especially New York, with a huge impact on tourism to the United States. The ensuing conflict in Afghanistan had a profound global impact on all facets of the tourism industry.

Destination authorities at the national level need to be supportive of the local and regional tourist authorities most directly affected by a crisis. Support may be in the form of direct grants or marketing subsidies, giving the region a higher marketing profile in advertising and marketing campaigns. The destination authorities should encourage a broader industry focus on an affected locality or region. In New York City, Delta Airlines provided 10 000 free seats to passengers from all over the United States to visit New York City. Global tour operator Insight Vacations, in conjunction with Egypt Air, value-added a one-week package in Egypt, including a tour of Luxor for the equivalent of US$1 in association with its European product as part of Egypt's recovery programme following the 1997 Luxor massacre.

Regular liaison between national, local and regional tourism authorities is vital during a crisis. In Britain, rural tourism operators and regional bodies criticised the British Tourist Authority during the foot-and-mouth crisis. They felt alienated by what they claimed was the BTA's abandonment of rural Britain in favour of promoting urban attractions during the crisis. The Croatian Ministry of Tourism sought to subsidise the marketing programs of less-visited areas of the country during its postwar recovery phase from 1996.

GOVERNMENT ADVISORIES AND TRAVEL INSURANCE

A critical and often neglected area of crisis management is the establishment and maintenance of an ongoing liaison between destination authority representatives and foreign ministries in the governments of their source markets. A destination's image and tourist accessibility can be severely damaged by government advisories which caution citizens to avoid or defer travel to a destination or describe a multitude of threats which deter travellers from considering this destination. The primary significance of travel advisories is that travel insurance coverage for that destination is based on the wording of the advisory, which greatly influences the marketability and saleability of a destination.

A destination authority has little direct influence over another country's travel advisories, but they can adopt a consultative role and be treated as a credible source of information. Few nations have a diplomatic presence in every country, and foreign ministries sometimes rely on second- and thirdhand advice in formulating a travel advisory. This sometimes results in serious inaccuracies. Effectively managing the delicate communication with foreign ministries requires consistency, persistence and a commitment to a long-term consultative relationship.

During a crisis, many destinations subject to a negative government advisory, especially from a strategically or commercially important source, react with anger and seek to overtly impose pressure or overturn the advisory. Confrontational tactics are rarely, if ever, successful. No government is prepared to defer to foreign pressures on matters relating to the perceived security of its citizens.

ALLIANCES WITH TOUR OPERATORS, AIRLINES AND HOSPITALITY INDUSTRY REPRESENTATIVES SERVICING THE DESTINATION IN SOURCE MARKETS

One of the most important tasks destination marketers undertake as an ongoing concern is the establishment, development and maintenance of business alliances with tour operators, travel agents, wholesalers, airlines, hoteliers, car rental firms and other principals which service, promote or sell the destination in key source markets. Most national, state and regional tourism offices work in conjunction with these allies at all times to promote the destination to the trade and the consumer market. During a crisis situation, these allies assume a pivotal role in assisting the marketing activities of destination authorities. They are the prime movers in facilitating a recovery.

Many destination authorities provide marketing subsidies to such principals based on product specifically directed to that destination. The policy of the Israel Government Tourism Office is typical. If an operator produces a brochure in which Israel content comprises 50 per cent of the brochure, then subsidy support will be assessed on that 50 per cent of the content.

During Israel's crisis since September 28, 2000, the percentage of subsidy support available to tour operators marketing Israel has increased. Similar practices are common among national tourist authorities. Most destination authorities ensure that their allies are regularly briefed on the situation during a crisis. Where possible, briefing visits are offered to the management of key allied organisations, providing them with necessary first-hand knowledge.

The allied organisations play a critical role in transmitting information provided by the destination authorities to their client base. In turn, destination authorities rely on their allies to assist in hosting and facilitating familiarisation visits for media, key consumer opinion leaders and influential travel industry professionals who provide a source of credible testimonials stimulating pull and push marketing programs. Cooperative relationships between destination authorities and allied principals are based on the mutuality of self-interest. If a destination is a major source of income to the airline, operator or hotel, then it is manifestly in that company's interest to do whatever it can to boost confidence and demand in the destination during and after a crisis.

The effectiveness of the alliance between the destination authorities and their principal partners is a gauge of success or failure in restoring a destination's market following a crisis. The significance of these alliances is a common element in every case study analysed in this book. However, it is important to note that the most successful and rapid recoveries occur when there is a high level of unity of purpose and a commonality of recovery policy and tactics. In the area of media management, the role of liaison between destination authority and principal allies should be as centralised as possible.

All the elements discussed in Step 2 should be incorporated by destination authorities as integral elements of a crisis contingency plan. The crisis management team must be prepared to act immediately a crisis occurs. Delays in mobilising a crisis management campaign after the crisis has begun are detrimental to all parties with a vested interest in marketing the destination.

STEP 3: PROMOTING THE DESTINATION DURING AND AFTER A CRISIS

The approach to the promotion of a destination during

and after a crisis varies according to the duration. During short-term crises such as the August 1999 Izmit earthquake in Turkey, or the 1996 Port Arthur massacre, it is appropriate to suspend destination advertising briefly and to focus on a post-crisis marketing campaign.

In both cases, the destination authorities actually redesigned their destination marketing to promote the subliminal message that the crisis had passed.

There are some cases in which the duration of a crisis situation is so lengthy that the destination authorities maintain a marketing profile despite the crisis. The underlying assumption of this approach is that the attractions of the destinations and tourism product will override the risk factors which tourists may face.

Such approaches, especially when the destination refuses to acknowledge the crisis, are accompanied by ethical problems. This strategy remains and is still practised by some destinations.In cases where the crisis is of indeterminate duration, several marketing methodologies may be employed. They include the following:

ISOLATION MARKETING

This methodology involves the separation of the trouble spot from the remainder of the destination, which is depicted as safe and attractive to visit. Israel took a further step when a specific region of the country (the Red Sea port of Eilat) was promoted as a destination in its own right. In Britain during the foot-and-mouth crisis, emphasis was placed on promoting urban and cultural attractions at the expense of rural Britain. The Turkish government, during its recovery phase after the 1999 Izmit earthquake, distinguished between the earthquake zone and the accessibility and safety of the major tourist attractions elsewhere in the country.

Segmenting the market into stalwarts, waverers and disaffected:

During an extended crisis, some destination authorities will prioritise their marketing and promotional activities and budgets according to the propensity of specific market segments to visit or support the destination during challenging periods. There are three key categories. Their naming is arbitrary but easily understood.

- *Stalwarts*: The stalwart market comprises those with a strong affinity or feeling of solidarity to the destination. During a crisis, many destination authorities seek to elicit the support of the domestic market. In the United States after September 11, 2001, the US travel industry sought to encourage American citizens to visit their own country and considerable emphasis was given to New York City. Some countries draw on specific foreign source markets with a special affinity to the destination. Israel has sought to promote solidarity tourism from Diaspora Jews and Christian Zionists. The Philippine tourism authorities encouraged expatriates to make a home visit. VFR (Visiting Friends and Relatives) tourism has been a significant market for many destinations cited here, including Croatia, the United Kingdom and South Africa, all of which have large communities of nationals or former nationals living abroad. The expatriate population is often exhorted to visit a destination during a crisis, or as an expression of solidarity during the recovery phase. The stalwart market may be deterred due to the crisis, but if the destination is marketed effectively many will continue to visit. In most cases, such marketing will appeal to their sense of affinity while overcoming their major concerns. Clearly, this group would be subject to intense advertising and promotion during a crisis situation and the recovery phase.
- *Waverers/fair weather friends*: In DESTCON 5 (normal) circumstances, this group would form the mainstay of the market to the destination. It comprises people who would normally visit or conduct business, and who have a broad sense of affinity with the destination short of an ideological, ethnic or spiritual commitment. The crisis situation casts a question over

their decision to visit the destination at the time of the perceived crisis. This grouping is normally the first to resume travel after the crisis is resolved.

In the event of a short-term crisis, destination authorities may wait until the crisis situation is deemed to be over and conduct an intensive marketing campaign to lure this market back by reassurances that the destination has returned to normal and offers of incentives.

This group represents the prime target market in the post-crisis recovery and restoration phase. In the event of a long-term crisis, this group requires attention and assurance that the region experiencing the crisis does not necessarily compromise the safety or viability of travel to those parts of the destination which normally attract this segment. In the Croatian case study, many well-informed Europeans continued to visit Croatia's northern Adriatic resorts during the 1992–95 war because they were assured of the relative safety of this region.

- *Disaffected or discretionary market*: Predominantly, this segment of the market chooses to see the destination as a holiday destination and will understandably be deterred by anything which may be perceived as complicating, undermining security or adding stress to their visit. Media reporting of a crisis situation readily influences this market and until they can be convinced that the destination is trouble-free they will choose an alternative destination. This segment is the largest travel market in the world. The dramatic slump in international travel during the 1990–91 Gulf War and the last quarter of 2001 was largely based on a twin fear of air travel *per se* (especially in 2001) and the perception that a vast region of the world was a potential danger area. This did not mean that people stopped travelling. However, during both periods travellers tended to stay closer to home than usual and favour destinations perceived as far removed from any threat. These patterns were especially evident among US and Japanese travellers.

Destination authorities have a number of options in marketing to this large group of people. Ignoring this market is *not* an option. In the midst of a crisis, destination authorities need to signal to all sectors of the market that they are committed to their destination and have the confidence to promote it. The intensity of promotion during a crisis to the discretionary market may be reduced, but a visible presence should be maintained through advertising campaigns which counter negative perceptions and highlight the positive reasons to continue travel.

A visible presence at consumer tourism promotional events where destination authorities can engage in dialogue with prospective travellers, coupled with utilising media coverage and positive testimonials, can help challenge negative perceptions. It is the disaffected/discretionary segment which provides the greatest potential for market growth, especially during the restoration and recovery phase.

Marketing campaigns isolate trouble spots from the overall appeal of the destination, and feature images that contradict the media's focus on the crisis. A special effort is required to instil the travel industry with confidence to sell and promote the destination.

INCENTIVES TO RESTORE THE MARKET

Destinations which have experienced crisis need to ensure that the recovery process is as rapid as possible. A post-crisis marketing approach requires the ability to restore market confidence in the destination through positive media coverage, maintaining an informed travel industry and wide dissemination of the recovery process to the consumer market.

During the intensive phase of the recovery process, normally within three to six months of the actual or announced 'end' of the crisis, marketing incentives should be offered. These may come in the form of discounts, value-added extras, competitions with a trip to the destination as the main prize and other marketing and promotional tactics which will stimulate demand and create a sense of urgency to return to the destination. Ideally, the incentives should cover as wide a spread of tourism product as possible, including airfares, hotel accommodation, tours, attractions and restaurants. During a crisis, every aspect of the tourism industry will have shared in the downturn and the destination authority should show a commitment to encouraging all elements to benefit from the recovery phase. The most rapid market recoveries have taken place when *all* segments in the industry are seen to be acting in concert. This was effectively illustrated in both the Fijian and Turkish case studies.

Once the restoration process is advanced, incentives are gradually phased out. This process should implemented and closely monitored in accordance with the duration of the recovery process.

MAINTAINING AN EFFECTIVE WEBSITE

Many destination authorities now realise that an effective website is one of the most cost-effective marketing tools they have. It is an especially useful marketing aid during and after a crisis. The media are heavily reliant on websites with visuals as a source of news and feature articles on tourism. The British Tourism Authority is one of many national tourist authorities which have used websites as a means to transmit crisis management information to the media, the travel industry and a growing portion of the public.

The website serves as an integrated marketing medium featuring information on sites, operators, special deals and events. The qualities of a good website are ease of access and the comprehensive and up-to-date provision of information. During a crisis and the recovery phase, the website is rapidly replacing the traditional press release as a means of updating all concerned parties.

ENSURING THAT OPINION LEADERS IN SOURCE MARKETS SEE FOR THEMSELVES

During a crisis and in a post-crisis recovery phase, the most brilliant marketing campaigns and the most comprehensive websites are no substitute for firsthand independent testimonials from opinion leaders in source markets. Influential travel writers, travel-orientated television, radio programs and influential travel industry identities reporting a positive impression from eyewitness accounts of visiting the destination, especially during the restoration phase, are an important element in recovery stimulation.

STEP 4: MONITORING RECOVERY AND ANALYSING THE CRISIS EXPERIENCE

Destination authorities need to carefully monitor statistical trends and the duration of both crisis and recovery process. In doing so, they should include as many factors as possible. Market research should be a continual task for destination authorities. Monitoring source market and segmentation within each provides an understanding of the market, and enhances the development of strategies to effectively target each market segment with the most appropriate message. For destinations in which tourism is a strategically and economically significant industry, effective market research and detailed statistical monitoring are vital.

During a crisis and recovery process, analysis of source markets which under- or over-performed during the crisis assists the destination authorities to determine the allocation of marketing resources to each market. Market research gauges the effectiveness of marketing campaigns on source markets and segments within those markets.

For all the negative aspects of a destination crisis, effective analysis of a crisis presents an opportunity for a destination authority to adjust and alter market strategies. The Tasmanian and Turkish case studies are examples in which a crisis led to a reimaging of a destination.

One critical aspect of monitoring destination crisis and restoration marketing management is understanding how other destinations managed their own crises. A common popular expression in business management is 'world's best practice'. This concept is simply applying the world's most effective practice used in a specific field of endeavour. It applies to all fields of business, and tourism marketing is no exception. Each of the following case studies includes initiatives worthy of emulation and application, and errors that should be avoided.

Destination authorities managing a crisis should undertake a regular SWOT analysis of the management of their crisis and recovery process. The analysis of their strengths, weaknesses, opportunities and threats enables them to assess their performance according to the criteria of crisis and restoration management discussed in this chapter.

Professional crisis and restoration management is based on the ability to treat these issues as an operational and management contingency. While it would be unreasonable for any destination authority to have a management scenario for all crisis typologies, they must have readily accessible plans prepared for implementation of the events they are most likely to encounter.

The Destcon ranking and implementation of the steps outlined in this chapter will be a guide to effective crisis management. The ability of a destination authority to be prepared for any crisis scenario can impact on millions of people whose livelihood are dependent on or linked to a prosperous inbound tourism industry.

Certain countries such as Vietnam have successfully created an economic boom (following extended periods of warfare) based upon heavy reliance on the tourism industry as the fulcrum of their national economic recovery. The case study of Croatia reflects the importance of a tourism restoration strategy as a core element in its national economic recovery.

Chapter 3

The Tourist Industry

Tourism is defined as the act of travel with the intentions of recreational pleasure. The World Tourism Organization defines a tourist is someone who travels at least 50 miles or 80 kilometers away from their home, for the purpose of entertainment and pleasure.

There are a variety of ways that a traveller can get to their intended destinations. Shorter distances may be reached by automobile or bus, where longer distances can be reaches by airplane, train or boat. A newer form of travel that has recently become available involves having *outer space* as an option. From a tourism viewpoint, the division of the world into tourist-generating and tourist-receiving countries is not as sharp as one might imagine.

Tourism is a give and take traffic, which presupposes an exchange of tourism arrivals between countries although to varying extents. Nevertheless, economic realities show that the industrial states with the highest standard of living (mostly Western) are the main tourist generators in the world. Statistics show that 75% of the world tourism traffic is generated by twelve Western countries only, which get at the same time about 84% of the international tourism movement. Developing countries in Africa, the Middle East, Asia and Latin America get about 7%, if we leave room for countries in-between like Japan, Australia and those of Eastern Europe.

India is a country having a great potential of tourism during vacation in the country. Tourism in the country has received a major boost in the past decade. There are lots of options in the country appealing tourists from world over. The country has right potential of tourism and attractions to captivate all kinds of tourists even the most negative tourist.

Adventure tours, cultural expeditions, wildlife expedition, beach tourism, pilgrimage tours, heritage tourism, medical tourism, monsoon tourism, rural tourism, etc are prime elements of tourism in India that enthralls a great influx of tourists from all over the world. Traveling in different parts, states and cities of India gives tourists cultural and geographical richness of the country.

Geographically, the country of India has been divided in the four parts – North India, East India, West India and South India. And part is known for own charm of culture and rich tourism potential. The country of India has 28 states and 7 union territories. Each state of India has its own charm and fascination and gives tourists something new and something extra. Rajasthan, Jammu & Kashmir, Uttar Pradesh, Uttarakhand, Himachal Pradesh, Goa, Maharashtra, Kerala, Tamil Nadu, Andhra Pradesh, are some of states of India known for their rich tourism potential.

These popular states of India offer tourists real charm of India tourism combing together culture & heritage tourism, adventure tourism, hill station tourism, beach tourism, rural tourism, monsoon tourism and medical tourism.

If you are interested in heritage of India you, travelling through Indian states like Rajasthan, Uttar Pradesh, Maharashtra, Andhra Pradesh, Kerala, etc can be exciting experience. If you are interest in wildlife tourism exploring wildlife destination like Ranthambhore, Sariska, Gir Forest, Corbett, Bharatpur, Kanha, Pench, Panna, Bandhavgarh and Periyar can be thrilling experience you will love to cherish whole life long.

If you are interested hill tourism, nature tourism or adventure tourism then go to states like Assam, Sikkim, Himachal Pradesh, Jammu & Kashmir, etc; you will have truly a memorable experience of Inde tourisme. If you are beach lovers then Goa and Kerala have some finest beaches in the world where you can make your vacation in a cheerful way enjoying awesome beach tourism and fun activities.

If you want to take a deep insight of rich culture and great Indian hospitality you should visit Rajasthan – the royal state of Rajasthan and Delhi with the capital city New Delhi. Rajasthan is widely known for it rich culture, great hospitality and glorious past. Delhi has some of magnificent monuments like Red Fort, Jama Masjid. Taj Mahal in Agra is not to be missed attraction of Inde voyage.

Varanasi, Pushkar, Ajmer, Amritsar, Vaishno Devi, Tirupati, Shirdi, Khajuraho, Deoghar, Rajgir, Bodhgaya, Konark, etc are popular destinations known for their religious significance. Kerala, Goa, and Uttarakhand have some of world class ayurvedic and spa resorts offering excellent accommodation and ayurvedic and spa experience as well with modern amenities.

The royal state of Rajasthan has some of world famous heritage hotels where tourists find ethnic & age old ambiance with modern amenities. In general, India is a perfect destination for perfect vacation with right tourism potential. And tourism in India during India vacation never fails to grab the attentions and steal the heart of tourists and vacationers.

TRAVEL ELEMENTS

When traveling, tourists must keep in mind and plan for:

- Accomodation: a place to stay while traveling, whether it is a hotel, motel, apartment, resort, inn, hostel or guest house.
- Foods and beverages.
- Tours: getting to know the surrounding area that has been visited. This can be achieved through a walking tour, bus tour, coach tour, boat tour, even by helicopter.
- Souvenirs: bringing home a memory from the trip, such as a postcard, shot glass, keychain or snow globe.

Other elements of tourism might involve insurance, safety, security, culture, language and currency exchange. Many tourists travel for a number of reasons, including relaxation, escape, adventure, as well as experiencing new and different cultures.

Cultural heritage tourism or heritage tourism is a niche element of the overall tourism spectrum. It is meant to gain an appreciation of the past or something we have got in legacy. It is one of the oldest forms of travel, and involves heritages of all kinds – colonial heritage, urban renewal, religious tourism, genealogy, industrial heritage, and ethnicity. Thus a visit to Cellular Jail in Port Blair, or to Haldighati and Ellora Caves constitute heritage tourism in the Indian context.

Heritage tourism is difficult to segregate from other elements of tourism. Tourists interested in other areas, like adventure, religion and leisure also visit different Indian heritage sites; with monuments like Taj Mahal, Humayun's Tomb, Red Fort, Sarnath, Kaziranga, Tirupati, Varanasi, Rameshwaram, and Ajanta Caves being quite popular. UNESCO has identified 27 heritage sites in India as world heritage, and has collaborated with state government authorities to develop several themed itineraries, like linking Buddhist holy places, legends of Shiva, yoga, and ayurvedic healing.

More than five million foreigners visited India in 2007, and out of these, at least, three million visited heritage sites in India. Number of domestic tourists outnumbered foreign travelers by more than 60 times in 2007. The share of cultural heritage tourism in the overall tourism figures in India, be it domestic or foreign travelers, is over 60 per cent, according to various estimates.

India needs quite a lot of effort and professional touch to keep its heritage sites intact. While government authorities have been mainly responsible for this, heritage management in India has started seeing the participation of big players like Tata, Oberoi, Indian Oil Corporation, and others, on the lines of European countries and the US. Heritage hotels, another colour in the spectrum of heritage tourism, are quite popular among tourists, with celebrities like Amitabh Bachchan and Richard Gere also voicing their preference for them. Barring most of major hotel players like Taj, Oberoi, and ITC, there are several heritage hotels owned by the descendants of former rulers and aristocrats.

Not everything is, however, honky dory in the field of heritage tourism. Services at heritage sites are nowhere compared to those at similar sites in countries like Italy, UK, China and Spain. Foreign tourists often feel cheated as they pay several times more entrance fees compared to Indians. They often feel disappointed by the shabby treatment they receive at the hands of the vendors, whose only agenda seems to be to extract the maximum possible money from the tourists. Tourists are also miffed at the lower levels of services offered by several heritage hotels, tour operators, transporters and others.

Be it the exquisite marble inlay work of the Taj Mahal or the titillating sculptures of the Khajuraho temples or the excellent fusion of science and art in Konark Sun Temple, Indian heritage sites manifest their richness everywhere. Taj Mahal, the most popular heritage of India, alone attracts some 2.5 million tourists every year.

According to various estimates, heritage tourism contributes well over 60 per cent to the overall share of tourists in India, both domestic and foreigners. An interesting aspect of this, however, is that almost 80 per cent of foreign tourists visiting India restrict themselves to the Golden Triangle (Delhi-Jaipur-Agra) and Rajasthan, areas quite rich in heritage monuments.

This comes as a surprise considering places like Bihar, Tamil Nadu, Kerala, Andhra Pradesh, Uttar Pradesh, Madhya Pradesh have so many beautiful heritage monuments. This, however, also spells huge untapped opportunities heritage tourism presents. Even if a fraction of the potential of these states is tapped, it can do wonders. Aditya Nath, managing director, Apass India Leisure Solutions, a Delhi-based tour operator, says, "A package for the Golden Triangle can easily be sold.

Everyone wants to make easy money. Convincing tourists to visit other places will require more efforts." Nath says, "Rajasthan looked at heritage tourism as an opportunity to shed its BIMARU (Bihar, Madhya Pradesh, Rajasthan, and UP) tag. Better marketing strategy backed by focus on infrastructure development and creating safe environment for tourists in the state have proved the differentiator."

Rajasthan has been systematic in promoting its heritage sites. It has been flexible with time as well. While till a few years ago the state was busy promoting better known places like Jaipur, Udaipur and Jaisalmer, now attempts are successfully being made to market lesser known places, often in hinterlands, like Sawai Madhopur, Kumbhalgarh, Kota, Sariska, Alwar, Bundi, Barmer, and Dungarpur.

Required Factors

In order to travel, a person must possess four essentials:

- Disposable Income: money that can be spent on pleasure items.
- Time.
- Means of transport.
- Accommodation arrangements.

The history behind tourism and travel first referred to wealthy people who were interested in visiting distant parts of the world in order to view historic buildings or other works of art, as well as to learn a new language or sample foreign foods. The terms tourist and tourism were first recognized in 1937 by the League of Nations, whose definition involved a person who traveled abroad for more than 24 hours.

TYPES OF TOURISM

There are different types of tourism that can be enjoyed. Some are listed below:

- Adventure tourism: involves travel to rugged regions so that tourists can participate in adventure sports such as hiking or climbing mountains.
- Cultural Tourism: involves visiting historical or intersting cities, such as Paris, Shanghai, Beijing or Warsaw. This is when tourists engage in cultural experiences, like visiting an art museum, theater or opera.

- Ecotourism: involves traveling that does not pose a threat to the environment, such as safariing in Kenya.
- Gambling Tourism: visiting destinations for the purpose of gambling, to places such as Las Vegas, Atlantic City or Monte Carlo.
- Sport Tourism: involves travel with the thought of a particular sport in mind, such as a ski trip during the winter season.

World events, the economy, tastes and trends and the technology of travel—all of these and more have an effect on global tourism. And despite a decline in American travel in recent years, the website peopleandplanet.net reports, "By some measure, tourism may already be the world's largest industry, with annual revenue approaching $500 billion." A major in tourism will get you a foot in the door to this ever-booming industry. And the sky's the limit—quite literally—on where you go from there. Tourism majors aim to discover the world's top destinations and how best to encourage people to visit them.

From the dreamy, steamy islands of the South Pacific to Sweden's Icehotel, you'll learn how to make guests feel welcome and enjoy a safe and memorable stay. A tourism major covers the whole spectrum of travel—you'll study everything from the booking of flights to facilitating operations at a resort hotel.

You'll use the tourism industry's most prevalent electronic databases and discover how to navigate other travel-related computer programs and systems.

Count on learning how to market and sell travel destinations and products, including how to promote tourism in new places and how to sustain interest in classic tourist destinations. In addition, you'll examine how Internet technology is affecting the Tourism industry and how to use this technology most advantageously. Your tourism major should also touch on the effect tourism has on the environment—and how certain aspects of the industry are working to minimize those effects.

Tourism is more global than ever and this major will

explore the role it plays in the world—how it affects cities and countries both economically and culturally. You'll learn where the industry has been and where it might go in the future. (Is a moon resort really viable? *You'll* be able to tell *us*.) Before you graduate, you should be a pro at giving knowledgeable and friendly customer service and managing all aspects of the travel experience. After college, you'll have the skills you need to pursue a career for an airline, a travel agency, or many other sorts of travel service organization.

Tourism is an interdisciplinary major and your course work will draw from accounting, marketing, communication and other business courses, as well as courses in geography and specific elements of tourism.

Tourism Overview in 2005-06

Tourism in India has registered significant growth in the recent years. In 1951, International Tourist Arrivals stood at around 17 thousand only while the same has now gone up to 3.91 million in 2005. The upward trend is expected to remain firm in the coming years. Tourism is the third largest net earner of foreign exchange for the country recording earnings of US $ 5731 million in 2005, a growth of 20.2% over 2004. it is also one of the sectors which employs the largest number of manpower.

The first ever Tourism Satellite Accounts for India compiled by NCAER for the year 2002-03 showed that tourism employed 38.8 million persons, directly and indirectly, which was 8.3% of the total employment in the country and who contributed 5.8% of the GDP. These figures are estimated to have increased to 41.85 million employed in 2003-04 with a GDP contribution of 5.9%. Various studies have also shown that tourism generates the highest employment per unit of investment for the skilled, semi-skilled and unskilled. The World Travel and Tourism council (WTTC) has identified India as one of the foremost growth centers in the world in the coming decade.

While the growth in tourism has been impressive, India's share in total global tourism arrivals and earnings in quite insignificant. It is an accepted fact that India has tremendous potential for development of tourism. The diversity of India's natural and cultural richness provides the basis of a wide range of tourist products and experiences, which embrace business, leisure, culture, adventure, spirituality, eco-tourism and many other pursuits.

Apart from acknowledging the traditionally recognized advantages of developing tourism for the promotion of national integration, international understanding, earning of foreign exchange and vast employment generation, it can play a major role in furthering the socio-economic objectives of nation.

The Ministry of Tourism adopted a multi-pronged approach in order to achieve this growth. Providing a congenial atmosphere for tourism development, strengthening the tourism infrastructure and hospitality related services, integrated development of identified destinations and circuits, integrating elements of tourism, emphasizing on culture and clean civic life marketing of tourism products a focused manner along with a branding exercise and positioning India as a high value destination in the new key markets and giving thrust on the human resource development activities have been the hallmarks of this strategy.

The focus of product development in the States also underwent a change by enhanced outlays for 'destination development up to an amount of Rs. 5 crore and 'circuit development' up to an amount of Rs. 8 crore. A new proposal was moved to allocate up to Rs. 50 crore for individual destinations with high tourist footfalls in order to totally redesign the experience of the tourist through greater organization and provision of civic facilities

The important initiatives taken by the Government to improve the flow of foreign tourists into the country and thereby increasing the country's share in the world tourism included the following:-

- Beginning of cruise tourism by an international shipping firm.
- Direct approach to the consumers through electronic

and print media through the "Incredible India" Campaign called "Colours of India".

- Creation of World Class Collaterals.
- Centralized Electronic Media Campaign.
- An integrated campaign in South East Asia to promote Buddhist sites in India.
- Direct co-operative marketing with tour operators and wholesalers overseas.
- Greater focus in the emerging markets particularly in the region of China, South Korea, Japan and South East Asia.
- Participation in over 185 Trade Fairs and Exhibitions all over the world.
- Optimizing Editorial PR and Publicity.
- Use of Internet and Web marketing.
- Generating Tourist Publications.
- Re-enforcing hospitality programmes including grant of air passages to invite media personnel and tour operators on familiarization tours to India to get first hand knowledge on various tourism products.
- Launching of Road Shows in key source markets of Europe, America, South East Asia and the Middle East.
- Focusing on growth of hotel infrastructure particularly budget hotels.
- Enhancing connectivity through augmentation of air capacity and improving road infrastructure to major tourist attractions.
- Introduction of the Medical Visa.
- Guidelines formulated for the classification of Time Share Resorts, Serviced Apartments, Guest Houses and Home Stay accommodation.

Impressive strides were made in the field of Human Resource Development. The Institute of Hotel Management continued to be the backbone of manpower training for hospitality industry in the country.

The Diploma courses offered by these Institute were upgraded to a Degree course. The scheme of 'Capacity

Building for Service Providers' also continued to be implemented for providing basic skills to unorganized sector service providers engaged in activities having direct interaction with the tourists. The first Phase of the "Atithi Devo Bhava" Programme was completed during which over 26,000 stakeholders in seven cities were trained.

The allocation of plan funds was raised from Rs.500.00 crore in 2004-05 to Rs.786 crore in 2005-06. The new priorities and initiatives have been actuated with a sound backing of a National Tourism Policy. With the significant positive trends in the year 2005, the Tourism industry is poised for a brighter 2006.

URBAN TOURISM

The demand for travel to cities has greatly increased over the last few decades. While many travel for business or convention purposes, others are traveling on leisure time to learn about other cultures, to develop their specific interests and to seek entertainment. But what exactly are the specific elements of the urban tourism product that determine the attractiveness of a city for visitors?

Christopher Law examines the relationship between tourism and urban areas. He distinguishes between primary, secondary and additional elements of a city's tourism resources. Primary elements provide the main reasons why tourists visit cities.

Secondary elements such as accommodation and shopping as well as additional elements like transportation or tourist information are also very important for the success of urban tourism, but are not the main attractor of visitors. The following are key elements that can enhance the visitor friendliness in urban areas.

Historic attributes of buildings, streetscapes, neighbourhoods and special landmarks emphasize the local character of an area. Historic districts are generally very pedestrian friendly with a mix of attractions and amenities that are easily accessible. Beyond their educational component, they also generate a sense of place and provide the urban visitor with memorable experiences. Thus, cities blessed with heritage as a selling point are advantaged when looking to develop their tourism product.

Approximately 80 % of Europe's population lives in towns and cities, making Europe the world's most built-up continent and the urban question one of the major issues for future years. Urban conurbations mirror the problems that face European society as a whole: traffic gridlock, pollution, lawlessness and unemployment. They are not just the main places in which wealth is created and the focus of cultural and social development, however, but places where people live and work, shop and enjoy leisure pursuits.

Renewed interest in urban tourism since the beginning of the 1980s has brought about a sharp upturn in this kind of tourism. Various interlinked factors have undoubtedly played a part in this: the need to breathe life back into and rehabilitate the historic centres of towns and cities, wider-ranging and more diversified cultural pursuits, consumers' interest in the heritage and urban development and their search for things to do and for spending opportunities. The fact that people are taking more, but shorter holidays, the advent of the single market and the general increase in mobility have also helped to build up urban tourism in Europe.

The broader range of activities and leisure pursuits that visitors are seeking is extending what is on offer. This diversification is also due to a growing awareness of tourism among political decision-makers who are increasingly keen to promote it as a key factor in economic development bringing wealth and employment. Tourism is being seen as a cornerstone of a policy of urban development that combines a competitive supply able to meet visitors' expectations with a positive contribution to the development of towns and cities and the well-being of their residents.

Integrated quality management (IQM) offers an opportunity to act on both these fronts: economic development, on the one hand, and urban development, on the other. It does this by offering visitors a unique and original experience and by trying as far as possible to satisfy residents' rightful aspirations for harmonious economic and social development which shows concern for the environment.

Taking 15 case studies of European urban tourist destinations as a starting point, this publication highlights factors that have helped to make such strategies successful, looks at methods and procedures and shows what resources have been implemented and what results have been obtained. This publication is for everyone, whether in the public or private sector, involved in managing urban destinations.

Not just those in charge of or providers of tourist services or products in destinations, but also those responsible for urban development (planning and urban development departments, development and environmental agencies, etc.). The case studies and recommendations may also provide food for thought for local, regional and national public authorities, the tourism industry and in particular SMEs which are the driving force behind and the cornerstones of an urban destination's quality initiatives.

The publication also looks at the ways in which tourism enterprises can help individually or collectively to improve a destination's quality. Urban destinations from the whole of the European Economic Area that are being promoted as tourist destinations, have been studied. They include small towns and large cities, towns with a tradition of tourism and towns where tourism is a more recent development, as well as towns active in various urban tourism markets (cultural cities, leisure centres, business centres, trade fair and conference towns). Residential towns and towns with fewer than 20 000 inhabitants were excluded as case studies.

This publication is the result of a study conducted by the Belgian contractor OGM ('Organisation Gestion Marketing') for the Tourism Unit of the Enterprise Directorate-General of the European Commission. Information gathered from European, national and regional organisations and an assessment of the replies to a self-evaluation questionnaire sent out to 171 urban destinations in the European Economic Area provided a starting point for identifying and selecting the 15 case studies.

A panel of experts initially selected a long list of 28 destinations which, following further examination, were reduced to a final list of 15 destinations for detailed study (in particular through a visit to the destination). The 15 destinations finally selected reflect the diversity of European urban tourist destinations from the point of view of their location, size, openness to and reliance on tourism and the progress that has been made with quality initiatives and the ways in which such initiatives can be implemented, as well as their objectives and strategies. While these may not be unique situations, they do illustrate real experiences and can in no way be considered to be models.

Waterfronts

Not matter if it is for transportation, industry, or entertainment, urban waters have always attracted people out of necessity or pleasure. Lately, cities and private investors are paying increased attention to waterfronts because they pose a variety of opportunities for tourism, economic and community development.

San Antonio (TX) is probably one of the most classic examples in the US for successful riverfront development. San Antonio's capitalized on the city's main attraction, the water, which creates aesthetic and entertainment value while at the same time generating tourist dollars for the city.

Convention Centers and Exhibitions

Convention Centers and Exhibitions are often regarded as one of the staples of city tourism. In some cities, up to forty per cent of those staying overnight have come for this type of business tourism. Convention Centers and Exhibitions are perceived to be strong growth sectors in which the visitor spends an above average amount and which operate for most of the year.

Employment, publicity, image improvement and urban regeneration are benefits that generally justify the big financial investment for those centers. Besides these advantages, it is important to remember that the conference business cannot be separated from the rest of the tourism industry particularly because most participants are also seeking urban amenities in an exciting environment.

Festivals and Events

Festivals and Events have become an increasingly popular means for cities to boost tourism. They range in size and scale from one time events like the World Exhibition or the Olympics to annual events like Folk Music Festivals or Gallery Nights. Spectacles like that are important, however, their impact upon the city's tourist industry depends on the attendance and the type and number of outside visitors

Special Visitor Districts

Special visitor districts are places where a combination of visitor attractions such as cultural, amusements, or sports facilities is clustered in one location. These districts are not merely a strategy to attract tourists and provide better amenities for local residents, but one that can be used to facilitate urban renewal.

Special visitor districts enable visitors to move easily from one attraction to another and, if this is known in advance, may encourage more visitors to come to the city due to a critical mass of attractions.

In many parts of the world, special visitor districts have been the anchor for regenerated dockland zones. In Baltimore, for instance, the Inner Harbor was planned with three such attractions: an aquarium, a science museum and a viewing platform at the top of the World Trade Centre. According to the Baltimore Area Convention and Visitors Association, the total number of out-of-town visitors was almost 12 million. These guests spent an estimated $2.9 billion.

Tourism Employees

Friendliness is probably one of the most important sociocultural features of the tourism product. Professionalism and excellence of service offered to visitors start with friendliness. Key factors in visitor's decision to visit a place are friendly, hospitable people. That's what people remember and that's what they come back for. Responsibility for the "Welcome", however, does not rest solely with tourism employees.

Each and every person working and living in the city, who has contact with visitors, should market themselves to the kind of visitors needed to bring more dollars to restaurants, hotels, museum and other entertaining places. If urban tourism wants to continue to grow and prosper, everyone, from the cab driver to the store-owner and the resident, should act as a tourism agent and provide their guests with positive memorable experiences.

Retail and Catering Facilities

Although shopping and restaurants are regarded as a secondary element of tourism, it is still an important part of the tourism economy since visitors spend a significant amount of time and money on shopping and eating. Shopping, for instance, has for some visitors become a leisure activity where they tour stores with no specific purpose in mind.

For others, it is more like a sport where they go from store to store and see if there are different goods on sale at the destination compared to home. Cities that add retail stores or restaurants to their downtown or to special facilities like airports, train stations, or casinos, experience positive economic impacts that not only apply to one location, but spill over and trickle down to other areas of the city.

REQUIREMENT OF VISA

Foreigners desirous of visiting India can do so after obtaining a visa from the Indian Mission in the country of their residence. They should posses a valid National passport-except in the case of nationals of Bhutan and Nepal, who may carry only suitable means of identification. Any foreigner who wants to enter into India must have a valid visa affixed on his or her passport. This can be obtained from the Indian Consulate in your country. Foreign nationals of Indian origin, their spouses and children can obtain visas from the Consulate. Foreign nationals of Indian origin, their spouses and children can obtain Entry Visas valid upto 10 years.

Tourist Visas can be obtained for six months, one year and 10 years. Visas of the appropriate type should be obtained by students, businessmen, journalists and others who want to visit India for professional purposes.

All types of visas are valid for the indicated period from the date of issue (and not repeat not from the date of first entry into India). Post-dated visas are not issued at any case. All applicants for Entry and Tourist visas are required to fill out an application form and provide one recent passport size photograph. Applicants for Business, Research, Journalist and some other types of visas are required to submit two forms duly filled in and two pictures.

Visas can also be issued to persons who normally do not live in the jurisdiction of this Consulate (this also includes people holding Tourist/Business visas) after obtaining clearance from the Indian Mission under whose jurisdiction the applicant normally resides. This however takes a few weeks. The applicant may, however, pay an additional charge for clearance by fax or telex.

Persons desiring to go to a restricted area should fill in special forms and apply well in advance as clearances are required before a permit can be issued to travel to these places. It takes at least 6 to 8 weeks to receive the Government of India's clearances in such cases.

Firm letters of admission from Universities, recognized Colleges or Educational Institutions in India are required for issuance of Regular Student Visas. Applicants are also required to produce satisfactory evidence of financial support. In case of admission in a medical or a para-medical course, the applicant has also to produce a 'No Objection Certificate' from the Ministry of Health, Government of India, to obtain a Student Visa.

Applicants for Student Visas who want to pursue graduate or post-graduate studies in Engineering/Technology are required to produce a similar 'No Objection Certificate' from the Ministry of Human Resource Development

(Department of Education). Provisional Student Visas for a period of 6 months can however be issued on production of a Provisional Admission Certificate issued by a University/ recognized Educational Institution in India. It can be changed to a regular student visa in India itself subject to completion of the formalities listed above. However, no change of institute/ purpose is allowed.

The entry of foreigners, stay, movements and departure is regulated by the Acts passed by the Indian Parliament and rules framed hereunder by the Central Government from time to time. Foreigners who enter India should have a valid passport, visa or other accredited travel documents. All foreigners should enter India through authorized check post or airport only. They are subjected to immigration check at the airport or check post.

All foreigners who enter India or depart from India either by air or sea shall furnish a true statement of particulars setting it out in form 'D' embarkation card. The civil authority under Foreigners Order 1948 has powers to impose restrictions on the movement of any foreigner in India.

The authority can also refuse a foreigner entry into India if he/she does not posses a valid passport, or is insane or is suffering from any infectious disease or has been convicted for an extradition offence or if his/her entry is prejudicial to the interest of the country.

All foreigners who desire to stay in India beyond 180 days have to register themselves at the Foreigners Registration Office within two weeks of their arrival. Those who intended to stay for less than 180 days but ended up staying longer also have to register themselves.

Any violation of this provision makes them liable for prosecution under section 5 of the Registration of Foreigners Act, 1939.

The State Registration Officer in the State capital functions as the liaison office between the Foreigners Registration Officers (FRO) and the government. The Foreigner Registration Officer is the primary agency to regulate the registration, movement, stay, departure and also for recommending the extension of stay in India. A foreigner who enters India on a valid visa shall report before the Foreigners Registration Officer within two weeks of arrival and get himself registered.

He has to produce 6 sets of photos, passport copies, visa page, etc. Thereafter the FRO will issue registration certificate and a residential permit upto the validity of the visa period. A foreigner coming to India on a tourist visa valid for 6 months need not register his name. However this depends on the condition noted on the visa.

Children of foreigners under 16 years of age residing in India need not register their name as they are exempted from Registration (Exemption) Order 1957. But they will be issued a residential permit for their stay in India. They should also obtain extension for their stay from time to time.

Foreigners who wish to stay in India beyond the visa period should apply for extension of stay 90 days before his Residential Permit is due to expire. The Central Government has delegated limited powers to the FROs to grant extension of stay to foreigners and in all other cases the following documents are to be sent to the State government.

- Application duly filled and signed by the foreigner in duplicate.
- Photostat copy of the valid passport along with visa page.
- HIV certificate issued by a recognized medical institution.
- Copy of the registration certificate and residential permit.
- Financial guarantee given by an Indian citizen on a Rs. 10 stamp paper.
- Photostat copy of the bank account and remittance and letter given by the bank manager.
- Police report in English issued by the jurisdictional police station where the foreigner resides.
- Receipt for having paid the prescribed fee to the RBI under head of account OAS-0070.
- In case of businessmen, the agreement between the firm and the Government of India.

- In case of employment visa, letter of consent of the firm where the foreigner is employed.

Exemption from Registration

Foreigners coming to India on tourist visas for 180 days or a shorter period are not required to register themselves with any authority in India. They can move about freely in the country, except to restricted/protected areas and prohibited places.

Individuals without nationality or of undetermined nationality (stateless person; IRO refugees, persons receiving legal or political protection, holder of Nansen passport etc.) should have valid passport, identity documents or sworn affidavit with visa for which they should apply at least two months in advance.

LAND PERMIT FACILITY

Tourists may note that no Landing Permit Facility is available to any foreign tourist landing without a visa. A limited facility exists only for group tours consisting of 4 or more members and sponsored by a travel agency recognized by the Government of India. Children below the age of 12 years of foreigners of Indian origin may be granted a landing permit by the Immigration authorities up to a period of 90 days to see their relatives, in case they happen to come without a visa.

Tourist Group

A tourist group arriving by air, ship or by a chartered or scheduled flight may be granted a collective landing permit for a period upto 30 days by the Immigration authorities on landing, provided the group is sponsored by a recognized travel agency, a predrawn itinerary is presented along with details of passport etc. of the members and the travel agency gives an undertaking to conduct the group together.

Extension of Visa

Facility exists for an extension of tourist visa beyond six months. In such a case, however, the foreigners' Registration

Officer throughout the country and obtain an extension of visa from him. All formalities of registration under the law would have to be fulfilled.

Other Types of Visas

If a foreigner wishes to come to India for a purpose other than tourism, he should come after obtaining an appropriate visit out of the following:

- *Business Visa*: A foreigner can obtain from an Indian Embassy abroad a multiple entry business visa valid for one year or five year but with a cumulative stay in India of not more than 180 days, provide he wishes to come for some business.
- *Student Visa*: A student visa can be obtained from the Indian Embassy on the production of proof of administration and means of sustenance while in India, etc. The visa is valid for one year but is extended in India for the duration of the course.
- *Conference Visa*: Delegates coming to attend International Conferences in India can be granted "Conference Visas" to cover the conference as well as tourism in India. Delegates are advised to apply to the Indian Embassies well in advance.
- Foreigners wishing to undertake trekking, botanical expeditions, mountaineering expeditions, canoe-rafting, etc., in a team may be granted visas for the required duration on presentation of full details of he touring members, nature of the event, area to be visited and any other tourist information that may be asked for by the Indian Embassy.
- Sports teams or individual sportsmen wishing to participate in international sports events being held in India may apply to an Indian Embassy/Mission for the grant of visa for the necessary duration. Requests for such visas may be made well in advance.
- Foreign journalists, media men, documentary and feature filmmakers may obtain necessary visas after due formalities from the Indian Embassy.

- *Yoga*: Visa for study of Yoga, Vedic Culture, dance, music etc. Foreigners wishing to come to India to study these subjects are required to apply well in advance with all necessary particulars. The Indian Embassies may grant visas for a period of one year which may be extended on an annual basis in India.

CURRENCY REGULATIONS

There are no restrictions on the amount of foreign currency or travellers' cheques a tourist may bring into India provided he makes a declaration in the Currency Declaration Form given to him on arrival. This will enable him not only to exchange the currency brought in but also to take the unspent currency out of India on departure. Cash, bank notes and travellers' cheques up to U.S.$10,000 or equivalent need not be declared at the time of entry.

Any money in form of travellers' cheque, draft, bills, cheques, etc. in convertible currencies which tourists wish to convert into Indian currency should be exchanged only through authorized money changers and banks who will issue an encashment certificate.

This certificate is required at the time of re-conversion of any unspent money into foreign currency. Tourists are warned that changing money through unauthorized persons is not only illegal but also an offence under Foreign Exchange Regulations Act 1973.It also involves the risk of receiving counterfeit currency.

Customs Formalities and Regulations

The usual duty free regulations apply for India.

- Alcoholic liquor and wine upto 1 litre each.
- 200 cigarettes or 50 cigars or 250 gms. of tobacco.

Visitors are generally required to make oral baggage declaration in respect of baggage and foreign currency in their possession. Visitors in possession of more than US$ 10,000 or equivalent thereof in the shape of travellers' cheque, bank notes currency notes are required to obtain a Currency declaration Form before leaving Customs. They should fill in the

Disembarkation Card handed over to them by the airlines during the course of the flight. There are two channels for Custom clearance:

Green Channel: for passengers not having any dutiable articles or unaccompanied baggage.

Red Channel: for passengers having dutiable articles or unaccompanied baggage or high value articles to be entered on Tourist Baggage RE-Export Form.

IMMIGRATION

Passport: Citizen of all countries require a valid national passport or valid travel documents and valid visa granted by Indian Mission abroad for entering India Except Nepalese or Bhutanese citizens who when proceedings from their respective countries need no passport or visa should possess suitable documents for their identification.

Illegal immigration is a serious political problem in India, with widely differing estimates of the number of such migrants. In places this has led to outbreaks of xenophobic violence, particularly against those perceived to be Bangladeshi.

In 2003, former Indian Defence Minister George Fernandes alleged that there are there are more than 20,000,000 illegal Bangladeshi immigrants in India. The Government of Bangladesh claims that "there is not a single Bangladeshi migrant in India".

It is extremely hard to distinguish between illegal Bangaldeshis and local Bengali speakers. The Hindu has reported a case where Bangladeshis have been able to secure ration and voter identity cards.

Assam spent Rs.1.7 billion between January 2001 and September 2006, which resulted in identification of 9,149 foreigners, only 1,864 could be deported back to Bangladesh. This amounts to Rs. 180,000 spent to deport an illegal Bangladeshi. India is building a fence along its entire border with Bangladesh.

The Centre for Women and Children Studies estimated in 1998 that 27,000 Bangladeshis have been forced into prostitution in India. Ahmedabad Crime Branch (ACB) has investigated a prostitution racket run by a Bangladeshi couple living in Ahmedabad. It believed over 500 women had been coerced into prostitution by illegal Bangladeshi agents in Gujarat.

Indian newspapers reported that "the state government has reports that illegal Bangladeshi migrants have trickled into parts of rural Bengal, including Nandigram, over the years, and settled down as sharecroppers with the help of local Left leaders. Though a majority of these immigrants became tillers, they lacked documents to prove the ownership of land".

Allegations exist that other parties such as the Bharatiya Janata Party and the Indian National Congress have discriminated against Bengali-speaking Muslims.. Even though it must be noted that the number of Bengali-speaking Muslims has increased multifold since independence, suggesting that many of these Bengali-speaking Muslims are maybe illegal Bangladeshi immigrants.

In August 2008, the Delhi High Court dismissed a petition by a Bangladeshi national against her deportation. The High Court ruled that the illegal Bangladeshi immigrants "pose a danger to India's internal security".

Arrival Formalities

If the visa for stay in India is more than 180 days, registration Certificate and Residential Permit should be obtained from the nearest Foreigners' Registration Office within 7 days of arrival. Personal appearance is absolutely necessary at the time of registration, extension or exit as required by the Law of the Land. Four photographs/pictures are also required for registration. The foreigners are registered at Foreigners' Registration.

The foreigners registered at Foreigner's Registration Office are required to report change of their addresses. Departure from India All persons except nationals of Nepal and Bhutan leaving by roads or rail have to fill an Embarkation Card at the time of departure. All tourist visitors holding Registration Certificate are endorsed by the appropriate registration authorities before departure. Registration Certificates and Residential permits are to be surrendered at the Registration Office.

None for holders of Entry Visas (Except tourist/Transit Visa Holders). All visitors holding Registration Certificate have to obtain, before departure, exit endorsement from the Registration Officer of the district in which they were registered

INCOME TAX CLEARANCE

If a person not domiciled in India intends to stay in the country for more than 120 days, an Income Tax Clearance' certificate is required in order to leave the country. This document will prove that the person's stay in India was financed by his own money and not by working or selling his goods.

The foreign section of the Income Tax Department at Delhi, Calcutta, Madras and Bombay issues these certificates on being shown the person's passport, visa extension form and the currency exchange receipts, which have been used by the person.

FOREIGN TRAVEL TAX

Passenger embarking on journey to any place outside India from a Customs airport/seaport will have to pay a Foreign Travel Tax (FTT) of Rs. 500 and Rs. 250 on journeys to Afghanistan, Bangladesh, Bhutan, Burma, Nepal, Pakistan, Sri Lanka and the Maldives. No tax is payable on journeys performed by ship from Rameshwaram to Talaimanar and in case of transit passenger, provided they do not leave the Customs barrier.

Transit passenger travelling by air who have to leave the airport on account of mechanical trouble provided they continue their journey by the same aircraft and the same flight number by which they arrive are also exempted from FTT. Transit sea passenger leaving the ship for sightseeing, shopping etc, during the ship's call at any of the Indian ports will not be required to pay FTT.

INLAND AIR TRAVEL TAX

An Inland Air Travel Tax is leviable at 10 per cent of the

basic fare on all passengers paying their airfare in foreign exchange will be exempted from payment of this tax.

In addition infants, cancer patients, blind persons and invalids (those on stretchers) are also exempted from this tax after fulfilling certain conditions stipulated in the relevant notifications.

GUIDES

Trained English speaking guides are available at fixed charges at all important tourist centres. The Government of India Tourist Offices can be contacted by tourists for these. French, Italian, Spanish, German, Russian and Japanese speaking guides are available at some cities.

Please consult the nearest Government of India Tourist Office. Unapproved guides are not permitted to enter protected monuments and tourists are, therefore, advised to ask for the services of guides who carry a certificate issued by the Department of Tourism/Archaeological Survey of India.

HEALTH REGULATIONS

Foreign tourists should be in possession of Yellow Fever Vaccination Certificate conforming to International Health Regulations, if they are originating or transitting through Yellow Fever endemic countries (Africa and South America).

INTERNATIONAL AIRPORT FACILITIES

The international airports offer a range of services ensuring that the traveller on business can continue working while waiting to catch an international connection, or when transferring between international flights.

These include gourmet restaurants, business centres and are equipped with state of the art equipment including word processors and telefax. Airports also provide the tourist with such facilities for leisure as duty-free and handicrafts shopping, informal snack bars, nursery and baby care rooms and even an art gallery. Duty-free prices in the airport shops are very competitive, offering you bargains on international merchandise.

INLAND TRAVELS

Indian Airlines

Ranked as the world's second largest domestic IATA airlines outside USA, Indian Airlines commands a large and modern fleet of A300, A320 and B737 aircraft. Indian Airlines (IC) network, spanning the country's 3,000 km from Leh in the north to Thiruvananthapuram in the south and about the same from east to west, covers all important places of tourist interest linking 55 cities in India and 17 in fourteen neighbouring countries: Afghanistan, Bangladesh, Maldives, Nepal, Pakistan, Singapore, Sri Lanka and Thailand. Also included is Kuwait and Kuala Lumpur.

Fares: IC offers a variety of special fares aimed at encouraging tourist travel within the country. These include:

Discover India, US$750, permits unlimited travel within India for 21 days.

India Wonderfares, US$300, permits unlimited travel within India for 21 days.

South India Excursion, 30 per cent discount on US$ tariff for travel on specific South Indian Sectors.

Youth Fare, 25 per cent off on US$ tariff for all tourists between the ages of 12 and 30.

Reservations: Reservations on IC can be made from any where abroad in a matter of minutes through the SITA Airlines Communications System which is linked to the airline's Real Time Computer Reservation System.

IC has inter-line agreements with over 120 airlines worldwide and the offices of any of these airlines or their agents have been enabled to issue tickets on IC flights. To facilitate group tourists in obtaining reservations, IC is guaranteeing confirmed seats to all foreign tour groups of 10 or more passengers provided booking is requested more than four months in advance on all Airbus and selected B737 tourist services.

Private Airlines

Jet Airways and Sahara Airlines are two major private

carriers. They operate metro routes, tourist circuits and also offer special fares to discover India. Smaller airlines like Archana and Jagsons in the north and Gujarat Airways in the west provided feeder services to smaller towns. Jet and Sahara have either their own offices or representative offices in major countries abroad.

Railways

The Indian Railways system is the largest in Asia and the second largest it the world among systems under a single management. Daily, ore than 11 million people or more than 1.4 per cent of India's population board the trains.

Everybody more than 1 million tonnes of freight traffic are lifted by Indian Railways. Nearly 11,000 trains crisis-cross about 62,500 kilometers of rail route, connecting 7,084 railway stations scattered over the far-flung parts of the vast country.

Indrail Pass

Indian Railways have introduced the facility of Indrail Passes which offer all budget visitors the facility to travel as they like over the entire Indian railway system without any route restriction and within the period of validity of he ticket. Indrail passes are sold only to foreign nationals and Indians residing abroad holding valid passports.

Payment is accepted only in US Dollars and Pound Sterling. A tourist travelling on Indrail pass is exempt from paying reservation fees, sleeper charges and extra supplementary charges for travelling by Superfast trains which are otherwise chargeable in the case of ordinary tickets.

RESTRICTED AND PROTECTED AREAS

Military installations and areas, defence organisations and research organisations are considered protected areas, where permits are generally not given to foreigners.

PHOTOGRAPHY RESTRICTIONS

Photography is prohibited in places of military importance, railway stations, bridges, airports and other military installations.

EXPORT OF ANTIQUITIES

Antiquities include sculpture, painting or other works of art and craftsmanship, illustrative of science, art, crafts, religion of bygone ages and of historical interest which have been in existence for not less than one hundred years. Also manuscripts, or other documents of scientific, historical, literary or aesthetic value in existence for not less than seventy five year art treasures not necessarily antiquities but having regard to the artistic and aesthetic value cannot be exported out of India.

For farther clarification on the antiquity of an artefact, the tourists can contact the authorities and get information on the Acts and Rules governing Antiquities and Art Treasures Act, 1972.

Govt. of India is concerned about the conservation of its endangered and rare fauna. With this view, export of all wild animals indigenous to the country and articles made from such listed animals like skin, pelts, furs, ivory, rhino horns, trophies etc have been totally banned.

Tourists are also advised to acquaint themselves with the provisions of Convention on International Trade of endangered species of wild fauna and flora. All the member countries of the convention allow import of the articles covered by convention on the strength of a certificate of export from the country of origin.

CLIMATE

India has three major seasons: winter, summer and the monsoon. The winter months (November-March) are pleasant throughout India with bright sunny days. In the northern plains, the minimum temperature may vary between 4 to 10 degree Celsius and there is snowfall in the hills. In the west, south and the east, however, December and January are pleasantly cool, never really cold. The summer months (April-June) are hot in most parts of India and it is during this season that hill resorts such as Shimla, Musoorie, Nainital, Kullu and the Kashmir valley, Darjeeling, Shillong, Octacamund, Kodaikanal, Pachmarhi and Mount Abu provide cool retreats.

The south-west monsoon usually breaks about the beginning of June on the west coast and reaches elsewhere later. With the exception of the south-eastern areas, India receives the major share of its rainfall from the north-east monsoon between mid-October and December-end. Traditionally, India had been popular in the winter months. However, with easy availability of air-conditioned hotels, transport and leisure facilities (such as dining and shopping), the summer months too have become popular and India has become a year-round tourist destination.

The climate of India defies easy generalisation, comprising a wide range of weather conditions across a large geographic scale and varied topography. Analysed according to the Köppen system, India hosts six major climatic subtypes, ranging from desert in the west, to alpine tundra and glaciers in the north, to humid tropical regions supporting rainforests in the southwest and the island territories. Many regions have starkly different microclimates. The nation has four seasons: winter (January and February), summer (March to May), a monsoon (rainy) season (June to September), and a post-monsoon period (October to December).

India's unique geography and geology strongly influence its climate; this is particularly true of the Himalayas in the north and the Thar Desert in the northwest. The Himalayas act as a barrier to the frigid katabatic winds flowing down from Central Asia. Thus, North India is kept warm or only mildly cold during winter; in summer, the same phenomenon makes India relatively hot. Although the Tropic of Cancer—the boundary between the tropics and subtropics—passes through the middle of India, the whole country is considered to be tropical.

As in much of the tropics, monsoonal and other weather conditions in India are unstable: major droughts, floods, cyclones and other natural disasters are sporadic, but have killed or displaced millions. India's long-term climatic stability is further threatened by global warming. Climatic diversity in India makes the analysis of these issues complex.

During the Late Permian (some 260–251 Ma), the Indian

subcontinent was part of the vast supercontinent Pangaea. Despite its position within a high-latitude belt at 55–75° S (as opposed to its current position between 5 and 35° N), latitudes now occupied by Greenland and parts of the Antarctic Peninsula, India likely experienced a humid temperate climate with warm, frost-free weather, though with well-defined seasons. Later, India joined the southern supercontinent Gondwana, a process beginning some 550–500 Ma.

During the Late Paleozoic, Gondwana extended from a point at or near the South Pole to near the equator, where the Indian craton (stable continental crust) was positioned, resulting in a mild climate favourable to hosting high-biomass ecosystems.

This is underscored by India's vast coal reserves—much of it from the late Paleozoic sedimentary sequence—the fourth-largest reserves in the world. During the Mesozoic, the world, including India, was considerably warmer than today. With the coming of the Carboniferous, global cooling stoked extensive glaciation, which spread northwards from South Africa towards India; this cool period lasted well into the Permian.

Tectonic movement by the Indian Plate caused it to pass over a geologic hotspot—the Réunion hotspot—now occupied by the volcanic island of Réunion. This resulted in a massive flood basalt event that laid down the Deccan Traps some 60–68 Ma, at the end of the Cretaceous period. This may have contributed to the global Cretaceous-Tertiary (K-T) extinction event, which caused India to experience significantly reduced insolation.

Elevated atmospheric levels of sulphur gases formed aerosols such as sulfur dioxide and sulfuric acid, similar to those found in the atmosphere of Venus; these precipitated as acid rain. Elevated carbon dioxide emissions also contributed to the greenhouse effect, causing warmer weather that lasted long after the atmospheric shroud of dust and aerosols had cleared.

Further climatic changes 20 million years ago, long after India had crashed into the Laurasian landmass, were severe enough to cause the extinction of many endemic Indian forms. The formation of the Himalayas resulted in blockage of frigid Central Asian air, preventing it from reaching India; this made its climate significantly warmer and more tropical in character than it would otherwise have been.

India is home to an extraordinary variety of climatic regions, ranging from tropical in the south to temperate and alpine in the Himalayan north, where elevated regions receive sustained winter snowfall. The nation's climate is strongly influenced by the Himalayas and the Thar Desert.

The Himalayas, along with the Hindu Kush mountains in Pakistan, prevent cold Central Asian katabatic winds from blowing in, keeping the bulk of the Indian subcontinent warmer than most locations at similar latitudes. Simultaneously, the Thar Desert plays a role in attracting moisture-laden southwest summer monsoon winds that, between June and October, provide the majority of India's rainfall.

Four major climatic groupings predominate, into which fall seven climatic zones that, as designated by experts, are defined on the basis of such traits as temperature and precipitation. Groupings are assigned codes according to the Köppen climate classification system.

A tropical rainy climate covers regions experiencing persistent warm or high temperatures, which normally do not fall below 18 °C (64 °F). India hosts two climatic subtypes that fall under this group. The most humid is the tropical wet monsoon climate that covers a strip of southwestern lowlands abutting the Malabar Coast, the Western Ghats, and southern Assam. India's two island territories, Lakshadweep and the Andaman and Nicobar Islands, are also subject to this climate. Characterised by moderate to high year-round temperatures, even in the foothills, its rainfall is seasonal but heavy—typically above 2,000 millimetres (79 in) per year.

Most rainfall occurs between May and November; this is adequate for the maintenance of lush forests and other vegetation throughout the remainder of the year. December to March are the driest months, when days with precipitation are rare. The heavy monsoon rains are responsible for the extremely biodiverse tropical wet forests of these regions.

In India, a tropical wet and dry climate is more common. Significantly drier than tropical wet zones, it prevails over most of inland peninsular India except for a semi-arid rain shadow east of the Western Ghats.

Winter and early summer are long, dry periods with temperatures averaging above 18 °C (64 °F). Summer is exceptionally hot; temperatures in low-lying areas may exceed 50 °C (122 °F) during May, leading to heat waves that can each kill hundreds of Indians. The rainy season lasts from June to September; annual rainfall averages between 750–1500 millimetres (30–59 in) across the region. Once the dry northeast monsoon begins in September, most precipitation in India falls on Tamil Nadu, leaving other states comparatively dry.

A tropical arid and semi-arid climate dominates regions where the rate of moisture loss through evapotranspiration exceeds that from precipitation; it is subdivided into three climatic subtypes. The first, a tropical semi-arid steppe climate, predominates over a long stretch of land south of Tropic of Cancer and east of the Western Ghats and the Cardamom Hills. The region, which includes Karnataka, inland Tamil Nadu, western Andhra Pradesh, and central Maharashtra, gets between 400–750 millimetres (16–30 in) annually.

It is drought-prone, as it tends to have less reliable rainfall due to sporadic lateness or failure of the southwest monsoon. North of the Krishna River, the summer monsoon is responsible for most rainfall; to the south, significant post-monsoon rainfall also occurs in October and November. In December, the coldest month, temperatures still average around 20–24 °C (68–75 °F). The months between March to May are hot and dry; mean monthly temperatures hover around 32 °C, with 320 millimetres (13 in) precipitation. Hence, without artificial irrigation, this region is not suitable for permanent agriculture.

Most of western Rajasthan experiences an arid climatic regime. Cloudbursts are responsible for virtually all of the region's annual precipitation, which totals less than 300 millimetres (12 in). Such bursts happen when monsoon winds sweep into the region during July, August, and September. Such rainfall is highly erratic; regions experiencing rainfall one year may not see precipitation for the next couple of years or so. Atmospheric moisture is largely prevented from precipitating due to continuous downdrafts and other factors.

The summer months of May and June are exceptionally hot; mean monthly temperatures in the region hover around 35 °C (95 °F), with daily maxima occasionally topping 50 °C (122 °F). During winters, temperatures in some areas can drop below freezing due to waves of cold air from Central Asia. There is a large diurnal range of about 14 °C (57 °F) during summer; this widens by several degrees during winter.

East of the Thar Desert, the region running from Punjab and Haryana to Kathiawar experiences a tropical and sub-tropical steppe climate. The zone, a transitional climatic region separating tropical desert from humid sub-tropical savanna and forests, experiences temperatures that are less extreme than those of the desert. Average annual rainfall is 30–65 centimetres (12-26 in), but is very unreliable; as in much of the rest of India, the southwest monsoon accounts for most precipitation. Daily summer temperature maxima rise to around 40 °C (104 °F). The resulting natural vegetation typically comprises short, coarse grasses.

Most of Northeast India and much of North India are subject to a humid sub-tropical climate. Though they experience hot summers, temperatures during the coldest months may fall as low as 0 °C (32 °F). Due to ample monsoon rains, India has only one subtype of this climate, *Cfa* (under the Köppen system). In most of this region, there is very little precipitation during the winter, owing to powerful anticyclonic and katabatic (downward-flowing) winds from Central Asia.

Humid subtropical regions are subject to pronounced dry winters. Winter rainfall—and occasionally snowfall—is associated with large storm systems such as "Nor'westers" and "Western disturbances"; the latter are steered by westerlies towards the Himalayas. Most summer rainfall occurs during powerful thunderstorms associated with the southwest summer monsoon; occasional tropical cyclones also contribute.

Annual rainfall ranges from less than 1,000 millimetres (39 in) in the west to over 2,500 millimetres (98 in) in parts of the northeast. As most of this region is far from the ocean, the wide temperature swings more characteristic of a continental climate predominate; the swings are wider than in those in tropical wet regions, ranging from 24 °C (75 °F) in north-central India to 27 °C (81 °F) in the east.

India's northernmost areas are subject to a montane, or alpine, climate. In the Himalayas, the rate at which an air mass's temperature falls per kilometre (3,281 ft) of altitude gained (the adiabatic lapse rate) is 5.1 °C/km. In terms of environmental lapse rate, ambient temperatures fall by 0.6 °C (1.1 °F) for every 100 metres (328 ft) rise in altitude. Thus, climates ranging from nearly tropical in the foothills to tundra above the snow line can coexist within several dozen miles of each other.

Sharp temperature contrasts between sunny and shady slopes, high diurnal temperature variability, temperature inversions, and altitude-dependent variability in rainfall are also common. The northern side of the western Himalayas, also known as the trans-Himalayan belt, is a region of barren, arid, frigid, and wind-blown wastelands. Most precipitation occurs as snowfall during the late winter and spring months.

Areas south of the Himalayas are largely protected from cold winter winds coming in from the Asian interior. The leeward side (northern face) of the mountains receives less rain while the southern slopes, well-exposed to the monsoon, get heavy rainfall. Areas situated at elevations of 1,070–2,290 metres (3,510–7,510 ft) receive the heaviest rainfall, which decreases rapidly at elevations above 2,290 metres (7,513 ft).

The Himalayas experience their heaviest snowfall between December and February and at elevations above 1,500 metres (4,921 ft). Snowfall increases with elevation by up to several dozen millimetres per 100 metre (~2 in; 330 ft) increase. Elevations above 5,000 metres (16,404 ft) never experience rain; all precipitation falls as snow.

The India Meteorological Department (IMD) designates four official seasons:

- Winter, occurring between January thru March. The year's coldest months are December and January, when temperatures average around 10–15 °C (50–59 °F) in the northwest; temperatures rise as one proceeds towards the equator, peaking around 20–25 °C (68–77 °F) in mainland India's southeast.
- Summer or pre-monsoon season, lasting from March to June (April to July in northwestern India). In western and southern regions, the hottest month is April; for northern regions, May is the hottest month. Temperatures average around 32–40 °C (90–104 °F) in most of the interior.
- Monsoon or rainy season, lasting from June to September. The season is dominated by the humid southwest summer monsoon, which slowly sweeps across the country beginning in late May or early June. Monsoon rains begin to recede from North India at the beginning of October.
- Post-monsoon season, lasting from October to December. South India typically receives more precipitation. Monsoon rains begin to recede from North India at the beginning of October. In northwestern India, October and November are usually cloudless. Parts of the country experience the dry northeast monsoon.

The Himalayan states, being more temperate, experience an additional two seasons: autumn and spring. Traditionally, Indians note six seasons, each about two months long. These are the spring (*Sanskrit: vasanta*), summer (*grîcma*), monsoon season (*varcâ*), early autumn (*œarada*), late autumn (*hemanta*), and winter (*œiœira*). These are based on the astronomical division of the twelve months into six parts. The ancient Hindu calendar also reflects these seasons in its arrangement of months.

Once the monsoons subside, average temperatures gradually fall across India. As the Sun's vertical rays move south of the equator, most of the country experiences moderately cool weather; temperatures change by about 0.6 °C (1.35 °F) per degree of latitude. December and January are the coldest months, with mean temperatures of 10–15 °C (50–59 °F) in Indian Himalayas. Mean temperatures are higher in the east and south, where they reach 20–25 °C (68–77 °F).

In northwestern India, virtually cloudless conditions prevail in October and November, resulting in wide diurnal temperature swings; as in much of the Deccan Plateau, they range between 16–20 °C (61–68 °F). However, from March to May, "western disturbances" bring heavy bursts of rain and snow. These extra-tropical low-pressure systems originate in the eastern Mediterranean Sea. They are carried towards India by the subtropical westerlies, which are the prevailing winds blowing at North India's range of latitude.

Once their passage is hindered by the Himalayas, they are unable to proceed further, and they release significant precipitation over the southern Himalayas. The three Himalayan states (Jammu and Kashmir in the extreme north, Himachal Pradesh, and Uttarakhand) experience heavy snowfall; in Jammu and Kashmir, blizzards occur regularly, disrupting travel and other activities.

The rest of North India, including the Indo-Gangetic Plain, almost never receives snow. However, in the plains, temperatures occasionally fall below freezing, though never for more one or two days. Winter highs in Delhi range from 16 °C (61 °F) to 21 °C (70 °F). Nighttime temperatures average 2–8 °C (36–46 °F). In the Punjab plains, lows can fall below freezing, dropping to around "6 °C (21 °F) in Amritsar. Frost sometimes occurs, but the hallmark of the season is the notorious fog, which frequently disrupts daily life; fog grows thick enough to hinder visibility and disrupt air travel 15–20 days annually.

Eastern India's climate is much milder, experiencing moderately warm days and cool nights. Highs range from 23 °C (73 °F) in Patna to 26 °C (79 °F) in Kolkata (Calcutta);

lows average from 8 °C (46 °F) in Patna to 14 °C (57 °F) in Kolkata. Frigid winds from the Himalayas can depress temperatures near the Brahmaputra River. The two Himalayan states in the east, Sikkim and Arunachal Pradesh, receive substantial snowfall. The extreme north of West Bengal, centred around Darjeeling, also experiences snowfall, but only rarely.

In South India, particularly the hinterland of Maharashtra, Madhya Pradesh, parts of Karnataka, and Andhra Pradesh, somewhat cooler weather prevails. Minimum temperatures in western Maharashtra, Madhya Pradesh and Chhattisgarh hover around 10 °C (50 °F); in the southern Deccan Plateau, they reach 16 °C (61 °F).

Coastal areas, especially those near the Coromandel Coast, and low-elevation interior tracts are warm, with daily high temperatures of 30 °C (86 °F) and lows of around 21 °C (70 °F). The Western Ghats, including the Nilgiri Range, are exceptional; there, lows can fall below freezing. This compares with a range of 12–14 °C (54–57 °F) on the Malabar Coast; there, as is the case for other coastal areas, the Indian Ocean exerts a strong moderating influence on weather.

Summer in northwestern India lasts from April to July, and in the rest of the country from March to June. The temperatures in the north rise as the vertical rays of the Sun reach the Tropic of Cancer. The hottest month for the western and southern regions of the country is April; for most of North India, it is May. Temperatures of 50 °C (122 °F) and higher have been recorded in parts of India during this season.

In cooler regions of North India, immense pre-monsoon squall-line thunderstorms, known locally as "Nor'westers", commonly drop large hailstones. Near the coast the temperature hovers around 36 °C (97 °F), and the proximity of the sea increases the level of humidity. In southern India, the temperatures are higher on the east coast by a few degrees compared to the west coast.

By May, most of the Indian interior experiences mean temperatures over 32 °C (90 °F), while maximum temperatures often exceed 40 °C (104 °F). In the hot months of April and

May, western disturbances, with their cooling influence, may still arrive, but rapidly diminish in frequency as summer progresses. Notably, a higher frequency of such disturbances in April correlates with a delayed monsoon onset (thus extending summer) in northwest India. In eastern India, monsoon onset dates have been steadily advancing over the past several decades, resulting in shorter summers there.

Altitude affects the temperature to a large extent, with higher parts of the Deccan Plateau and other areas being relatively cooler. Hill stations, such as Ootacamund ("Ooty") in the Western Ghats and Kalimpong in the eastern Himalayas, with average maximum temperatures of around 25 °C (77 °F), offer some respite from the heat.

At lower elevations, in parts of northern and western India, a strong, hot, and dry wind known as the Loo blows in from the west during the daytime; with very high temperatures, in some cases up to around 45 °C (113 °F); it can cause fatal cases of sunstroke. Tornadoes may also occur, concentrated in a corridor stretching from northeastern India towards Pakistan. They are rare, however; only several dozen have been reported since 1835.

The southwest summer monsoon, a four-month period when massive convective thunderstorms dominate India's weather, is Earth's most productive wet season. A product of southeast trade winds originating from a high-pressure mass centered over the southern Indian Ocean, the monsoonal torrents supply over 80% of India's annual rainfall. Attracted by a low-pressure region centered over South Asia, the mass spawns surface winds that ferry humid air into India from the southwest.

These inflows ultimately result from a northward shift of the local jet stream, which itself results from rising summer temperatures over Tibet and the Indian subcontinent. The void left by the jet stream, which switches from a route just south of the Himalayas to one tracking north of Tibet, then attracts warm, humid air.

The main factor behind this shift is the high summer temperature difference between Central Asia and the Indian

Ocean. This is accompanied by a seasonal excursion of the normally equatorial intertropical convergence zone (ITCZ), a low-pressure belt of highly unstable weather, northward towards India. This system intensified to its present strength as a result of the Tibetan Plateau's uplift, which accompanied the Eocene–Oligocene transition event, a major episode of global cooling and aridification which occurred 34–49 Ma.

The southwest monsoon arrives in two branches: the Bay of Bengal branch and the Arabian Sea branch. The latter extends toward a low-pressure area over the Thar Desert and is roughly three times stronger than the Bay of Bengal branch. The monsoon typically breaks over Indian territory by around 25 May, when it lashes the Andaman and Nicobar Islands in the Bay of Bengal. It strikes the Indian mainland around 1 June near the Malabar Coast of Kerala.

By 9 June, it reaches Mumbai; it appears over Delhi by 29 June. The Bay of Bengal branch, which initially tracks the Coromandal Coast northeast from Cape Comorin to Orissa, swerves to the northwest towards the Indo-Gangetic Plain. The Arabian Sea branch moves northeast towards the Himalayas. By the first week of July, the entire country experiences monsoon rain; on average, South India receives more rainfall than North India.

However, Northeast India receives the most precipitation. Monsoon clouds begin retreating from North India by the end of August; it withdraws from Mumbai by 5 October. As India further cools during September, the southwest monsoon weakens. By the end of November, it has left the country.

Monsoon rains impact the health of the Indian economy; as Indian agriculture employs 600 million people and composes 20% of the national GDP, good monsoons correlate with a booming economy. Weak or failed monsoons (droughts) result in widespread agricultural losses and substantially hinder overall economic growth. The rains reduce temperatures and replenish groundwater tables, rivers, and lakes.

During the post-monsoon months of October to December, a different monsoon cycle, the northeast (or "retreating") monsoon, brings dry, cool, and dense Central Asian air masses to large parts of India. Winds spill across the Himalayas and flow to the southwest across the country, resulting in clear, sunny skies. Though the India Meteorological Department (IMD) and other sources refers to this period as a fourth ("post-monsoon") season, other sources designate only three seasons.

Depending on location, this period lasts from October to November, after the southwest monsoon has peaked. Less and less precipitation falls, and vegetation begins to dry out. In most parts of India, this period marks the transition from wet to dry seasonal conditions. Average daily maximum temperatures range between 28 °C and 34 °C (82–93 °F).

The northeast monsoon, which begins in September, lasts through the post-monsoon seasons, and only ends in March, carries winds that have already lost their moisture while crossing central Asia and the vast rain shadow region lying north of the Himalayas. They cross India diagonally from northeast to southwest.

However, the large indentation made by the Bay of Bengal into India's eastern coast means that the flows are humidified before reaching Cape Comorin and rest of Tamil Nadu, meaning that the state, and also some parts of Kerala, experience significant precipitation in the post-monsoon and winter periods. However, parts of West Bengal, Orissa, Andhra Pradesh, Karnataka and North-East India also receive minor precipitation from the northeast monsoon.[46]

Shown below are temperature and precipitation data for selected Indian cities; these represent the full variety of major Indian climate types. Figures have been grouped by the four-season classification scheme used by the IMD; year-round averages and totals are also displayed.

Climate-related natural disasters cause massive losses of Indian life and property. Droughts, flash floods, cyclones, avalanches, landslides brought on by torrential rains, and snowstorms pose the greatest threats. Other dangers include frequent summer dust storms, which usually track from north to south; they cause extensive property damage in North India and deposit large amounts of dust from arid regions. Hail is also common in parts of India, causing severe damage to standing crops such as rice and wheat.

In the Lower Himalaya, landslides are common. The young age of the region's hills result in labile rock formations, which are susceptible to slippages. Rising population and development pressures, particularly from logging and tourism, cause deforestation. The result, denuded hillsides, exacerbates the severity of landslides, since tree cover impedes the downhill flow of water. Parts of the Western Ghats also suffer from low-intensity landslides. Avalanches occur in Kashmir, Himachal Pradesh, and Sikkim.

Floods are the most common natural disaster in India. The heavy southwest monsoon rains cause the Brahmaputra and other rivers to distend their banks, often flooding surrounding areas. Though they provide rice paddy farmers with a largely dependable source of natural irrigation and fertilisation, the floods can kill thousands and displace millions. Excess, erratic, or untimely monsoon rainfall may also wash away or otherwise ruin crops.

Almost all of India is flood-prone, and extreme precipitation events, such as flash floods and torrential rains, have become increasingly common in central India over the past several decades, coinciding with rising temperatures. Mean annual precipitation totals have remained steady due to the declining frequency of weather systems that generate moderate amounts of rain.

Tropical cyclones, which are severe storms spun off from the Intertropical Convergence Zone, may affect thousands of Indians living in coastal regions. Tropical cyclogenesis is particularly common in the northern reaches of the Indian Ocean in and around the Bay of Bengal. Cyclones bring with them heavy rains, storm surges, and winds that often cut affected areas off from relief and supplies.

In the North Indian Ocean Basin, the cyclone season runs from April to December, with peak activity between May and November. Each year, an average of eight storms with sustained wind speeds greater than 63 km/h (39 mph) form;

of these, two strengthen into true tropical cyclones, which have sustained gusts greater than 117 km/h (73 mph). On average, a major (Category 3 or higher) cyclone develops every other year.

During summer, the Bay of Bengal is subject to intense heating, giving rise to humid and unstable air masses that morph into cyclones. The 1737 Calcutta cyclone, the 1970 Bhola cyclone, and the 1991 Bangladesh cyclone rank among the most powerful cyclones to strike India, devastating the coasts of eastern India and neighboring Bangladesh.

Widespread death and property destruction are reported every year in the exposed coastal states of West Bengal, Orissa, Andhra Pradesh, and Tamil Nadu. India's western coast, bordering the more placid Arabian Sea, experiences cyclones only rarely; these mainly strike Gujarat and, less frequently, Kerala.

Cyclone 05B, a supercyclone that struck Orissa on 29 October 1999, was the deadliest in more than a quarter-century. With peak winds of 160 miles per hour (257 km/h), it was the equivalent of a Category 5 hurricane. Almost two million people were left homeless; other 20 million people lives were disrupted by the cyclone. Officially, 9,803 people died from the storm; unofficial estimates place the death toll at over 10,000.

Indian agriculture is heavily dependent on the monsoon as a source of water. In some parts of India, the failure of the monsoons result in water shortages, resulting in below-average crop yields. This is particularly true of major drought-prone regions such as southern and eastern Maharashtra, northern Karnataka, Andhra Pradesh, Orissa, Gujarat, and Rajasthan. In the past, droughts have periodically led to major Indian famines. These include the Bengal famine of 1770, in which up to one third of the population in affected areas died; the 1876–1877 famine, in which over five million people died; the 1899 famine, in which over 4.5 million died; and the Bengal famine of 1943, in which over five million died from starvation and famine-related illnesses.

All such episodes of severe drought correlate with El

Niño-Southern Oscillation (ENSO) events. El Niño-related droughts have also been implicated in periodic declines in Indian agricultural output. Nevertheless, ENSO events that have coincided with abnormally high sea surfaces temperatures in the Indian Ocean—in one instance during 1997 and 1998 by up to 3 °C (5 °F)—have resulted in increased oceanic evaporation, resulting in unusually wet weather across India. Such anomalies have occurred during a sustained warm spell that began in the 1990s.

A contrasting phenomenon is that, instead of the usual high pressure air mass over the southern Indian Ocean, an ENSO-related oceanic low pressure convergence centre forms; it then continually pulls dry air from Central Asia, desiccating India during what should have been the humid summer monsoon season. This reversed air flow causes India's droughts. The extent that an ENSO event raises sea surface temperatures in the central Pacific Ocean influences the degree of drought.

India's lowest recorded temperature reading was –45 °C (–49 °F) in Dras, Ladakh, in eastern Jammu and Kashmir; however, the reading was taken with non-standard equipment. Further south, readings as low as –30.6 °C (–23 °F) have been taken in Leh, also in Ladakh. However, temperatures on the Indian-controlled Siachen Glacier near Bilafond La (5,450 metres (17,881 ft)) and Sia La (5,589 metres (18,337 ft)) have fallen below –55 °C (–67 °F), while blizzards bring wind speeds in excess of 250 km/h (155 mph), or hurricane-force winds ranking at 12 (the maximum) on the Beaufort scale.

It was those conditions, not actual military engagements, that were responsible for more than 97% of the roughly 15,000 casualties suffered by India and Pakistan over the course of conflict in the region. The highest reliable temperature reading was 50.6 °C (123 °F) in Alwar, Rajasthan in 1955. This mark was also reached at Pachpadra in Rajasthan. Recently, claims have been made of temperatures touching 55 °C (131 °F) in Orissa; these have been met with some skepticism by the India Meteorological Department (IMD), which has questioned the methods used in recording such data.

The average annual precipitation of 11,871 millimetres (467 in) in the village of Mawsynram, in the hilly northeastern state of Meghalaya, is the highest recorded in Asia, and possibly on Earth. The village, which sits at an elevation of 1,401 metres (4,596 ft), benefits from its proximity to both the Himalayas and the Bay of Bengal.

However, since the town of Cherrapunji, 5 kilometres (3 mi) to the east, is the nearest town to host a meteorological office (none has ever existed in Mawsynram), it is officially credited as being the world's wettest place. In recent years, the Cherrapunji-Mawsynram region has averaged between 9,296 millimetres (366 in) and 10,820 millimetres (426 in) of rain annually, though Cherrapunji has had at least one period of daily rainfall that lasted almost two years. India's highest recorded one-day rainfall total occurred on 26 July 2005, when Mumbai received more than 650 millimetres (26 in); the massive flooding that resulted killed over 900 people.

Remote regions of Jammur and Kashmir, such as Baramulla district in the east and the Pir Panjal Range in the southeast, experience exceptionally heavy snowfall. Kashmir's highest recorded monthly snowfall occurred in February 1967, when 8.4 metres (331 in) fell in Gulmarg, though the IMD has recorded snowdrifts up to 12 metres (39 ft) in several Kashmiri districts. In February 2005, more than 200 people died when, in four days, a western disturbance brought up to 2 metres (7 ft) of snowfall to parts of the state.

Current sea level rise, increased cyclonic activity, increased ambient temperatures, and increasingly fickle precipitation patterns are effects of global warming that have impacted or are projected to impact India. Thousands of people have been deplaced by ongoing sea level rises that have submerged low-lying islands in the Sundarbans. Temperature rises on the Tibetan Plateau are causing Himalayan glaciers to retreat, threatening the flow rate of the Ganges, Brahmaputra, Yamuna, and other major rivers; the livelihoods of hundreds of thousands of farmers depend on these rivers. A 2007 World Wide Fund for Nature (WWF) report states that the Indus River may run dry for the same reason.

Severe landslides and floods are projected to become increasingly common in such states as Assam. Ecological disasters, such as a 1998 coral bleaching event that killed off more than 70% of corals in the reef ecosystems off Lakshadweep and the Andamans, and was brought on by elevated ocean temperatures tied to global warming, are also projected to become increasingly common.

The Indira Gandhi Institute of Development Research has reported that, if the predictions relating to global warming made by the Intergovernmental Panel on Climate Change come to fruition, climate-related factors could cause India's GDP to decline by up to 9%. Contributing to this would be shifting growing seasons for major crops such as rice, production of which could fall by 40%. Around seven million people are projected to be displaced due to, among other factors, submersion of parts of Mumbai and Chennai, if global temperatures were to rise by a mere 2 °C (3.6 °F).

Such shifts are not new. Earlier in the Holocene epoch (4,800–6,300 years ago), parts of what is now the Thar Desert were wet enough to support perennial lakes; researchers have proposed that this was due to much higher winter precipitation, which coincided with stronger monsoons. Kashmir's erstwhile subtropical climate dramatically cooled 2.6–3.7 Ma and experienced prolonged cold spells starting 600,000 years ago. Thick haze and smoke, originating from burning biomass in northwestern India and air pollution from large industrial cities in northern India, often concentrate inside the Ganges Basin. Prevailing westerlies carry aerosols along the southern margins of the steep-faced Tibetan Plateau to eastern India and the Bay of Bengal.

Dust and black carbon, which are blown towards higher altitudes by winds at the southern margins of the Himalayas, can absorb shortwave radiation and heat the air over the Tibetan Plateau. The net atmospheric heating due to aerosol absorption causes the air to warm and convect upwards, increasing the concentration of moisture in the mid-troposphere and providing positive feedback that stimulates further heating of aerosols.

Citizens of all countries, except Nepal and Bhutan, require a valid national passport or valid travel documents and a valid visa granted by Missions abroad for entering India. Nepalese or Bhutanese citizens need no passport or visa but should possess suitable documents for their identification when proceeding from their respective countries.

Foreigners desirous of visiting India can do so after obtaining visa from the Indian Mission in their country of their residence. They should possess a valid National Passport except in the case of nationals of Bhutan and Nepal, who may carry only suitable means of identification. Usually, a multi-entry visa, valid for a period of 180 days, is granted for the purpose of tourism.

The visa is valid from the date of issue. The facility also exists for the issue of collective visas to group tours consisting of not less than four members and sponsored by a travel agency recognized by the Government of India. Such groups may split into smaller groups for visiting different places in India after obtaining a collective "license to travel" from the immigration authorities in India. However, they must reassemble and depart as the original group.

Transit visas are granted by Indian Missions abroad for a maximum period of 15 days. Foreigners coming to India on tourist visas for 180 days or shorter period are not required to register themselves with any authority in India. They can move about freely in the country, except to restricted/protected areas and prohibited places. Nationals of Bangladesh are exempted from registration upto six months.

If their stay exceeds six months, they have to register themselves. Individuals without nationality (stateless persons; IRO refugees, persons receiving legal or political protection.) should have valid passports, identity documents or sworn affidavits along with the visa for which they should apply two months in advance. Family passports issued by other governments are recognized without discrimination.

Tourists may note the no *Landing Permit Facility* is available to any foreign tourist landing without a visa. A limited facility exists only for group tours consisting of four or more members and sponsored by a travel agency recognized by the Government of India. Children of foreigners of Indian origin below the age of 12 may be granted a landing permit by the immigration authorities' upto a period of 90 days to see their relatives, in case they happen to come without a visa.

A tourist group arriving by air, ship or by a chartered or scheduled flight may be granted a collective landing permit for a period of upto 30 days by the immigration authorities on landing, provided the group is sponsored by a recognized travel agency and a pre-drawn itinerary is presented along with details of passport etc. of the members and the travel agency gives an undertaking to conduct the group together.

As a rule no extension of stay is granted on a Tourist Visa. Other Types of Visas: If a foreigner wishes to come to India for a purpose other than tourism, he should come after obtaining one of the following visas.

A foreigner can obtain one from an Indian Embassy abroad. A multiple entry visa is valid for 5 years, provided he wishes to come for some business. Foreigners of Indian origin can obtain a 5 year multiple entry visa for business, to meet their relatives etc.

A student visa can be obtained from the Indian Embassy on the production of proof of admission and means of sustenance while in India, etc. The visa is valid for one year but can be extended in India for the duration of the course. Delegates coming to attend international conferences in India can be granted Conference Visa to cover the conference as well as for tourism in India.

Delegates are advised to apply to Indian Embassies well in advance. Foreigners desirous of coming to India for taking up employment should apply for an Employment Visa, which are issued by Indian Missions abroad. Initially granted for a period of one year, it can be extended in India upto the period of contract. Recreation: Foreigners wishing to undertake any international sporting event, trekking, botanical expeditions, yoga, journalists, media men, documentary and feature film makers may obtain visas after due formalities from the Indian Embassy.

Customs Formalities and Regulations

Visitors are generally required to make an oral baggage declaration in respect of baggage and foreign currency in their possession. They are also required to obtain the Currency Declaration Form from the Customs. They should fill in the Disembarkation Card handed over to them by the airline during the course of the flight.

For passengers not in possession of any dutiable articles or unaccompanied baggage. For passengers with dutiable articles or unaccompanied baggage or high value articles to be entered on the tourist Baggage Re-Export Form.

Currency Regulations

There are no restrictions on the amount of foreign currency or travelers' cheques a tourist may bring into India provided he makes a declaration in the Currency Declaration Form given to him on arrival. This will enable him not only to exchange the currency bought in, but also to take the unspent currency out of India on departure. Cash, bank notes and travelers' cheques up to US$ 1,000 or equivalent, need not be declared at the time of entry.

Any money in the form of travellers' cheques, drafts, bills, cheques, etc. in convertible currencies, which tourists wish to convert into Indian currency, should be exchanged only through authorized money changers and banks who will issue an encashment certificate that is required at the time of re-conversion of any unspent money into foreign currency. Exchanging of foreign currency other than banks or authorized money changers is an offense under Foreign Exchange Regulations Act 1973.

ARRIVAL FORMALITIES

If the visa, for stay in India, is for more than 180 days, a Registration Certificate and Residential Permit should be obtained from the nearest Foreigners' Registration Office within 15 days of arrival. All persons including Indian nationals are required to fill in a Disembarkation Card, at the time of arrival. Four photographs are also required for registration. The foreigners registered at Foreigners' Registration Office are required to report change of their addresses.

Departure from India

All persons, except nationals of Bhutan and Nepal, leaving by air, road or rail have to fill in an Embarkation Card at the time of departure.

Exit Formalities

Every foreigner who is about to depart finally from India shall surrender his Certificate of Registration either to the Registration Officer of the place where he is registered or of the place from where he intends to depart or to the Immigration Officer at the Port/Check post of exit from India.

HEALTH REGULATIONS

Foreign tourists should be in possession of their Yellow Fever Vaccination Certificate conforming to International Health Regulation, if they are originating or transiting through Yellow Fever endemic countries.

AIRPORTS

The international airports in the metro cities offer a range of services ensuring that the traveller on business can continue working while waiting to board an international connection, or when transferring between international flights. These include restaurants, business centers, rest rooms and handy telephones booths. Business centers are equipped with state-of-the-art equipment including word processors and tele fax.

Airports also offer tourist dutyfree and handicrafts shopping, informal snack bars, nursery and baby care rooms and even an art gallery. Duty-free prices in the airport shops are very competitive, offering you bargains on international merchandise.

Foreign Travel Tax

Passengers embarking on journeys to any place outside India from a Customs airport/seaport will have to pay a Foreign Travel Tax (FTT) of Rs. 500 and Rs. 150 on journeys to Afghanistan, Bangladesh, Bhutan, Myanmar, Nepal, Pakistan, Sri Lanka and Maldives. No tax is payable on journeys performed by ship from Rameshwaram to Talaimanar and in case of transit passengers, provided they do not leave the customs barrier.

Transit passengers traveling by air who have to leave the airport on account of mechanical trouble but continue their journey by the same aircraft and the same flight number by which they arrive are also exempt from FTT. Transit sea passengers leaving the ship for sightseeing, shopping etc. during the ships' call at any of the Indian ports will not be required to pay FTT.

During the 1990s, Turkey's inbound tourism industry underwent massive growth, catapaulting the country from a middle range tourist destination to one of the top 20 most popular tourist destinations in the world. Statistically, inbound tourism grew from 5.389 million in 1990 to 10.428 million in 2000. There has been considerable speculation about the reasons for Turkey's sudden burst of popularity at the end of the twentieth century.

The most credible explanation is that, during the 1990s, Turkey mounted an aggressive and professional promotional campaign to showcase the country's many compelling tourist attractions to its key source markets.

Geographically and culturally, Turkey straddles the two continents of Europe and Asia. Its largest city, Istanbul, bridges both continents. Turkey is a country of many paradoxes. Almost 99 per cent of Turkey's 66 million people are Muslim, but its political orientation is democratic, secular and Western-orientated. Turkey is a member of NATO and—unusually for a predominantly Muslim nation—enjoys cordial relations with

Israel and has actively sought membership of the European Community.

Conversely, Turkey has often maintained tense relations with its neighbouring Arab states of Syria and Iraq to its south, problematic relations with Iran to its east, and there has been traditional tension in Greek-Turkish relations to Turkey's west. Historically, in the days of the Ottoman Empire (1500–1917), Turkey dominated much of what is referred to today as the Middle East, including Syria, Iraq, Lebanon, Israel and Egypt. The Ottoman Empire also dominated Bulgaria, Greece and parts of the former Yugoslavia to the west. In a region where political memories are long, there is lingering resentment between many Arab countries and their former Turkish overlords.

To its northeast, Turkey borders the two newly independent states of Armenia and Georgia, formed as a result of the collapse of the former Soviet Union. Relations with Armenia in particular are coloured by Armenian claims of genocide which allege that between 1 million and 1.5 million Armenians were killed by the Turkish army during World War I. The Turks hotly deny claims of genocide and state that the numbers involved were far smaller and most Armenian deaths resulted from a military response to Armenian insurgency during that war.

The establishment of an independent Armenian state in 1990, bordering on Turkey, has led to the first tentative attempts to resolve this historic chasm between the two countries. The collapse of the former Soviet Union enabled Turkey to establish diplomatic and economic relations with many of the predominantly Muslim republics in what was the southern part of the Soviet Union.

The major source of recent and contemporary political conflict in the eastern and southern frontier regions of Turkey has been the challenge of Kurdish separatism. The Kurds are a stateless ethnic group numbering 25 million, most of whom live at the confluence of Turkey, Syria, Iraq and Iran. The Kurdish plight has rarely been reported in the Western media and only came to prominence during the 1991 Gulf War when the United States-led coalition established a 'safe haven' for them in Northern Iraq, an area which has been variously attacked by Iraqi and Turkish forces.

Both countries accuse the Kurds of undermining their sovereignty. US government foreign policy towards the Kurds has at best been confusing: Kurdish nationalism is viewed positively by the US as a source of opposition to Saddam Hussein's regime in Iraq and viewed negatively when it is in conflict with its ally, Turkey.

Kurdish nationalist and territorial claims have long been consistently vague and subject to internal debate among the various Kurdish factions. Some Kurdish factions seek statehood, while others want autonomy in the countries in which they live or simply seek rights as a minority. Kurdish separatists have been in conflict with the governments of all the countries in which they reside.

The confrontation between Kurdish nationalists and Turkey, home to half the Kurdish population, has been especially bitter. Between 1991 and 2001 there were many instances of Kurdish orchestrated terrorism in Turkey aimed at attracting international attention to Kurdish nationalist claims. Some terrorist acts were targeted at tourists, which has presented a continuing problem for the Turkish government and Turkey's image as a safe and desirable tourist destination.

Although this chapter will focus on the impact of the 1999 earthquake on tourism to Turkey, Turkish tourism authorities have regarded Kurdish terrorism as an impediment to the uninterrupted growth of its tourism industry, though a lesser threat than natural disasters.

One of the compelling attractions of Turkey as a tourist destination has been the impact the cross-currents of human history have wrought upon the country's cultural landscape. Modern Istanbul is one of the great urban chameleons of history: it was known as Byzantium during the days of Roman dominance, and was a bulwark of emerging Christian power; after the fall of Rome and the rise of Islam, the city was named Constantinople, the capital of an empire which encompassed Egypt, the Levant and spread into Greece, Bulgaria and the

Balkans. From the rise of the Ottoman Empire, it became known as Istanbul. The city was the setting for the rise of secular nationalism led by Kemal Ataturk at the end of World War I.

All over Turkey, there is evidence of indigenous societies and the influence of empires ranging through Greek, Hittite, Assyrian, Roman, Persian, Babylonian and Sumerian. St Paul (born the Jewish Saul of Tarsus in Southern Turkey) traversed Turkey during his journey throughout the Roman Empire to spread Christianity. It is said by some New Testament scholars that Jesus's mother Mary died in Ephesus.

The Turkish town Catalhoyuk is claimed by Turks to be the oldest known human urban settlement on earth, dating back 9500 years—a title traditionally challenged by Jericho. Since the September 2001 discovery of a town in Israel on the shores of the Sea of Galilee dating back 23 000 years, both claims are now redundant. However, there is no dispute that the history of human civilisation in Turkey is long, varied and fascinating.

The city of Troy, one of the world's most famous archaeological treasures, is located in western Turkey. Capadoccia, curious rock formations of conical peaks, were hollowed out as homes to thousands of people 4000 years ago in southern central Turkey. Nearby Pamukkale is a series of calcium-rich bleached thermal springs millions of years old, which have formed a series of terraced pools along the slopes of a mountain.

Geographically and scenically, Turkey is a country of immense contrasts and beauty. The mountainous east is dominated by the country's highest peak, Mt Ararat, fabled resting place of the biblical Noah's Ark. Turkey is girded by 8000 kilometres of coastline on the Black Sea, Sea of Mamara, Aegean Sea and the Eastern Mediterranean. Turkey's 775 000 square kilometres range from deserts to lush and fertile lands. In recent years, the Turkish Ministry of Tourism has become increasingly effective in communicating the variety and quality of the country's scenic, historical and cultural attractions.

The curse of Turkey's geographical location is that it is

situated at the epicentre of a series of fault lines caused by the pressure exerted by three major plates of the Earth's crust. The Arabian, African and Eurasian plates literally squeeze Turkey from north, south and east.

The convergence of these tectonic forces on Turkey has caused frequent earthquakes over the centuries, some of which have been highly destructive and inflicted many thousands of casualties. During the twentieth century alone 96 major earthquakes in Turkey caused 100 000 deaths. The two most destructive earthquakes in Turkey during the twentieth century were the Erzinkan earthquake of 1939, which caused 32 000 deaths, and the Izmit earthquake of August 17, 1999, which resulted in 17 000 deaths. The Izmit earthquake is the focal point of this case study.

Turkey's tourism industry was one of the few success stories of Turkey's troubled economy during the 1990s. As described at the beginning of this chapter, inbound tourism numbers almost doubled between 1990 and 2000. Tourism receipts increased from US$2.705 billion in 1990 to US$7.636 billion in 2000. In 2000, the Turkish tourism industry employed at least 2.5 million people in Turkey, although unofficial estimates are double this figure when taking into account Turkey's large black economy (business conducted without records and in cash only to avoid taxes) and the many merchants who derive much of their living from selling goods and services to tourists.

The tourism industry was estimated to contribute 2.1 per cent of Turkey's GNP in 1988. By 1997, tourism's contribution to GNP had more than doubled to 4.5 per cent, or 25 per cent of export earnings.

During the decade 1990–2000, tourism matured to become a significant and strategically vital element in Turkey's economy. The major source market was Europe. Turkey successfully marketed the destination worldwide and attracted a growing diversity of source markets. In 2000, the total inbound tourism numbers reached 10.428 million.

The largest single source market was Germany, primarily driven by the 'visiting friends and relatives' (VFR) market drawn from the 3 million Turks living in Germany at that time. Turkey's ease of access from Europe by road, rail, air and sea, coupled with the modest prices (by European standards) of its accommodation, shopping and internal transport, made it an increasingly popular destination for tourists of all types, ranging from backpackers to luxury travellers.

The growth of Turkish tourism during the 1980s was driven by government-funded developments and marketing initiatives based on a series of five-year plans. These included infrastructure development projects exemplified by the establishment of the Turkish Riviera based on the southern Mediterranean port of Antalya. In the city of Antalya, the opening of a series of casinos (the only legal casinos in the Muslim world) attracted large numbers of tourists from the former Soviet Union and Israel especially, who took advantage of low-priced package tours to the Antalya area.

The casinos were closed in the late 1990s due to religious opposition, but by that time the region was well established as a sun-and-fun resort area with or without the dubious attractions of legal gambling. As prices in Greece began to steadily increase, the high-quality, low-priced Mediterranean resorts of southern Turkey were marketed as an attractive alternative.

Turkish tour operators and developers established ski resorts and a well-defined series of tour programs, which included many of Turkey's historical, scenic and cultural attractions. The industry diversified to promote eco-tourism and adventure tourism; Christian, Jewish and Muslim pilgrimage tourism; and educational, archaeological and historically-oriented tours. The international marketing of destination Turkey was coordinated by the Turkish Ministry of Tourism, based in the capital of Ankara. Turkish information offices were located in 23 countries by 2000. The activities of Turkish tourism offices were actively supported by the national carrier, Turkish Airlines, and a growing number of Turkish and internationally based tour operators, all of which were able to take advantage of marketing subsidies available from the Turkish Ministry of Tourism.

During the 1990s, the Turkish Ministry of Tourism was utilising the marketing consultancy services of international PR consultants PPK. The strategic and high-quality advertising of Turkey in leading publications and television stations in key source markets was improving destination awareness. The advertisements featured diverse images of Turkey to reinforce the message that Turkey was a destination that appealed to many market segments.

Certain niche marketing programs were also developed, ranging from promotions to Christian pilgrims in the years leading to 2000 (Christianity's bi-millennial); business travellers from Russia and the Arab world; war veterans and their descendants, packages which had strong appeal to sections of the British and Australasian markets; golfing for the Japanese; and sporting and adventure travel options which appealed to the European and North American markets.

A special campaign was conducted to appeal to the large UK and European academic and schools tour markets, promoting Turkey's many pricecompetitive and well-preserved historical, cultural and archaeological sites. Turkey was increasingly incorporated into multi-destination European package tours.

At the luxury end of the market, Istanbul was featured as the true end of the line on the fabled Orient Express, which until the 1990s only went as far as Venice. Overall, the prime marketing message was the promotion of the diversification of Turkey's appeal as a destination and the capacity of its tourism infrastructure to meet varied tastes and budgets. During the 1990s, the Turkish government upgraded and expanded the main international gateway airports of Istanbul, Ankara and Antalya to more efficiently manage increased demand and also to improve the image of these gateway points.

Turkish Airlines services 113 destinations worldwide and plays an important role in Turkey's destination marketing. Its recent opening of a route from Istanbul to Shanghai is indicative of increasing awareness of the potential importance of a rapidly growing outbound market from China (PRC) which also has a government policy of 'approved destinations' based in part on a proviso that the approved destination must have a direct air link with China.

The Turkish Ministry of Tourism and Turkish tourism offices worldwide actively sponsored familiarisation trips and hostings for travel agents and travel journalists to assist in spreading the marketing message. The Ministry also sought to overcome the powerful negative images portrayed in the highly successful 1978 Hollywood film *Midnight Express,* which depicted two American tourists incarcerated on charges of drug smuggling in Turkey, and that affected a large segment of young American and Western European markets. The film, which depicted cruelty and corruption in Turkey, coloured negative Western—and especially American—images of Turkey for many years, a stereotype that the Turkish tourism industry was anxious to alter.

The growth of high-quality hotel and resort accommodation in Turkey's major cities, resort areas and tourist attractions was beginning to lure the big-spending but fickle markets of the United States and Japan, where travellers sought new and different destinations which offered high-quality accommodation and service. By 2001, Istanbul alone had 5000 five-star hotel rooms operated by most leading international hotel chains.

In their tourism marketing, Turkey's tourism authorities were careful, almost to the point of paranoia, to depict Turkey as a European destination and anxious to avoid being labelled or depicted as a Middle Eastern destination. Turkey did, however, accept being defined in certain markets—such as Eastern Asia and Australasia—as an Eastern Mediterranean destination, provided it was promoted in conjunction with primarily European countries in that region. This attitude was a marketing position and reflected Turkey's geopolitical alignments.

The overall picture of Turkish tourism during the decade 1990–2000 was one of considerable growth. The diversification of Turkey's tourism infrastructure and its weak currency meant that Turkey was a relatively inexpensive destination for foreign visitors, irrespective of the standard of travel, tourist services and accommodation required.

The key interruptions to Turkey's inbound tourism growth in 1991 were attributable to the Gulf War (Operation Desert Storm) and Turkey's actual and perceived proximity to the war zone. Although the war between the coalition and Iraq was officially over by early March 1991, there was an extended period of Turkish involvement in the Kurdish dominated region in northern Iraq.

In 1993, Turkey experienced internal political instability and there was an upsurge in Turkish-Kurdish conflict which impacted on tourism during that year. However, the largest downturn in Turkish tourism numbers during the decade was directly linked to the August 1999 earthquake, which occurred during the height of the summer tourism season and led to a substantial reduction in inbound tourism numbers in late 1999.

The August 1999 Izmit earthquake was one of the most destructive and costly natural disasters afflicting Turkey during the twentieth century, both in terms of human casualties and destruction of residential and industrial property. The exceedingly rapid recovery of tourism to Turkey after this wellpublicised disaster was partly because most of Turkey's major tourist attractions were spared damage from the quake but due mainly to the highly effective campaign to restore the tourism market after the disaster.

On August 17 at 3.00 a.m. local time, an earthquake measuring 7.4 on the Richter scale with an epicentre near the Turkish city of Izmit, 100 kilometres east of Istanbul in the Marmara region of northern Turkey, devastated a large area. Seismologists defined the earthquake as a *shallow quake.* This maximised the destruction to buildings. Casualties were estimated to be 20 000 dead and 50 000 injured. The region in which the earthquake struck was a heavily populated and highly industrialised region of the country. According to a UN report, 350 000 housing units and business premises were damaged or destroyed. Many of the dead and injured were buried in the rubble of their homes while they were sleeping.

The earthquake met with a massive international response

of sympathy and support. In addition to the mobilisation of thousands of local rescue workers and medical professionals, rescue and medical aid teams from Israel, the United Kingdom, the United States, Greece, Kuwait, Germany and nineteen other countries arrived at the scene within 72 hours.

There was an international effort involving 64 countries to provide food, medical assistance, temporary shelter and clothing aid to the victims. Rescue and aid teams were hampered by the extensive damage to roads and bridges and the on-site difficulty of access to victims trapped among the rubble of collapsed multi-storey buildings. While the rescue efforts were both heroic and extensive, the reactive nature of response to the Izmit earthquake revealed an ongoing problem of disaster management in Turkey.

Turkey's vulnerability to earthquakes and floods has been a fact of life for thousands of years, yet there appears to have been little done to develop contingency plans and measures which could have assisted in casualty and damage minimisation. A common observation of rescue and relief teams, engineers, financial planners and others involved in assessing the impact of the Izmit earthquake was that there was little or no indication of readiness for earthquakes.

There was little evidence of legislation or enforcement of building regulations to protect structures against the impact of earthquakes. Most private residences and business premises were uninsured. Emergency facilities were poorly equipped or non-existent. There were few if any procedural guidelines to facilitate rescue or evacuation from danger zones. In fact, only since the 1980s had the Turkish government devoted resources to establish seismic stations and it was only as recently as 1998 that early warning systems for floods and other natural disasters were developed.

In November 1997, the Turkish government, in association with the United Nations Disaster Relief Programme, established the Disaster Management Implementation and Research Centre. The DMIRC was established concurrently with the foundation of the General Directorate of Disaster Affairs as a Branch of the Turkish Ministry of Public Works and Settlement. The two organisations were empowered to research and develop contingency plans to deal with disasters and establish early warning systems.

The General Directorate of Disaster Affairs had in fact proposed a series of building codes in early 1999, but by August 1999 they were not subject to legislation—and even if they had been, it would have been unlikely that more than a small fraction of existing structures could have been altered to meet the technical requirements. Turkey's rapidly growing population and residential and industrial building requirements were met by rapidly and poorly built, cheap and usually flimsy buildings.

The Izmit disaster and the criticism levelled at the Turkish government's lack of preparedness by the United Nations, the World Bank, the media and some of the rescue teams led to Turkey upgrading its disaster management infrastructure. In fact, the global effort to assist Turkey led to Ankara hosting the Global Disaster Information Network Conference in April 2000, which resolved to implement global cooperation in the prevention, contingency management, information-sharing, financing, and rescue and recovery procedures for major natural disasters.

The human cost of the Izmit earthquake was massive. However, the financial cost all but crippled the Turkish economy, which had been burdened by 50 per cent per annum inflation, poor balance of payments, massive external debt and a government hampered by ongoing deficit budgeting. The Izmit earthquake ruined much of Turkey's productive industrial heartland. The World Bank's assessment of the Izmit disaster suggested that the net cost of the earthquake would be in the region of US$3.6–6.5 billion, or between 1.5 and 3.3 per cent of GDP in 1999–2000. The assessment was based on increased output in unaffected regions and external financial support. The report was critical of Turkey's lack of preparedness for the disaster in relation to the paucity of enforceable building codes, poor insurance cover and a shortage of contingency measures.

It did, however, praise the Turkish government's

preparedness to increase tax to finance social welfare measures to assist the 500 000 homeless and to provide social security, educational and medical services and housing to the families of the 20 000 killed and 50 000 injured. The report called on the Turkish government to establish a centralised fund for disaster relief.

The Centre for Strategic International Studies in Washington DC published a detailed paper by Rusdu Saracoglu, a former Governor of the Turkish Central Bank and Minister of State for the Economy. Saracoglu observed that, during the 1990s, Turkey had experienced high GNP growth coupled with high inflation and a large number of outstanding government and private-sector loans. He described the Turkish financial system as small and weak by world standards.

Saracoglu believed that Turkey needed to operate under tighter controls such as those enforced by the International Monetary Fund. A more disciplined fiscal system would lead to control of interest rates and reduction in inflation and government deficits. In his view, the Izmit earthquake was evidence that these measures needed urgently to be implemented by the government.

The Izmit earthquake generated a vast amount of media coverage, much of it sympathetic to Turkey and especially the plight of the victims. The rescue and recovery effort did a great deal to build bridges between Turkey and the nations involved in providing assistance. The Izmit earthquake was a scene of cooperation of rescue teams from Israel and Arab states and the extensive involvement of US military rescue teams reinforced the Turkey-United States alliance. The political dividend from the US perspective was Turkey's vocal and strategic support for the US 'war against terrorism' following the September 11, 2001 attacks against New York and Washington DC. Turkish support was politically valuable for the United States in seeking to galvanise support from predominantly Muslim countries.

A positive outcome was a thawing in relations between Turkey and Greece. The Greek government provided considerable assistance to Turkey and sent rescue teams.

Turkish rescue teams reciprocated when Greece experienced a severe earthquake in 2000. Cultural links and other bilateral contacts increased between Greece and Turkey following the earthquake.

The initial impact of the Izmit earthquake was devastating and immediate. From all key source markets, there were cancellations and a reduction of forward bookings to Turkey. The media coverage at the time of the earthquake painted a picture of Turkish devastation. The normally sobre BBC reported that even central Istanbul was badly hit—though these reports were eventually revised when the actual extent of damage was realised.

The eastern outskirts of Istanbul were indeed affected by the quake, but not the central part of the city. The UK Foreign Office established an update line. On August 18, 1999, the Association of British Travel agents warned British travellers to 'reconsider' visits to Istanbul in the days immediately after the earthquake.

John Cunningham, reporting in *The Guardian* (London), summed up the response of many would-be tourists to the Turkish earthquake: 'after empathising with the victims ... is to wonder whether it is safe to go or holiday there'. His article went on to discuss the impact of disasters, be they terrorism, war or natural disaster, on all destinations. The blanket coverage of global media TV services including BBC, CNN and Deutsche Welle had a particularly profound and negative impact on tourism from Turkey's three largest source markets: Germany, the United Kingdom and the United States.

The impact was magnified when the largest Kurdish resistance movement PKK (Kurdistan Workers Party) issued statements in October 1999 warning tourists to avoid Turkey and threatened attacks on tourists who visited the country.

Although there was intense media interest in the Izmit earthquake at the time of the event, media coverage ran its course and waned within one month. Unlike some other countries discussed in this book, Turkey does not have a large permanent contingent of foreign correspondents and media coverage is subject to far stricter controls than in Western

European countries or North America. Other stories such as the onset of the millennium and the great scare of the 'Y2K Bug' rapidly replaced the Izmit earthquake in Western media headlines.

Even the PKK's genuine threats against tourists, which were tactically timed to gain media coverage while world attention was focused on Turkey, failed to stir a great deal of media interest—much to the relief of the Turkish government and the chagrin of the Kurds.

In the months between August and December 1999, inbound tourism figures were 30 per cent down on comparable months of 1998. Within a month of the earthquake, Turkish tourism authorities began the task of restoring the market.

The main tasks were:

- Highlighting the minimal earthquake damage to most visited tourist sites in the country and the tourist attractions of Istanbul;
- Encouraging the travel industry to demonstrate support for Turkey by urging their clients to visit;
- Stressing the overall safety of Turkey as a destination;
- Organising familiarisation visits by travel industry and tourism journalists to see Turkey first-hand and pass the message on to their clients/readers/listeners/viewers;
- Cooperate with allied tour operators in the various source markets to help disseminate a positive message about turkey.

The success story of the restoration of Turkey's tourism market in 2000 had a great deal to do with the professionalism of the Turkish Ministry of Tourism's marketing management and the onset of 2000, so frequently and incorrectly described as the 'New Millennium'.

The Turkish Ministry of Tourism was provided with strong moral and financial support by the Turkish government, enabling it to embark on a marketing restoration programme after the Izmit earthquake. The Turkish government recognised that tourism was a strategically important source of foreign exchange and goodwill. Turkish ethnic communities worldwide were encouraged to support the country during the emergency period and to assist in encouraging foreigners to visit.

The first priority for Turkish tourism offices was the mobilisation of media and travel agency hostings to Turkey facilitated by the Turkish Ministry of Tourism with the cocperation of Turkish Airlines and the major tour operators servicing Turkey. Television crews, journalists and travel agents were invited to see the extent of earthquake damage and then visit the main tourist areas to reinforce the message that they were largely untouched by the quake.

This strategy sought to convey a dual message of support for the victims of the quake by spending tourism dollars in Turkey. The Ministry also increased marketing subsidies to operators promoting Turkish tourism product.

The Turkish Ministry of Tourism established a crisis management team immediately after the earthquake to control press releases and messages tailored to the travel industry, the public and the media. The excellent Turkish Tourism website was utilised to reinforce the prime messages that tourism infrastructure was undamaged, access to the country and popular sites was unaffected and that tourists were safe if they visited.

While it is impossible to give a statistical measure of the success of these PR activities, there is no doubt that by January 2000 inbound tourism to Turkey had reached and surpassed the levels of the pre-earthquake period of 1999.

Turkey also actively promoted itself, sometimes in conjunction with Israel and Italy, as a key destination for Christian pilgrims during Christianity's bimillennial in 2000. During Pope John Paul II's series of visits to Christianity's holiest sites during the 2000 Holy Year declared by the Roman Catholic Church, Turkey was an integral part of the Pope's eastern Mediterranean itinerary.

Mr Erdal Aktan was appointed in 2001 to manage the Turkish Tourism Office in Australia. He had served in London during the early 1990s and was involved in the PR campaign to thank rescue teams in Turkey during 2000. As a gesture of the Turkish government's appreciation for their efforts Mr Aktan organised the hosting in Turkey of members of rescue teams from the 24 countries that provided rescue and medical teams during the earthquake crisis.

According to Mr Aktan, these hostings were warmly welcomed by the invitees and generated considerable positive publicity about Turkey in the countries which had provided the teams. The hostings also included reunions between rescuers and the people and communities they had assisted and helped publicise the recovery of devastated areas.

The Turkish Ministry of Tourism, with the assistance of its marketing consultants DDB Dreamworks, designed a new logo for Turkish tourism and released a new advertising campaign in 2000. The campaign focused on traditional themes of the diverse attractions of destination Turkey, but it also emphasised spirituality, 'green' and environmentally sensitive themes. The campaigns of 2001 were ethereal compared with the simple message of the 1990s, which was that Turkey was a jigsaw of attractions.

Considerable emphasis was placed on finding testimonials from people who had visited after the earthquake and whose opinions would carry weight in source markets. Concerts were staged in Turkey featuring European and American celebrities who could show their concern for the victims of the earthquake and then see Turkey and pass on the message to their audiences that it was safe to visit—a popular, mutually beneficial and effective public relations strategy.

The combination of creating a new marketing image, reassuring travellers and travel agents, and promoting a new millennial interest in Turkey all contributed to the acceleration of Turkey's tourism restoration. Overall, the combination of strategies was highly successful.

The other element which helped to achieve rapid recovery was the working alliance between the national tourism authority, airlines servicing Turkey (especially Turkish Airlines), and the Turkish and overseas tour operators marketing Turkey. Turkey's phenomenal growth as a destination during the 1990s provided considerable business for many private companies, hoteliers, charter carriers, and transport and tour operators servicing Turkey.

Apart from a genuine concern about speeding the recovery of Turkish tourism for all these businesses, there was a powerful element of enlightened self-interest to facilitate and accelerate the recovery.

Of the case studies in this book, the recovery of Turkey's tourism industry from the devastating Izmit earthquake was one of the most rapid and complete marketing restoration campaigns. While the Izmit earthquake represented a single incident, it was one of a series of earthquakes which Turkey, due to its geological structure, will regrettably continue to experience.

Turkey's strength, in common with that of Fiji, involved a well coordinated marketing campaign combining the resources of the government and private sector. A distinguishing factor of the Turkish recovery was the welltargeted and effective PR campaign directed at the travel industry from major source markets and the media. In the future, Turkey's position in a geologically and politically volatile part of the world will almost certainly require Turkey's tourist authorities to maintain their crisis management contingency plans in good working order.

Chapter 4

Tourism Policy and International Organizations

So much has been said about globalization and the need for corrective policies at this crossroads in history, that the demand for solid institutions to design, apply and develop these policies has all too often been overlooked. It was only in the late 1990s, with the Asia-Pacific economic crisis, the situation in Russia and other countries of the former communist bloc - Bosnia, Kosovo or Chechnya - that the mainstream of thought was admitting to the need for second generation reforms, that is to say, policies aimed at reinforcing institutions.

Given this situation, theoretical thinking in tourism and actual tourism policies are still somewhat behind the times. The need for an explicit national tourism policy is at times questioned: such tourism powers as the United States have dismantled their central tourism agencies; others, like the European Union, assign their tourism policy to small departments with absurd budgets, inadequate staff resources and incoherent programmes.

In some countries, especially in those which have recently become active in tourism, interventionism is practised, while others employ the discredited if well-intentioned formula of leaving business to the businessmen, while the public administrations carry out the promotion.

The panorama is even more baffling at the international level. While all main agents of tourism - airlines, hotel chains, tour operators, tourism administrations, etc. - discuss and/or defend globalization, little is done to analyse its contents and implications. In this regard, much less has been done to propose frames and instruments of action for international tourism policy and, beyond that, global institutions committed to the development and coordination of world tourism.

In some cases, it seems that the concept of globalization is introduced to justify non-action or, more specifically, the dismantling of national and international *public* tourism policy. Somehow, the argument goes, the market forces will find a way, and it will be to the benefit of consumers.

In spite of that business philosophy, this chapter deals with public sector intervention, through a specific sectoral policy, tourism policy, which responds to at least two crucial issues:

- The significant contribution of tourism activity to the general aims of economic policy - development, stability, efficiency, etc.; and
- The large component of public goods in tourism activity.

An overview of explicit tourism policy implemented in the last decade shows an evolution in its content, from interventionist attitudes and a focus on promotional mechanisms, to the creation of frameworks that foster the competitiveness of tourism clusters and the use of broad scope instruments, quite similar to those present in industrial policy.

Globalization - or rather, the growing trend towards globalization - increases the need for national and international tourism policies. But the question of who are to be the decision-makers of such policies, and what will be their substance, needs to be examined. Multinational/transnational enterprises will obviously play a role, and it will be naturally concerned with the efficiency and profitability of international tourism.

Non-governmental organizations will also want to intervene to ensure that tourism is compatible with their own agendas, with specific cultural, environmental or social objectives in mind.

Thus, it is vital to analyse what is the role of governments and intergovernmental organizations in global tourism and what may be the adequate substance of international global tourism policy, regarding both the development of tourism and its contribution to global society.

GLOBALIZATION AND TOURISM: THE NEW AGE

In recent years, reference to globalization in the academic and professional world is constant. The notable interdependence between economies and the trend towards greater similarity of lifestyles are two conventional points of reference in the globalization concept. Nevertheless, globalization, under other names, is not a new concept but rather an acceleration of trends that have been active for decades and even centuries.

In fact, in the twentieth century, apart from technological advances and the political and social transformations of the past few decades, there had not been a great advance of this trend. It can even be said that financial and economic institutions in the second half of the nineteenth century were more internationalized than at the beginning of the twentieth century.

What is often understood as globalization comprises diverse economic, social and political phenomena. The intensification of commercial exchanges, marked by the progressive dismantling of protectionist barriers, the growing integration of financial markets, the presence of new industrialized countries and technological developments, especially in the area of know-how and information, are affecting both the national economies and the lifestyles of societies.

All of this is creating the basis for a global system or organization, distinctly characterized by a high level of economic, socio-cultural and environmental interdependence. In the latter area, some authors have pointed to the problems caused by the global warming, pollution and the danger of nuclear war as factors which accelerate globalization. The development of these and other phenomena on a global scale clashes with the entrenched policies and institutions designed for national frameworks, as public policies, debated and occasionally agreed upon in international fora as they may be, still lack the global dimension.In this context, it is not remarkable that tourism activity is both the cause and effect of accelerated globalization. It is useful to point out three essential elements of contemporary tourism:

- The extension of tourism demand throughout the world: the increase in intra- and inter-regional travel - although many strata of the population are still travelling only locally or are strangers to tourism.
- Similarity of tourism demand: convergence of consumer preferences, tastes and lifestyles - although the type of travel is segmented.
- Concentration and similarity of tourism supply: expansion of distribution systems, business mergers, etc. - although new specialists agents are appearing on the scene.

To all of this it must added without doubt the impact of new technologies on tourism, which is even more significant than that of changes in consumer taste or in institutional structures. The traditional tourism resources, the comparative advantages (climate, landscape, culture, etc.), are becoming less and less important compared with other factors in tourism competitiveness.

Information (or rather, the strategic management of information), intelligence (innovative capacity of teams within an organization) and knowledge (know-how, or a combination of technological skills, technology and organizational culture - *humanology*) now constitute new tourism resources and key factors in the competitiveness of tourism organizations (enterprises, destinations and institutions).

The major (most-visited) tourism destinations of the world are no longer the famous beaches or traditional cultural capitals, but rather man-made products, such as Orlando or Las Vegas. In fact, the greatest foreseeable competition in the medium term for the present tourism activity is not the appearance of new exotic resorts, but instead the massive use of the increasingly accessible and efficient information and communication technologies for new leisure products: virtual travel and experiences.

Tourism thus finds itself in a situation, which Kuhn (1962) would clearly define as a paradigm shift, and which is not casually related to or far from the globalization process of economy and society in general. The concept of a business paradigm, understood as a set of theories, values, attitudes, methods and instruments, rules and practices, is useful when analysing business strategy in given framework conditions.

Thus, it is increasingly seen that, in recent decades, mass tourism business strategies (the Fordian Era of Tourism) - and especially profit-making through economies of scale and the consequent standardization of rigid tourism packages - are giving way to a new paradigm shaped by the segmentation of the new consumer demands, new technologies, new forms of business production and management and new framework conditions.

This new post-Fordian business paradigm in tourism, which Fayos-Solà (1994) called the *New Age of Tourism*, has repercussions on business strategy, and also very profound ones on the policy and even the organization of tourism administrations.

The main objective of tourism policy is to improve the conditions under which tourism activity is carried out. In the Fordian era, increase in tourism activity required a quantitative type of action - which goal was maximizing the number of visitors. In this paradigm, the emphasis on attracting demand corresponded well to the then traditional type of economic policy, based on Keynesian mainstream thinking. Tourism receipts enhanced foreign currency earnings and the creation of employment, so that the success of this sectoral tourism policy allowed other economic policy objectives to be reached, especially those related to economic growth and full employment.

The Keynesian-style policies are based on handling the components of aggregate demand: consumption, investment, public expenditure and net exports (exports minus imports). In this intervention framework, tourism expenditure is considered as an item within exports. The income multiplier - i.e. the mechanism which explains how an increase of the variables of aggregated demand (investment, public expenditure and exports) creates an increase in income which exceeds the initial effort - has constituted the central explanatory and justifying mechanism of demand policies.

The transmissions and leakages in the multiplier chain depend on the marginal propensity to consume (the part of each increment in income destined to consumption), on the marginal propensity to import, and the average tax rate. These last two elements constitute leakages in the Keynesian model: the greater these two elements are, the less the multiplier effect in the domestic economy is.

Interior tourism expenditure (domestic plus incoming - traditionally considered under exports) favours the initial effort in the chain. Outgoing tourism expenditure (national less domestic - usually considered under imports) diminish, cancel or make this initial effort negative. The capacity of the national economy to supply the needs of tourism activity affects the marginal propensity to import, increasing or diminishing the final effect of income creation.

Within this theoretical framework we should emphasize how Keynesian-style economic policy makes full sense within a framework of nation-states, where the effects of these policies are highly predictable and controllable. However, this model lost validity after the financial and economic crises at the end of the 1970s, its theoretical base weakened by the difficulty of applying Keynesian formulas when facing wage-price spiralling inflation - stagflation - and a growing internationalization of the economy.

The dismantling of international trade restrictions (tariffs, import duties, etc.) stimulated by the GATT strongly modified the preconceptions on marginal propensity to import. Imports have become less expensive and the previously described chain of induced consumption was easily channelled towards 'foreign' products. 'National' economic areas are now more receptive to foreign products. The leakages of the model described have increased considerably.

In addition, in international tourism markets the emergence of new destinations and products with competitive prices has been constant since these years, and is a strong threat to traditional destinations. With growing competition, it has been necessary to undertake the restructuring of traditional offers.

Within this setting, it is logical that tourism administrations since the 1980s have switched their emphasis to supply policies. The main aim of aggregated supply policies is to increase and improve the productive capacity of a country. Without abandoning supply policies, it is necessary to point out the change in perspective caused by this shift, since it was no longer only a question of creating internal or external demand, of improving demand conditions, of fostering their increase or moderation in accordance with the current economic cycle; or of tourism administrations concentrating on promotion.

From this time, the need to improve tourism production to meet with an ever growing competition was felt. This implied the dismantling of sub-sectors, enterprises and unproductive products, a greater research and development (R&D) effort in education and training, in the business quality clusters, in the infrastructure, public services and goods for the sector, etc.

This change, from a tourism policy based on demand to supply models, takes into consideration that the basic problem is not tourism demand, which will continue to grow according to all forecasts. Globalization and the increased competition in tourism markets after the 1980s has required a consistent improvement in the price/product-characteristics ratio, that is to say, a continuous striving towards quality and efficiency. The Spanish case provides a good example of the new approach to tourism policies, which prioritizes action on the quantity and, especially, quality of tourism supply, making available to businessmen the necessary mechanisms to increase competitiveness:

- Improving know-how by fostering R&D, tourism education and training, and information management;

- Diversifying the supply, with new products and destinations;
- Physical modernization of installations and infrastructure;
- Improving business clusters, encouraging action by ancillary businesses, associations and the *coopetition* (cooperation-competition) between private agents and the public sector;
- Improving promotion, with greater quality (responding to promotion needs of the actual, existing supply) and efficiency;
- Conservation and regeneration of tourism areas; and
- Improving horizontal (interdepartmental) and vertical (local-regional-state-intergovernmental) coordination of public administrations for tourism policy.

Globalization, governance and the nation-state: implications for national tourism policies

As several authors have pointed out, the discussion on globalization often covers up highly ideological visions of the future; there is no true evidence that globalization has gone beyond the acceleration of political, economic and cultural internationalization processes which began in many cases centuries ago, and in any case, it does not appear to be totally just to use this concept to defend a radically anti-political vision of the world in the twenty-first century.

It is obvious that the debate on globalization has rekindled extreme right and left ideological points of view. For the former, globalization will offer new hope (after the failure of the monetary experiences of the 1970s and 1980s) for a world where free trade, world capital markets and transnational organizations can fully use productive resources without the clumsy interference of governments.

For the radical left (also affected by the fall of state socialism and the anti-imperialist movements of past decades), globalization of capitalism indicates the uselessness of social-democratic style 'welfare' initiatives carried out at a national level.

If we examine the general role of the state at present before defining its tourism policy functions, it is quite obvious that its capacities have been redefined. The *sovereignty*, exclusive control (excluding other authorities) of a territory no longer exists. The capacity to 'defend' its citizens from macro-conflicts has been questionable since the era of nuclear arms.

The claim to standardize and control culture within borders is also no longer justifiable; citizens of the world establish cultural affinities and links through means of communications that escape the control of nation-states and almost any censoring attempt. Finally, and this has been remarked previously, economic internationalization makes it practically impossible to carry out autonomous economic policies.

But all this does not signify either the disappearance of the political role of nation-states, or a great change in international relations. Perhaps it should be recalled that in the first place the very sovereignty of states, as defined in the seventeenth and eighteenth centuries, has always depended on their international recognition. The guarantee of non-intervention by other states allowed the consolidation of sovereignty in the state itself.

Also, although nation-states have seen their capacity for exclusive control of a *territory* enormously diminished, what is true is that they still have a central role in the control of the *population* of this territory, taking into account that it is much less mobile than either information or economic flows.For this reason, it seems that the issue under debate is not the avowed disappearance or reduction to a minimum of the role of the nation-state in a 'globalized' world, but rather the question of governance in a more integrated society at world level and the role of governments in this society.

There is no doubt that the nation-states have a vital role in this process: they still possess a great deal of the power and, in any case, maintain the legitimacy of representing the populations that live within their frontiers; and beyond having an unquestionable role as 'local' suppliers of certain public goods in the world context, they are the natural interlocutors in intergovernmental organizations that can possibly make advances in the task of designing, proposing and maintaining standards (voluntary, agreed or legislated) for the functioning of international and/or global systems.

Although there may be other protagonists in the creation of framework conditions - multinational companies for example - it does not seem that they can claim a greater representation of the world's citizens, and the authentic multinational nature of many companies - which in reality are strongly established in one of the developed regions of the world and also have operations and subsidiaries in other countries and regions - is questionable.

In any case, it seems evident that the *second generation* tasks, to which the introduction of this chapter refers - the creation and strengthening of responsible international and global institutions in charge of these framework conditions - will in great part depend on the collaboration between nation-states and other major protagonists on a world level.

Within the area of tourism activity, and, as has been previously indicated, the transition from national policies almost exclusively quantitative in dimension (maximizing the number of tourists through promotion), to others stimulating competitiveness (quality and efficiency) in an international context, entails a change of traditional functions in the tourism public sector.

This change can be summarized as follows:

- First, the transition from a situation where the public sector owns and operates all types of tourism facilities and intervenes customarily in the direct provision of goods and services, to a role of coordinator of private and public actions in tourism.
- Second, the opening up of the goals and means of tourism policy, from an almost exclusive promotional content (generic advertising, trade missions and exhibits, publications, etc.), to a broad range of instruments to foster and facilitate the activities of tourism decision-makers.
- Finally, the evolution, from a philosophy of rigid

regimentation of entrepreneurial activities, to deregulation and privatization of tourism.

This ties in well with the new role of the nation-state: international representation of populations (and enterprises) located within its frontiers, concordance of interests which are not always in agreement - through the stimulation of associative and cooperative activity - and the improvement of the quality of life within its territorial limits.The implications for the formulation of national tourism policies are clear:

- The objectives of these policies must refer to the creation of competitive frameworks on a local-regional-national scale which, by improving the conditions of the economic, social and environmental framework, achieve contributions of the tourism sector to the well-being of the citizens.
- Although the use of promotional instruments by tourism administrations (communication, publicity, etc.) continues to be requested by decision-makers in tourism, its importance is decreasing. On the other hand, the need to coordinate promotion with a wider range of instruments in tourism policy has become evident.
- The new public instruments for tourism development and management are not fundamentally different from those used in sectoral industrial policy. Essentially, they foster the competitiveness of existing tourism clusters and the adoption of strategies for success in international markets of emerging destinations or those which are in the process of restructuring.

Although a study of the budgets of national tourism administrations indicates that public expenditure in tourism is still greatly concentrated in promotional instruments, in the area of competitiveness and strategy there is a growing dedication to Porterian-type instruments. Specifically, the new tourism policies of countries such as France, Spain, Italy, Germany, Canada, Australia and South Africa concur in the use of the following instruments:

Strengthening supply conditions:

- Human resource development in tourism. Education and training which is more in line with the short, medium and long-term needs of the tourism employers. Awareness of the need to anticipate the upsurge of new tourism professions and the continuous training of professionals in the sector.
- Fostering innovation and development (R&D) specifically for use by tourism enterprises. Awareness of the need to give priority to the R&D of tourism processes over the R&D directly applicable to products and services.
- Modernization of the productive plant, installations and infrastructure in tourism. Awareness of the need to make compatible the modernization of the supply of public and private goods and services, and to create lasting mechanisms to permanently (and not on a one-time basis) carry out this task.
- Impetus of diversification and specialization in tourism destinations, products and services, although taking into account that the competitive advantages are more easily achieved in the realm of tourism processes.
- Stimulus to the conservation of natural, cultural, urban or rural areas in which tourism is carried out, and of heritage sites sensitive to tourism use. Awareness that these areas form part of the consumer *tourism experience* and that there is no tourism product and destination quality without eco-tourism quality.
- Fostering a more even geographical distribution of tourism supply and demand, in support of other more generic objectives of public policy (e.g. an incomes policy for farming in disadvantaged areas). This has to be tightly coordinated with the responsible regional and local governments.

Strengthening the business fabric:

- Fostering of associative and cooperative initiatives between tourism enterprises and destinations.

Awareness of the need to cooperate and not only compete at the intra-cluster and inter-cluster level in the context of a national tourism policy.

- Stimulus to give tourism activities an adequate dimensional scope. Awareness that this dimensional scope depends on the nature of niche-markets and the (changing) state of available technology. New information and communication technologies allow for new solutions in this respect.
- Public and cooperative contributions to sectoral and sub-sectoral information management, useful for decision-making at the enterprise, sectoral association, *cluster*, tourism destination level or even at a macro-national level.
- Adaptation of the judicial and institutional framework to give confidence and greater efficiency to business decision-making. Awareness of the need to make this framework flexible so that it continuously adapts to rapidly changing circumstances.
- Contribution of the tourism administration and sectoral cooperation institutions to *strategic*decision-making, beyond considerations of short-or medium-term quality and efficiency and the search for excellence in established market niches.

Strengthening demand conditions:

- In the context of the Porterian paradox that a better informed, exigent and sophisticated demand favours competitiveness and strategic positioning of enterprises.
- Obtaining and disseminating market information on consumer groups typology and communication channels for this purpose.
- Improving the promotion policy, from an instrument based on passive information on the positive characteristics of products, destinations and cultural and environmental amenities, to a means of forming and modulating the expectations and even the perceptions of the clients.

- Support to marketing efforts of tourism enterprises and destinations. Awareness of the role of new technologies and stimulus to innovation in tourism marketing processes.
- Improving the tourism information milieu in which consumers, workers, enterprises and tourism administrations move. Awareness that the cost of obtaining this information for the individual decision-maker may be high and that it is therefore preferable to approach this matter as the provision of a public good.
- To strengthen tourism training and qualifications, not only within the business context, but also in that of the consumer and host societies.
- Protection of the consumer-tourist, improving the applicable standards and the inter-administrative coordination. Awareness that today's tourist demands a high degree of confidence in the quality of the product and in his personal safety as an essential condition to increasing his loyalty to tourism products, services and destinations.
- Integral management of tourism quality to increase the level of consumer satisfaction and the well-being of receiving societies. Awareness that it is essential to have existing client loyalty to be competitive in tourism destinations, and that this cannot be achieved only through aggressive commercial promotion aimed at new clients.

Strengthening of linked industries and services:

- Stimulus to the creation and adequate functioning of related industries and services in tourism clusters and destinations. Awareness of their relevance, both in the horizontal (complementary) and vertical (suppliers, sub-contractors and client companies) sense to achieve competitiveness.
- Coordination of public administrations concerned with tourism, both in the horizontal (departments within an administration) and vertical (local, regional

and national administrations) sense. Awareness that the public administration in general (and not only the *tourism* departments of the same) constitutes part of this institutional and business milieu essential for competitiveness in tourism.

- Stimulus to the re-engineering of the macro-processes within the tourism clusters and destinations. Awareness that it is possible to achieve the necessary quality objectives by improving the efficiency of the optional useable processes. Re-engineering of public administrative processes and their coordination with the private sector, improving their quality and dedication to service, usually is an important part of this instrument.

THE ROLE OF INTERGOVERNMENTAL ORGANIZATIONS IN TOURISM

In spite of abundant references in professional and academic literature to globalization in tourism, the fact is that the tourism business fabric is mainly made of sub-sectors with a large number of medium, small and micro industries, often of a marked local character.

The most notable exceptions are the air transport sub-sector in itself and the existence of some large enterprises in the hospitality (hotel chains), travel agency (certain tour operators) and entertainment (macro theme parks) sub-sectors. In fact, though, one of the best-known business lobbies in the sector, the World Tourism and Travel Council (WTTC), which defines itself as comprising the chairpersons and highest executives (CEOs) of the largest companies in the world, has only seventy-five members.

In addition, even when considering these large tourism enterprises, there is reason to question their status as *global* enterprises. Most frequently, they are strongly identified - by origin, business culture, major operations and decision-making strategies - with one of the countries of the G3 triad (North America, Europe and Japan), with their presence in other countries being as subsidiaries, franchises, etc.

For these reasons, it is difficult to agree with the statement that 'tourism is one of the most globalized industries'. The fact that many of the industry's clients have to cross borders to travel and that there are suppliers with products in several countries can grant it, at the most, a partially *international* character.

According to WTO estimates, only one in ten tourist movements is international, while the rest are domestic. Thus, although international tourism demand is already more than 650 million trips annually and is growing at an accumulative yearly rate of 4.3 per cent, most travel takes place within world-regions (Europe, North America-Caribbean, East Asia-Pacific) and within national borders. Additionally, tourism, unlike financial transactions or information flows, requires the physical transport of people, a characteristic which makes it highly controllable by the sovereignty, albeit residual, of nation-states.

Thus, it seems reasonable to defend the premise that the tourism industry is still in a phase of international activity, although it is also true that tourism is, on the other hand, contributing to the worldwide dissemination of cultural and social habits, and is therefore in this regard, a *factor* in the globalization process.

However, the importance and growing expansion of international tourism, its contribution to the development of regions and countries, to income and employment creation, its status, which has already been mentioned, as a transmitter of cultural identity images, all justify the attention it has merited and still merits from institutions on a worldwide scale as well as the existence of an intergovernmental organization (WTO) specifically dedicated to international tourism policy.

Neither an analysis, nor an exhaustive inventory of the international institutions, which have had or do have influence, either direct or indirect on tourism flows, is attempted here; the list is too long and the analysis complex. Many international organizations and agencies, from the OECD, with a tourism committee whose existence is now at risk, to the

World Bank, have given attention to some of the most relevant functions of tourism activity.

The European Union, in 1989 for the first time, granted responsibility for tourism policy to a specific department - its General Directorate XXIII - although the budgetary provisions given to the tourism unit were always minimal and the main part of the European budget had a much stronger impact on tourism activity through the structural funds, programmes for innovations and training or, in the case of third world countries, through development aid programmes.

Perhaps the most relevant issue, in the context of this chapter, is the substance of supranational intergovernmental action in tourism, i.e. *international tourism policy*, and the viability and pertinence of hypothetical global tourism policy.

Justification of an international tourism policy, apart from the arguments already indicated, is also based on the growing importance of the knowledge factor in the production of tourism services and *experiences*. Perhaps, somewhat paradoxically, the tourism industry, the origins of which tied it geographically to nature resources and/or historical or cultural heritage, has freed itself from these conditioning factors, to the extent where the most sought after tourism destinations at present are often totally artificial (man-made).

The use of communication in tourism, often tied to the leisure-entertainment industry, has shaped new consumer needs and created a demand for new tourism destinations in a process where communication-entertainment (the film industry, computerized games, the internet, television, publishing, etc.) has created expectations in potential tourists which are later satisfied (theme parks, theme hotels, dramatized tourism experiences, etc.) with major contributions from information-communication technology and the entertainment industry.

It is in this context, where one can see a rapid tendency towards globalization in the tourism industry, standardizing supply and demand and freeing them from the confines of stationary cultural or natural realities, and making it almost indistinguishable from the leisure industry, advancing towards a future of *virtual experiences* that could easily escape the control of the sovereignty of states. What should the substance of a contemporary international tourism policy be, and in what direction should this policy move, taking account of the previously mentioned tendencies towards future globalization?

The first issue should, without doubt, be to identify the players in tourism policy. If the globalization of tourism is not considered to have already happened, there is still time and the opportunity to identify those players who are more desirable and those who are less so. There is also time to favour the most sensible future scenarios, seen from the perspective of the contribution of tourism to the well-being of citizens, and their participation in the decisions as to what type of well-being they truly desire.

Far from accepting extreme positions on globalization - i.e. that it is already determined, that the decision-making power of multinationals/transnationals is above that of the traditional sources of governance - it is possible to determine explicitly the current players, and possibly future ones, of governance in general and tourism policy in particular:

- *Regional and local administrations*: Although their area of competence falls within the framework of higher level administrations, they have the effective advantage of being close to the citizen and the entrepreneurial units. They constitute the ideal public players to implement sectoral policies, which can be decided on occasion within the local and regional context or coordinated with the administrations having a wider scope of action. In the democratic context they are validated by the vote of their citizens.
- *National administrations*: They still have a wide magnitude of sovereignty. On occasion, they have devolved part of this to regional and local administrations and/or relinquished part to institutions or administrations with an international mandate. In the democratic context, they are

endorsed by the vote of their citizens and frequently discharge this representation within international institutions. The consequent limitations (free circulation of capital, elimination of tariffs, etc.) are accepted in view of the benefits expected from a better distribution of resources on an international/world scale, but other objectives of national economic policies can be in contradiction with this self-limitation.

- *Supranational administrations*: Their historical origin lies in commercial agreements. The European Union is the most significant experience in this sense. The size of this type of administration enables economic, social, environmental and sectoral policy objectives to be set, which are out of the reach of national administrations, and they can more successfully confront the undesirable aspects of the globalization process.
- Agreements between countries or even between blocks of countries (G3 or G7 type). These are established to confront specific problems (financial speculation, international crime, etc.) and sometimes lead to the creation of international legislation.
- International agencies and organizations created by a group of states to permanently handle specific issues arising from economic, social or environmental activities. In the field of tourism, the paradigmatic player in this category is the World Tourism Organization (WTO).

This final type of player is the one whose decisions on tourism policy are considered here, although the substance of the tourism policy which can evolve should be analysed within the context of other players in international governance.

Non-governmental organizations (NGOs) and private sector businesses and institutions are excluded here as principal players in governance, since they lack democratic representation, although their important role as partners or associates in governance by the previously mentioned players is obvious.The instruments which are useful to the international organizations usually belong to one of the following categories:

- *Legislation*: Agreements with a judicial scope to standardize the laws of member states and even of other states which may join the initiative. These agreements are directed at remedying the non-extraterritoriality of national laws and/or the lack of international legislation and/or the lack of enforcing bodies.
- *Agreements without a judicial scope*: Aimed at eliminating or lessening the repercussions of frontier restrictions by creating a framework for greater security in international transactions. These agreements have a technological, economic, social and/or ethical content. They are generally enforced through specific mechanisms to penalize infractions.
- *Voluntary quality standards*: These are proposed without the need of previous consensus, at the initiative of the organization in question or by a group of member states. They propose a model for conduct with regard to technological, economic, sociological and/or ethical matters. They do not usually have authority to penalize, but are intended rather to oversee or coordinate. They are accepted voluntarily due to the added value they give in terms of promotional image, facilitation in communication with other players in the market, interspatial and inter-temporal measurements, etc.

Given the demonstrated difficulty in establishing and developing the tourism policy instruments indicated in the first two categories, it can be said that international organizations specialized in tourism, and concretely WTO, are showing a growing tendency to use voluntary quality standard instruments.

This signifies, without doubt, an advance over the previous situation, where the insistence to establish legal agreements, or even simply enforceable agreements, led to a general impasse given the inability to achieve consensus or wide majorities because of:

- The diverse economic, social, cultural and political situations of the member states;
- The frequently heterogeneous nature of the member state's representation in the organization: Departments of Foreign Affairs, of Commerce and Tourism, of Culture and Tourism, of the Economy (Tourism Department), of Industry and Tourism, of Tourism, etc.;
- The variable importance of departments of tourism and of tourism affairs within governments of member states, where on occasion they play a minor role;
- With regard to legislative instruments, the difficulty that departments with competence in tourism have to influence sufficiently the deliberations and decisions of the national legislative powers.

The instruments in the voluntary quality standards category can point to models, of varying types, for flexible and rapid action, which can be gradually adopted by member states and even as a global voluntary standard. These models can successfully bring added value to international markets, which are potentially global, and can be adapted to different national situations.

Although the explicit adoption of a voluntary standard by a sovereign state facilitates its global establishment, this can be expedited, in the case of delay or a lack of will, if the standard is *de facto* adopted by the industry and/or citizens of the country in question. Furthermore, the standards proposed can also fail when their format is rejected or ignored by potential users.

Thus, in this context, it should be noted that the role of international organizations in tourism, and specifically that of WTO, is rapidly evolving, from the traditional one of a forum where countries meet, to that of serving as an information broker between the countries and of being responsible for carrying out economic development projects and giving specific assistance to countries, up to the present role of also serving as an institution where voluntary quality standards are created and implemented in such key areas of tourism as:

- The development of human resources for tourism - education, training, strategy, management and labour conditions;
- Statistical information;
- Market intelligence;
- Know-how in products, services and processes;
- Infrastructure, collective services and urban environments;
- Cultural and environmental aspects of tourism;
- Economic and social effects of tourism;
- Facilitation of international movements of travellers and tourists;
- Financing of tourism;
- Quality of products, services and tourism environments;
- Communication in tourism;
- Ethical aspects of tourism activity;
- Legislative processes and contents in tourism; and
- Coordination of administrations with competence in tourism - intra-administration, inter-administrations, and with the private sector.

The content of the tourism policy instruments being used in contemporary action is justified by the two major reasons for the existence of international organizations specialized in tourism (and that of the WTO itself):

- International and global public goods, externalities, market imperfections and merit and demerit goods.

To analyse the contemporary scope of this justification it must be realized that the foundations - i.e. the so-called resources - of tourism activity are rapidly changing. In principle, as has already been indicated, cultural and natural resources were those backing tourism development. The addition of financial capital and work efforts to these resources created tourism products. The comparative advantages of tourism destinations were based on the abundance and correct combination of these elements.

At present, the relevance of natural and cultural resources has diminished - except for world-class resources and in specialized niche markets - while the importance of financial capital and above all that of information, intelligence-creativity and know-how - used by human teams in business and organizational cultures prepared for competiveness and strategic success - has increased.

Given these circumstances, the role of international organizations specializing in tourism is clear:

- The provision of public goods which previously were the domain of the states, such as quality education and training, strategic information and basic know-how;
- The internalization of externalities in the planetary context, such as the costs of pollution or possible climate changes;
- The correction of imperfections in international markets such as the costs of information or the appearance of highly monopolized tourism operations; and
- The introduction of ethical criteria in carrying out tourism activity on an international scale (working conditions in tourism, sexual exploitation in tourism and the like).

This first justification of the activity of WTO or other international organizations clearly shows the differences between intergovernmental agencies or organizations - created by and responsible to a (large) group of states, and occupied with international governance - and other international organizations (such as NGOs, motivated by more specific aims), international business lobbies or large enterprises, whose objectives differ from, and on occasion are in conflict with, those mentioned above.

- The benefit to member states of exercising their sovereignty in optimal conditions and of supplementing it when it is questioned or proves inefficient in the globalization process.

This is where the traditional role of international

organizations is evolving towards greater technical contents, which give depth and relevance to the member states' fora of discussion. Without assuming a conceptual breach with this traditional role, it is obvious that the use of a voluntary standard type of instruments, already mentioned above, gives greater flexibility and scope to the resolutions discussed and adopted in these fora, which are later subjected to a validation process - through an appraisal of their value in the market and society and their acceptance or not by businesses, institutions and the citizen.

The acceptance and establishment of these standards, when it takes place, represents a real step towards international and global governance for:

- It makes it possible to have truly global rules (standards), backed by states, which are more representative than businesses or other types of organizations;
- This acceptance happens only when the standards create added value for a large enough number of social and economic players;
- It reinforces the role of the organizations creating and overseeing these standards as well as the capacity of such organizations to adapt them to changing circumstances with greater democratic legitimacy.

Although the concept of globalization is broadly used in academic and professional literature, its exact definition, its measurement and its effects are far from being clear. The mere reference to phenomena affecting the world is still conceptually weak and cannot be used as evidence of globalization without being qualified.

Economic, technological or cultural internationalization processes are not new, and their present acceleration does not imply that globalization is inexorable. Historically these processes have stopped and reversed several times.

It is also not evident that these processes and their future culmination in globalization imply the disappearance or impotence of the sovereignty of nation-states. This assumption on occasion responds to a highly ideological view of world society. States still have mechanisms to control large enterprises and to create new instruments for governance, guaranteeing democratic control of future scenarios compatible with the well-being of a majority of the citizens.

Multinational/transnational enterprises are not necessarily global, since their cultural and strategic bases and the greater part of their business volume are generally found in only a few countries, normally located in the area of the G3 (North America, Europe or Japan).

The phenomena related to globalization affect tourism differently, depending on whether demand or supply are being considered. Demand shows clearer globalization tendencies as consumer preferences and expectatives converge, even though the *type* of holidays sought is becoming more diverse. On the other hand, tourism supply is still far from being global; thus, multinationals in tourism have not permeated the markets, with a few exceptions such as airlines, and hotel chains.

The business fabric in almost all tourism sub-sectors is formed by hundreds of thousands of small and micro enterprises. In addition, international tourism, although significant and rapidly growing, only represents a minor part of the total volume of the tourism business, in the most part domestic. As tourism implies the physical movement of people, the capacity of the states to exercise their sovereignty in this activity is obvious.

National tourism policy will remain a key factor in the development of tourism in a majority of countries for at least the next decade, although devolution to regional and local governments may change its role in some areas. The importance of tourism and its economic, social and environmental implications, which affect governance and broader scope economic policy, speak in favour of establishing explicit national tourism policy frameworks.

This sectoral policy may then be implemented by regional and local administration, which is closer to concrete tourism destinations and business clusters. The question is therefore one of reassigning tasks and it does not imply the automatic weakening of national tourism administrations.

The substance of tourism policy in key countries has been broadly in line with other economic sectoral interventions, particularly industrial policy. Emphasis has shifted, from almost exclusive concern with promotion, to a wider range of instruments acting on productive conditions as well. However, the specific characteristics of tourism supply ask for special attention being put in certain elements of competitiveness.

The comparative advantages (natural and cultural resources) which used to be the base for the success of tourism destinations are giving way to *competitive* advantages in a new business paradigm (the New Age of Tourism) where information, inteligence and know-how play a vital role.

These national tourism policies increasingly have a central theme: the use of Porterian style instruments to foster the competitiveness of tourism clusters (destinations, sub-sectors and/or groups of enterprises).

These instruments belong to one or several of the following types:

- Strengthening the supply conditions;
- Strengthening the business fabric;
- Strengthening the demand conditions;
- Strengthening of linked industries and services.

Even though it may be premature thinking of tourism as an already globalized activity, the importance and expansion of international tourism does justify the treatment of tourism matters in international-scope organizations and the existence of an intergovernmental institution (the WTO) specifically dedicated to international tourism policy.

The work programme of any intergovernmental institution committed to tourism, and, in particular, that of WTO, must respond to two types of rationale:

- The importance in tourism of international and global public goods, externalities, market imperfections and merit and demerit goods; and
- The benefit to member states of exercising their sovereignty in optimal conditions and of

supplementing it when it is questioned or proves inefficient in the globalization process.

When in this context, tourism policy implemented by an intergovernmental organization represents a real step towards international and global governance.

International legislation or enforceable agreements are rather rigid instruments for international tourism policy. The evolution of national tourism policies - towards deregulation, privatization and a role coordinating public-private partnerships - leads the way to a more participative and less coercive kind of tourism policy.

The preferred type of instruments of such a policy is found in the realm of voluntary standards of quality; they can be very flexibly adopted by countries, destinations or the industry. These types of instruments adapt best to the difficulties found in developing international tourism policy given:

- The heterogeneous nature of government departments competent in tourism;
- The diverse economic, social, cultural and political conditions in nation-states;
- The variable importance of departments of tourism within governments of nation-states, where on occasion they play a minor role; and
- The difficulty that departments with competence in tourism have to sufficiently influence the deliberations and decisions of the national legislative powers.

The threats and opportunities characterizing the internationalization and globalization processes in contemporary society require, in tourism as well, responses beyond *ad hoc* legislation, treaties or agreements. International and global matters need international and global *institutions.*

The liberalization of trade and tourism, the removal of obstacles and the consequent improvement in the allocation of resources make for big improvements in the well-being of the peoples of the world. However, it is important to pay attention to the *actors* of the globalization processes.

Multinational/transnational companies and non-governmental organizations are without doubt very relevant decision-makers in the new realities - but they cannot play the leading role in representative governance, which is a question of increasing concern at world level.

Tourism, because of its importance in the development of regions and countries and its capacity to convey images of cultural identity - so deeply needed in the configuration of global society - requires international and global *representative* organizations, to play a key role in world governance.

Chapter 5

Tourism Demand and Competitiveness

Globalisation is already evident in most aspects of tourism activity. International tourism and hospitality enterprises have taken advantage of numerous factors to expand their operations globally. Globalisation has raised competitive pressures by bringing more entrants into the market and as a result enterprises have to compete within a much more complex environment. Emerging technologies enabled greater homogeneous control and operational systems as well as coordination with head office despite geographical location and distance.

Changes in the political and legal environment introduced greater freedom of trade and more specifically in travel deregulation of transportation and more flexible and adaptive international investment and development systems. A wide range of forms and arrangements is followed, from direct ownership, partnerships with local operators and/or governments, to franchising and marketing consortia. Labour mobility also enabled people to travel to different countries to manage properties and systems.

Perhaps more importantly the emerging multi-culturalisation of investors' employees generated through education and training, media reports, and extensive travelling experience developed a new breed of global enterprises which offer their products at a standard quality regardless of locality. As a result of the emerging globalisation new tools are required to manage processes, multi-ethnicity and culture and to support employees and enterprises in satisfying all their stakeholders. A whole range of changes in society and the global economy will need to be taken into consideration in planning and managing tourism destinations and enterprises in the era of globalisation.

This chapter concentrates on leisure tourism and identifies the main trends influencing demand. It illustrates that four main factors propel changes in the international tourism demand and explains that globalisation magnifies the scale and scope of the implications emerging.

The chapter illustrates that the most critical factors affecting demand are:

- Proliferation of technology both on transportation and information technology.
- Ecology and environmental concern.
- An increase of multicultural societies.
- A quest for edu- and enter-tainment, where education and entertainment merge to offer personal development opportunities.

The chapter suggests that tourism demand is going through a transformation which can be explained through the change of the 4Ss framework for seaside tourism: Sea-Sun-Sand-Sex; and the 4Ss framework for urban tourism; Sightseeing-Shopping-Shows-Short breaks, to Segmentation-Specialisation-Sophistication-Satisfaction. This framework should facilitate the interpretation of major demand trends in the international tourism arena in order to assist tourism managers to develop suitable solutions, which will delight, rather than just satisfy, all tourism stakeholders.

TOURISM DEMAND TRENDS AND GLOBALISATION

Tourism demand evolved rapidly in the 1990s altering conventional wisdom and changing a whole range of factors influencing tourism planning and management. Attempting to interpret tourism phenomena and forecast the future of international activity is similar to reading the 'crystal ball'. Tourism has grown enormously in the last half century and become the world's largest 'industry'. It has also developed a multidimensional and multidisciplinary character making the analysis of both demand and supply a complex task. The globalisation experienced alters the competitiveness of destination regions and provokes a whole range of new activities and requirements from the demand side.

Increasingly people are becoming more aware of their limited time and are looking for both value for time and value for money. Predicting international demand trends is therefore a very challenging task, as the dynamic nature of these developments clearly demonstrates that the only constant in tourism is continuous change.

Nevertheless, successful tourism management and planning will increasingly need to identify the factors changing demand trends. The industry should therefore offer meaningful tourism products and also provide strategic and operational tools, which can delight consumers and enhance the competitiveness of destinations and enterprises within the global market.

Workers have established their right for leisure time, dedicated to their recreation. Paid annual holidays of about four weeks are nowadays a right for most people in Western developed countries, and the rest of the world is gradually heading in this direction. Leisure time is also increasing gradually, as discussions are in progress in the European Union to reduce the working week to 35 hours and to establish a maximum of 48 hours per week. O'Brien (1996) explains that 'The West European leisure travel market is undergoing structural and cultural changes.

These changes are critical to the future demand for, and supply of, leisure products both to consumers and to intermediaries who distribute travel products.' The European market has experienced a certain level of maturity as the vast majority of North Europeans take annual holidays abroad. In contrast the majority of South European tourists as well as people in North America have traditionally consumed domestic tourism products for a variety of reasons.

A large proportion of these holidays is spent on

international trips, especially during the summer season, when people from northern climates traditionally visit southern resorts in order to enjoy the warm weather and waters. These leisure products are widely referred to as the '4Ss', i.e. Sun, Sea, Sand and Sex. Leisure 4Ss products are packaged together and consumers purchase a combination of transportation, accommodation and activities packaged together by tour operators. In addition, several other types of demand emerge, especially for short-break holidays, which tend to concentrate on sports and educational activity, hobbies and visiting cultural attractions. This kind of tourism is generally domestic and often takes advantage of resources located in urban environments (such as theatres, cultural centres) or rural areas (e.g. agriculture or heritage) in close proximity to the main residence of consumers.

In recent years, however, tourism demand started changing towards a new type of activity where the individuality and independence of travellers are placed at the heart of the leisure activities. An environmental awareness is evident and consumers are actively selecting destinations which manage their environmental resources properly. Moreover, 'a return to nature and its pace, the search for a measure of isolation, the concern for hygiene and health, the taste for do-it-yourself, home handicrafts and sport' can be observed along with an increasing interest in cultural issues. In this sense 'people prefer to live their holidays rather than to spend them'.

As a result, Goodall suggested that 'the days of 4S's holidays are numbered'. Buhalis proposed that the traditional 4S's for tourism (sea-sun-sand-sex) be transformed in 'specialisation-sophistication-segmentation-satisfaction'. This process started in the late 1980s and it is expected to dominate the transformation of tourism demand as well as the re-engineering of the industry during the next century.

As a result, both tourism destinations and enterprises will need to appreciate demand trends as well as the factors that affect them in order to predict the needs and want of their travellers and develop satisfactory tourism products.

CRITICAL FACTORS AFFECTING TOURISM DEMAND

A wide range of forces from the external environment propel the changes in tourism demand. The ones that are more critical are summarised in the following points.

Table: Forecast Growth of Worldwide Travel 1995-2010.

Volume of travel	Actual 1985	Actual 1995	Fore cast 2000	Fore cast 2005	Fore cast 2010
Trips abroad excl. day trips (millions)	307	535	632	782	964
Short/medium haul (millions)	272	455	518	617	724
Long haul (millions)	35	79	114	165	240
Nights abroad (millions)	2,828	4,571	5,518	6,903	8,654
Spending abroad (US$bn at 1995 prices)	206	393	516	686	922
Travel characteristics					
Nights per trip	9.2	8.5	837	8.8	9.0
Spending per trip (constant 1995 US$ excl. fares)	671	735	816	877	956
Spending per night (constant 1995 US$-excl. fares)	73	86	93	99	107
Growth rates %					
Trips abroad excl. day trips		5.7%	3.4%	4.4%	4.3%
Short/medium haul		5.3%	2.6%	3.6%	3.3%
Long haul		8.5%	7.5%	7.7%	7.7%
Nights abroad		4.9%	3.8%	4.6%	4.4%
Spending abroad (US$ at 1995 prices)		6.7%	5.6%	5.9%	6.1%

TECHNOLOGY IN GENERAL AND INFORMATION TECHNOLOGY INPARTICULAR

Table. Forecast Trips Abroad by Destination Region 1995-2010.

Trips (mn) Excl. day trips	Actual 1995	Of world (%)	Forecast 2000	Forecast 2005	Forecast 2010	Of world (%)	Growth pa, actual 1985-95 (%)	Growth pa, forecast 1995-2000 (%)	Growth pa, forecast 2000-05 (%)	Growth pa, forecast 2005-10 (%)
Europe/Mediterranean	379.6	71.0	412.2	489.5	566.7	58.8	5.1	1.7	3.5	3.0
North America	58.3	10.9	75.0	95.2	121.8	12.6	5.1	5.2	4.9	5.1
Caribbean	8.0	1.5	12.8	18.4	27.0	2.8	7.1	9.8	7.5	7.9
Central/South America	29.7	5.6	47.2	63.1	84.5	8.8	6.6	9.7	6.0	6.0
Africa (excl. North)	5.0	0.9	5.8	7.4	9.7	1.0	8.0	3.2	4.8	5.6
Middle East	4.2	0.8	5.5	6.2	7.5	0.8	7.6	5.5	2.4	3.8
South Asia/Indian Ocean	4.0	0.8	6.0	8.9	13.8	1.4	12.4	8.2	8.4	9.0
South East Asia	18.8	3.5	30.9	45.5	66.4	6.9	13.8	10.4	8.0	7.9
Australia/New Zealand	4.5	0.8	7.5	12.7	22.7	2.4	13.0	10.7	11.3	12.3
Far East/Pacific	22.3	4.2	29.4	35.3	44.3	4.6	8.8	5.6	3.7	4.6
Total	534.4	100	632.3	782.2	964.4	100	5.7	3.4	4.4	4.3

Bradley, Hausman and Nolan illustrate the profound role of technology on the competitiveness of organisations in the global economy, as they claim that 'globalisation and technology are mutually reinforcing drivers of change'. In addition, Metakides asserts that the global information revolution obliges enterprises to 'act local and think global', while transforming dramatically both production and consumption patterns.

The technological revolution since the 1970s has facilitated tourism activity and has enabled consumers to travel further afield at a fraction of the cost and time required earlier on. The proliferation of jet engines, the ubiquitous motor car and new technology vessels and trains have not only reduced money and time required but has also provided the infrastructure for more people to travel.

Consumers are also empowered by information technology. They not only require value for money, but also value for time for the entire range of their dealings with organisations. This reflects people's shortage of time, evident in Western societies. The emerging Internet tools enable consumers to search on-line for information and to undertake reservations. Increasingly, IT and the Internet in particular, enable travellers to access reliable and accurate information as well as to undertake reservations in a fraction of the time, cost and inconvenience required by conventional methods. IT can also improve the service quality and contribute to higher guest/traveller satisfaction.

The availability of information on everything conceivable enables consumers to personalise their tourism bundles and to purchase only the most suitable products. The usage of IT on the one hand is driven by both the development of the volume and complexity of tourism demand, and on the other hand it alters their characteristics and enables individuals to select a much more personalised bundle of tourism products.

Nobody really knows how many consumers are currently connected to the Internet and how many of them buy products electronically. It was estimated that 150 million people or 2 per cent of the global population used the Internet in the late 1990s. Most Internet users match the profile of the most desirable market segments: they are well-educated professionals who travel frequently and have a higher disposable income, as well as a higher propensity to spend on tourism products.

The proliferation of the Internet revolutionised communications as it enabled organisations to demonstrate their offerings globally using multimedia interfaces. Suppliers have an unprecedented opportunity to communicate with their target markets globally, to develop their global presence and to establish direct relationships with consumers. The WTO (1985) argues that 'the key to success lies in the quick identification of consumer needs and in reaching potential clients with comprehensive, personalised and up-to-date information'. The rapid growth rate and the expeditious increase of on-line revenue experienced in most industries, including tourism, illustrates that electronic commerce will dominate by the year 2005. This justifies massive investments by organisations to develop their electronic presence.

The Internet has revolutionised flexibility in both

consumer choice and service delivery processes. Every tourist is different, carrying a unique blend of experiences, motivations and desires often as a result of previous experience, background and social status. Increasingly customers become much more *sophisticated and discerning*.

Tourists become demanding, requesting high quality products and value for both their money and - perhaps more importantly - time. Having experienced several products the new/experienced/sophisticated/demanding travellers rely heavily on electronic media to seek information about destinations and experiences, as well as to be able to communicate their needs and wishes to suppliers rapidly.

Tourists are increasingly frequent travellers, linguistically and technologically skilled and can function in multicultural and demanding environments overseas. The Internet empowered the 'new' type of tourist to become more *knowledgeable* and to seek exceptional value for money and time. New consumers are more culturally and environmentally aware and they often would like a greater involvement with the local society.

ECOLOGY AND ENVIRONMENTAL CONCERN

Ecology and environmental concerns are increasingly becoming more important and attract a higher degree of interest by consumers. 'Green consumers' especially in Scandinavia and North Europe lead a new movement where regions and products, which fail to demonstrate a certain degree of sustainability, are increasingly becoming unacceptable in the marketplace. In tourism, there is a gradual growth of an environmentally friendly tourist who is often referred to as 'green', 'responsible', 'eco', 'ethical', 'alternative', etc. A wide range of considerations are related to green tourism which can influence the selection of destination, transportation modes, activities undertaken and products consumed during the holiday. As a result, a growing number of consumers are attracted to natural areas and ecotourism has emerged as one of the more significant powers of change in the international tourism industry.

Different consumers have dissimilar tolerance levels. As a result, Swarbrooke and Horner illustrate that there are shades of green tourism from 'very green' to 'not green at all'. Nevertheless, consumers are becoming less tolerant to environmental damage and actively seek unspoilt areas to spend their holidays. Escaping from environmentally unfriendly urban regions holidaymakers often require sustainable environments where they can relax and play.

Middleton and Hawkins explain 'there is overwhelming evidence of customer preference for product qualities that are unambiguously concerned with environmental quality at chosen destinations. Even more interesting is the clear evidence of growing preference among experienced travellers'. As a result, a new sector is emerging in the industry to offer green products and at the same time to preserve their sustainability.

However, the ability of destinations and enterprises to restrict themselves and to avoid overexploiting resources is questionable and often it is only a matter of time before greedy entrepreneurs and unwise planning procedures push a destination through the different stages of its life cycle to overdevelopment and oversupply forcing mass tourism. Nevertheless, environmental concern and preference will increasingly dominate consumer choice and it will also determine their willingness to pay as well-preserved destinations and facilities will be able to charge premium prices for the privilege.

MULTI-CULTURAL BACKGROUND

People increasingly live in a multi-cultural environment. A great labour mobility as well as immigration effectively means that societies are often composed of a multi-ethic population. Different cultural backgrounds often entail different customs and values which create dissimilar if not conflicting tourism needs and wants. Multi-culture is also promoted by the emerging global television channels, such as CNN, MTV, etc. which on the one hand broadcast global images and social behaviour paradigms, and on the other hand generate interest and curiosity for the 'global village'. As a consequence.

Consumers become more aware of other places, their political situations and special conditions. In addition, the exposure of consumers to many cultures through previous travelling experiences provides plenty of examples for comparisons and a wealthy basis for building expectations. Globalisation effectively implies that increasingly tourists and the industry need to interact in a culturally diverse environment and to learn how to manage, negotiate and compromise with people from different cultural backgrounds and experiences.

A whole range of new skills are therefore required by the industry to communicate with the entire range of customers as well as to interact with all stakeholders.

EDU- AND ENTER-TAINMENT

Consumers are also increasingly using their leisure time for personal development. Instead of lying by the swimming pool, there is evidence that a greater percentage of tourists use their time at destinations to learn about other cultures, history and customs. Special interest and activity holidays are attracting larger numbers of holidaymakers not only because people lack time to undertake these activities whilst at home, but also because they assume a more active and participative style of holidays where they take the opportunity for personal development and exploration.

Several levels of activity can be identified. People may use the time to practise their favourite sport, such as skiing, tennis, etc.; explore an area for a specific interest, e.g. archaeology, architecture; learn a new skill, such as cooking, painting; or simply interact with local people to meet, understand and appreciate the local culture.

THE TRANSFORMATION OF TOURISM DEMAND

The development of mass tourism, since the early 1950s, has been based on a combination of 'sea-sun-sand-sangria-sex' products for summer and sea-side holidays and on 'sightseeing, short breaks, shopping, shows, scotch whisky' for urban-based tourism. Holidaymakers from northern/cold regions traditionally 'escape' for a certain period to southern/ warmer destinations in order to relax, 'recharge their batteries', restore their physical and mental strength for another heavy winter and hard work at home. Tourists largely enjoyed a 'mass, standardised and rigidly packaged' holiday product, which enabled them to consume tourism products at reasonable prices due to economies of scale.

Recently, however, a shift can be identified in the marketplace, which takes customers away from the traditional tourism demand prototypes to the new era of tourism. The inclusive tour sector in the UK, for example, is set to experience the first decline since 1980, not just simply due to short-run factors or airport congestion and increased prices. A structural shift in consumer preference towards independent or semi-independent trips, and away from perceived mass tourism destinations can be observed.

Other Europeans, and particularly Germans and Danes, also move away from traditional mass destinations and select new, environmentally-friendly and more authentic regions for their holidays. O'Brien (1996) illustrates that across the West European market the estimated ratio of independent to package-booked travel is in the order of 70:30, with the majority of the French, Spanish, Italian and Greek markets arranging their travels themselves. In addition, consumers take a larger number of short holidays.

Consequently, they normally spend a couple of weeks away during the summer and also have two or three short breaks throughout the year. Holidays are not only regarded as opportunities to escape from the daily routine, but also as a personal development opportunity, where tourists can explore cultures and develop new skills, interests and hobbies. WTO (1985) claims that 'this non-mainstream tourism presently accounts for no more than 5% of the total tourism demand, but it is growing much more rapidly than traditional resort-based or round-tour tourism.

A ceiling of 10% of total tourism is forecasted by the travel trade for this new type of tourism, though this may rise over time as alternative becomes standard'.

Traditional destinations have been victims of their own success. They grew to attract a large amount of people and inevitably have become overcrowded. The development of facilities and services, which cater for the mass markets, has forced them to lose parts of their character and has reduced their appeal. Operating on low margins also prevented principals from reinvesting and regenerating their products. Hence, mass tourism products are often regarded as responsible for both the aesthetic and environmental degradation of various destinations. Failure to control tourism development and practices has had disastrous impacts on well-known resorts.

Thus, traditional tourism products and destinations have become outdated and have lost their ability to attract their intended market segments. Instead, they can attract consumers by reducing their prices and by developing a volume based product. Hence, they jeopardise their resources further and are unable to generate the positive impacts attributed to tourism. Marketing can therefore assist the management of tourism behaviour at the destination. Marketing should encourage a responsible attitude towards local resources.

FROM SEA-SUN-SAND-SEX-SANGRIA

The transformation of tourism demand follows a wide range of trends and developments, which propel several differences in consumer behaviour. The summer/sea-side holiday is changing due to a wide range of environmental and climatic reasons. Firstly, the *sea* in well-established resorts has often been polluted by sewage, waste leaked by leisure boats and litter left behind by holidaymakers. In addition, pollution caused by other industrial sectors as well as accidents in oil tankers, has also degraded the quality of the water environment.

A number of diseases and viruses can also be transformed through the sea, causing serious health problems. Examples include the algae in the Adriatic in 1989 and the pollution of the sea in several British seaside resorts. As modern tourists are reluctant to tolerate environmental pollution, the sea becomes less attractive at destinations that have failed to protect the natural environment.

Although the *sun* has been a prime motivation for sun-lust tourists, it becomes under attack as the Green House Effect and the Ozone Layer Loss have increased temperatures to uncomfortable levels. In addition, skin cancer from sun overexposure reduces its appeal as a tourism motivator, while Poon claims that 'the sun sets on tourism'.

Wall suggests that 'the Greenhouse Effect and the likely climate changes to which it will give rise will likely impinge upon tourism at a global scale and may lead to diverse and profound consequences of global climate change for tourism'. Consequently, these phenomena will probably change tourism demand patterns in the next century and lead tourists towards northern and cooler climates.

Sand has similarly been degraded since masses of tourists are normally packed into a limited space on beaches, and spoil the environment. Poon (1993) claims that 'degradation of beaches and soil erosion from construction too close to the shore line, for example, some hotels and resorts in the Caribbean region are experiencing a loss of sand and bathing area as the sea begins to reclaim some of the area, exposing ugly building foundations'.

In addition, sand has been identified as responsible for the transformation of various diseases and hence future tourists may avoid being exposed to the sand. Thus, excessive numbers of holidaymakers and tourism overdevelopment eventually destroy both the environment and the 'escape' element for consumers. In addition, the transformation of various diseases from sand starts being another negative factor against attracting tourists.

Sangria symbolises the tendency of traditional holidaymakers to consume great quantities of alcohol. New consumers use holidays as a form of personal development and hence alcohol will increasingly be less important. Excessive alcohol consumption is not only unhealthy and often responsible for accidents and injuries, but it also creates a range of social problems at destination areas. Frequently hooliganism and conflicts between locals and tourists are also attributed to excessive consumption of alcohol. New tourists will therefore need less alcohol in order to enjoy themselves.

Sex and romance have always been an important, but often untold, element of leisure and tourism activities. It may be one of the major motivations for 'sex-tourists', especially for some 'specialised' destinations or part of the sightseeing experience. Eroticism accompanies almost all tourism activities, and it has been extensively used for advertising purposes. Specific products have been developed to accommodate this type of demand.

For example holidays in particular clubs (e.g. the 18-30 Club or the Club Med.) traditionally had the image of the wild, care-free bachelors looking for companions while on holiday; various destinations (e.g. Amsterdam, Mykonos) are prime destinations for homosexuals; some Far East and African destinations have developed a prostitution industry which caters for wealthy Western tourists; whilst 'romantic' destinations fiercely target the 'couple/honeymooners' market. However, modern diseases (i.e. Aids) have increased public concern and have reduced sexual activity with non-regular partners during holidays.

This is influencing the tourism demand patterns. Destinations where sex is a primary activity or areas with a large Aids-sufferers population might face a decline in arrivals. In contrast, 'romance' destinations might gain a greater market share; tourism enterprises like the Club Med. have altered their image significantly and target different segments (i.e. family or sportive markets); while other clubs (e.g. Sandals) emerged to cater exclusively for couples.

It is quite apparent therefore, that the sex element in the traditional holiday patterns is also changing radically and it will influence the decision-making processes of future holidaymakers.

As a consequence of the above trends, Mediterranean destinations lose some of their market share and appeal. Trips from main European countries to this region are projected to fall from 45 per cent in 1995 to 38 per cent in 2010.

A combination of short breaks, sightseeing, shopping, shows and Scotch whisky has dominated urban tourism in the past. Often urban tourism is closely related with business travel (characterised by MICE [Meetings, Incentives, Conferences, Exhibitions]) as business travellers usually consume some leisure tourism products or they may stay for a few more days to enjoy the local resources.

Hence, urban tourism is often characterised by *short breaks,* sometimes combined or as an extension of business trips. Leisure tourists also tend to be curious to visit metropolitan centres which they are familiar with through the media. They also take advantage of the large amount of cultural and heritage resources often found in urban destinations, such as museums, galleries, theatres, cathedrals, monuments, etc. A wide range of facilities such as hospitals, centralised government agencies and educational establishments also act as attractions for consumers.

Often urban tourism is consumed through organised *sightseeing,* which aims to pack as many attractions as possible into the limited time available at the destination. Sightseeing is facilitated through transfers and guided tours. However, sightseeing programmes are often characterised by their rapidity and inflexibility. Consumers take specific interest in fewer but more personalised attractions and use their leisure time to concentrate on their interests.

They will be more interested in experiencing elements of the destination, rather than tick them off their 'must see' items. This will be particularly the case for repeat visitors to destinations who become familiar with local resources and people. Hence future tourists will need a greater flexibility and control over their time at the destination in order to explore in detail and experience resources of their choice. Thus they will need tailor-made sightseeing programmes which will enable them to increase their flexibility.

Shopping has dominated urban tourism as people from peripheral areas were lured by a great variety and often cheaper prices in urban centres. The proliferation of shopping malls out of city centres and the globalisation of manufacturing and retailing, as well as the distribution of products through the electronic media are expected to reduce the appeal of shopping as an attraction to urban destinations. Instead, shopping will be integrated with other attractions and experiences at the destination. Perhaps tourism shopping will be themed in relation to the local tourism product.

Another element of urban tourism has traditionally been shows of any kind, such as theatre, opera, cinema, circus, etc. Only cities have the infrastructure as well as the critical mass of consumers required in order to stage performances. However, the growth of electronic media and the development of facilities in peripheral regions as well as the maturity of the market demonstrate that it will be difficult to impress consumers in the future.

Even shows and entertainment activities will need to be customised to suit the feelings of consumers during their holiday. Similarly with sea-side tourism, *Scotch whisky* symbolises the contribution of alcohol to the urban tourism product. It can be observed that, although alcohol has been playing a significant role in urban tourism, health considerations as well as other life style influences discourage tourists from consuming large quantities of alcohol.

As a result, alcohol will be themed with the overall experience rather than being a stand-alone product. Examples of that can be demonstrated by the expansion of Irish pubs where Irish food and drinks can be consumed within a themed environment.

TOWARDS SOPHISTICATION-SPECIALISATION-SEGMENTATION-SATISFACTION-SEDUCTION

The shift of demand towards quality and value-for-money products is increasing rapidly in the tourism industry. Tourists demand higher quality products and services and real experiences during their holidays. The traditional annual family holiday in a seaside resort will play a less dominant role in the future. Multi-interest travel is therefore replacing part of the present bread and butter products of the industry. Future products will probably combine beach holidays with pleasure and special interest of some kind or culture. Future tourists will 'prefer to live their holidays rather than to spend them', and they do so by engaging in cultural, physical, educational and spiritual activities (WTO 1985).

Rigidly packaged tours are not in line with trends towards individual expression. As a result, the independently organised tourism segment emerges rapidly whilst there is a decline of the relative importance of packaged tours. O'Brien (1996) suggests that 'Growth in the inclusive tour market will continue, though at a much slower rate, but in the larger summersun markets, particularly Germany and the UK, the major IT operators will develop a wider product range to ensure that sales remain buoyant.'

One of the most important obstacles in organising individual tourism packages hitherto is the lack of economies of scale and bargaining power, which will enable the reduction of the individual package prices to affordable levels. WTO (1991:18) suggests that packaged tours are not in line with trends towards individual expression.

As a result, the decline of the relative importance of packaged tours is expected in favour of independently organised tourism. Bentley (1991:57) states that 'tour operators in the 1990s will seek to combine inclusive tour elements with individual variations, in order to satisfy the desire for an individual experience, but at a cost lower than an individually arranged holiday'.

Meanwhile, the tourism industry is moving towards the accommodation of activity/adventure/wildlife/culture/independent/special interest holidays. The new generation of tourists is more educated, experienced, sophisticated, knowledgeable and demanding. This is reflected in the kind of travel experiences they seek, their behaviour and preferences whilst at the destination and also in the information they require in travel decision-making.

The WTO (1985) estimates that 'ecotourism (or nature based tourism) is growing by 25-30 per cent per year while culture-based tourism is recording annual expansion of 10-15 per cent. Endemic tourism (based on the individual character of the locality or community) is expected to become an important means of differentiating tourist destinations and appealing to the 'new' types of tourism'.

SOPHISTICATION

Tourists in the post-industrial era are better prepared for living in an international world. Modern people are able to work and function in a demanding environment. They are often familiar and capable to cope with foreign languages, customs and cultures and as a result a 'new global lifestyle is emerging', often as a result of the globalisation of the media as well as the extensive travelling experiences of consumers.

The enhancement of the media, and especially television, has reduced the distances and increased the eagerness of modern people to approach and experience remote cultures and foreign areas. Bennett (1992:87) states that: educational improvements, together with enhanced communications have led to more sophisticated requirements from holidaymakers who are now looking for new activities to fill their leisure time and satisfy their cultural, intellectual and sporting interests. Increased linguistic ability among the younger generations, communication and financial services have made travel easier.

Hence, sophistication is a major element in the 'new types' of holidays and the products emerging to satisfy modern demand. Holidaymakers take advantage of their education as well as the availability of information through the new media and plan their holidays in advance. They are eager to approach and experience remote cultures and foreign areas in order to 'live their leisure time' and satisfy their cultural, natural, intellectual and sporting interests.

The linguistic abilities of younger generations (both hosts and tourists), as well as the prevalence of communication and financial services at a global level have made travel more accessible and easier.

Extensive travelling has also increased the required sophistication of the tourist product. As many modern travellers have been in several countries and treated by several tourism enterprises, they have developed a set of assessment criteria, which they utilise in order to compare their tourism experiences.

Moutinho (1992) illustrates that the 'sophistication of the customer will have an impact on all product development throughout the industry. There will be an increased requirement for high standards of product design, efficiency and safety'. Thus, people will seek more varied, personal and authentic experiences, while a wide range of new, imaginative, tourism products will be demanded. In addition, personal development and special interest travel are expected to provide rewarding, enriching, adventuresome experiences. Not only is mass tourism less able to satisfy a large proportion of the marketplace, it is also regarded as environmentally unacceptable and thus 'politically incorrect'. Moreover, Cooper and Ozdil (1992:378) suggest that:

In particular the realisation of the negative impacts of tourism on host environments and societies has prompted a search for alternative forms of tourism and a move away from 'mass' tourism. Indeed, this movement is largely consumer rather than industry driven and may lead to 'politically correct' or acceptable forms of tourism which will be chosen by the consumer in preference to more damaging forms.

Thus, adventure and green tourism are driven by consumer requirements, at the expense of mass and environmentally threatening tourism.

Tourist product sophistication should probably aim to deliver the appropriate product, at the appropriate time, at the appropriate price. The amalgamation of tourism products and the delivery of seamless travel experiences are increasingly important. Information technology facilitates the development of suitable businesses and communication networks for achieving these purposes. Modern travellers demand customer convenience in all aspects, while 'total consumer satisfaction' and enrichment of the holiday experience are required; all these at a competitive and fair cost.

The anticipated sophistication of the consumer will have

an impact upon product development as well as on customer retention throughout the industry. Not only will there be an increased requirement for high standards of product design, efficiency and safety, but also the tourist will be more critical of the product and will have the experience to compare offerings. Tourists' requirement for sophistication has recently initiated the demand for specialised products. Tourism motivation is a very complicated set of needs and desires, which differ for various people. Several motivators are consistently rated in a variety of consumer behaviour surveys.

However, tourism researchers are generally unable to identify the motivators and determinants of tourism activity with accuracy, as a result of the diversified needs, desires and decision-making criteria used by each individual consumer each time s/he selects a tourism product.

Hitherto, tourism products used to be general, unspecialised, with almost identical characteristics and have been traded as commodities rather than services for the satisfaction of specific needs. The mass tourism philosophy, where tourism products should appeal to all different tastes and should be as cheap as possible, in order to attract customers of all purchasing abilities and achieve economies of scale, used to dominate the marketplace. These products become less attractive as consumers are exceedingly conscious and keen to explore the cultural, social, gastronomical, political, and environmental aspects of destinations.

They are expected therefore to organise more independent activities, adventure and sport holidays and devote their holidays to special interest activities. As a result tailor-made travel arrangements are expected to grow at a faster pace than pre-packaged holidays over the next decade. Kotler (1988) suggests that 'each buyer is potentially a separate market because of unique needs and wants'. This statement could not be more valuable in any other industry than tourism. Technology makes possible more tailored products to meet individual tastes and hence we turn from mass production of all kinds to customisation.

One-to-one marketing initiatives emerge gradually to take

advantage of expressed consumer requirements and to develop individualised product solutions. Long-term customer segmentation will be based on the feeling of individual consumers at each particular moment, rather than on broad segmentation variables.

This will enable enterprises to offer instantaneous tourism products to satisfy the needs of consumers at each moment. Hence, the competitiveness of tourism organisations and destinations will depend on their ability to differentiate their product and serve individual consumer needs.

New specialised tourism products are marketed and distributed differently from ordinary offerings. Advertising will primarily be carried out in specialised media, while direct selling and relationship marketing will be utilised for understanding the consumer needs and promoting specialised products. The Internet and technology in general will facilitate one-to-one marketing, as specialised products will be distributed directly to the right market segments.

Offering specialised products on-line will not only improve the specialisation of the industry, but it will also enable the reduction of the brochure used for the promotion of tourism products, reducing both the printing cost as well as the environmental damage caused from the production and distribution.

Apart from including special interest activities in traditional holiday brochures, a wide range of new programmes emerge to cover these markets. New programmes such as 'Battlefields', 'Italian Cooking', 'Dutch Bulb-fields', etc. address specific interest markets and aim to provide a thematic tour. These new products are based extensively on activities that are undertaken during holidays, while accommodation and transportation arrangements are given less importance. Themed leisure activities are also expected to increase in order to satisfy the demand for specialisation. In the catering industry, for example, restaurants used to be specialised only in national cuisines (e.g. French, Chinese, Greek restaurants).

New themes are rapidly emerging based on the food served (e.g. Steaks: Aberdeen Steak House; Hamburger:

McDonald's; Chicken: Kentucky; Pizza: Pizza Hut); on the entertainment provided (e.g. Hard Rock Café or Planet Hollywood); the surrounding environment (e.g. Country pub: Bass Pubs or Rainforest Café); or on the life style and preferences (e.g. vegetarian or game restaurants) are continually emerging.

As a result, Lickorish (1990) predicts that the importance of the 'mini market segments' will increase rapidly. Independent holidays increase their market share in the international arena. In the UK for example they increased their contribution to 45 per cent of the total holidays abroad in 1994, from 37 per cent in 1983. Thus, Moutinho (1992) suggests that 'tourist innovation is more likely to be about un-packaging rather than packaging, providing more individual attention within a number of price bands'.

Eventually tourism marketing will move even further from one-to-one relationship marketing to the level of marketing towards how a person is feeling at a particular moment. This will be facilitated with the development of intelligent agents and push technology which will assess the situation and mood of a person and will promote the most appropriate products for that particular moment.

As a result, specialisation is expected to be a dominant element of holidays in the future. People will be able to select numerous specialised holidays all over the world. Both destinations and tourism enterprises should therefore identify their competitive advantage in offering specialised products and develop integrated and themed tourist experiences. For example, France could develop gastronomic themed activities, while Greece could emphasise themes based on archaeology-philosophy-culture. Orlando and Las Vegas in the USA, which are strongly themed towards Disneyland visitors and gamblers respectively, are good examples of specialised/themed tourism products which attract a large volume of visitors based on these attractions.

SEGMENTATION

Specialisation of tourism products entails a need for

segmentation of tourism markets. Since tourists no longer have single, standardised and rigidly packaged wants, segmentation offers the opportunity to provide appealing tourism products to well-defined markets.

Market segmentation can be defined as the grouping of individuals according to their preference or reaction to specific elements of the marketing mix, i.e. product, price, distribution and promotion or according to their characteristics. WTO (1991) claims that 'segmentation is the process by which a travel vendor, whether an airline, hotel or destination, identifies and attracts consumers who will be satisfied by the product or service the vendor offers'.

Traditionally, tourism marketers have been using geographic and demographic criteria in order to describe their markets, probably because these categories offer objective tangible and measurable variables.

However, as a number of phenomena could not be explained and interpreted, additional segmentation categories and methods have been added. Consequently, psychographics and behavioural criteria are used nowadays, in tourist segmentation, in order to provide detailed customer profiles, identify tourist motivations, needs and determinants, and offer an appropriate tourist product mix. Thus, life-style segmentation has gained ground in modern tourism marketing.

'Lifestyle is a way of living, characterised by the manner in which people spend their time (activities), what things they consider important (interests) and how they feel about themselves and the world around them (opinions)'. Although life-style segmentation is probably the most difficult and subjective method, it provides the best prediction and understanding of tourist activities.

Tourism destinations, enterprises and organisations will need to undertake thorough segmentation in order to ensure that they design suitable tourist products, use proper communication media and charge acceptable prices. Moreover, segmentation is essential for treating seasonality problems, as well as for mitigating tourism impacts at destinations.

Segmentation is also critical in bringing together the right types of consumers/tourists, as their interaction during the travel experience is largely responsible for the delivery and perception of tourism products.

For example, the demographic changes worldwide demonstrate the development of a new market segment of older/retired but active people who have plenty of time and often money to spend. Several operators currently develop suitable products for this market segment.

The UK company Saga Holidays specialises with holidays for the over 55s, while a new style of club is currently being developed by Mr Trigano, the ex Club Med. Chairman. The required sophistication and specialisation of tourism can only be offered to small segments of the market with very similar needs and motivations. Hence, customer satisfaction will largely depend on proper segmentation and achievement of a suitable customer mix.

SATISFACTION

Consumer satisfaction is the essence of most developments in tourism demand. Satisfaction 'occurs when consumer expectations are met or exceeded' and can be defined 'as an evaluation that the chosen alternative is consistent with prior beliefs with respect to that alternative'. Increasingly customer satisfaction will be inadequate for the fiercely competitive environment and thus 'delighting the customer' should become the target for all enterprises. Tourism satisfaction should be one of the strategic directions of every tourist enterprise, destination or organisation. This can be achieved by offering:

- At least the quality promised;
- Undertaking consumer research and formulating innovative tourism products;
- Improving services constantly;
- Adjusting tourism products to customer needs and feelings;
- Enriching the tourist experience; and
- Offering value for money.

Satisfying consumers, as well as providing sufficient value for both money and time, are also ethical obligations and responsibilities of tourist destinations and organisations. Satisfying consumers also makes financial/business sense.

- First, satisfied tourists are normally very loyal. The increasing sophistication of travellers, and the fierce competition in the international market make repeat business difficult to maintain. Therefore, it should be extremely welcome and appreciated by the tourism industry.
- Second, satisfied customers are always the best, most reliable and cheapest promotional medium, as they usually recommend tourist destinations/enterprises to friends through word of mouth. In contrast, dissatisfied travellers spread their complaints to potential customers. Bearing in mind that most people get advice for their travel plans from friends and relatives, the image of the destination depends heavily on the description of the previous visitors.
- Third, providing adequate services and satisfying the tourist will eliminate enterprises and destinations from potential legal actions and suits against them. Consumerism and consumer protection are international movements forced by various private and governmental organisations. The European Community Package Travel Directive, especially on the package and timeshare holidays, is expected to have major impacts on tourism enterprises in the near future.

Due to the fact that the tourism product is an amalgam of many products and services, which formulate the 'tourist consumption chain', each trip is assessed as a total experience. Hence, the satisfaction of tourists normally depends on the harmonic delivery of the product throughout the chain.

As destinations represent the 'raison d'être' for tourism, travel experience tends to be appraised at a destination level. Consequently, an integrated approach should be employed, by all enterprises and organisations involved at a destination level, in order to ensure that consumers are satisfied by the whole range of products consumed during their travelling experience.

Thus, all tourist enterprises should consider the needs and wants of their customers before, during and after the delivery of their own products to ensure that everybody involved in the tourism product delivery chain offers satisfactory services. The ultimate measurement of tourist satisfaction is probably hidden in the answer of two critical questions:

- Would the customer come back?
- Would the customer recommend the product/ destination to his/her friends?

SEDUCTION

Tourism providers need to 'seduce' tourists through the development and delivery of offerings and marketing mixes which reflect consumers' feelings at a particular moment and satisfy their entire range of needs and wants. The inconsistency and unpredictability of tourism consumers, which is emerging due to the dynamic nature of modern life and the overexposure of consumers to the media, illustrates that tourism marketing will become much more difficult for the future.

Tourism destinations and organisations that manage to seduce consumers will need to make them feel special at each stage of their travelling experience. Offering tailor-made tourism products and caring for the individual needs and wants of consumers will be one of the most critical attributes tourism organisations will need to have in order to attract and satisfy tourists in the future.

Extensive marketing research, using psychology methodologies will enable tourism organisations to explore consumer feelings and requirements whilst on holidays. Data mining on the information available through loyalty clubs, Passenger Name Records (PNRs), guest history, and other sources of information should be exploited in order to assess the needs and wants of particular consumers. Complex models of behaviour can then be developed in order to predict consumer requirements and develop instantaneous products before consumers require them. Developing relationship marketing will enable tourism organisations to establish a closer partnership with consumers. Destinations and organisations who manage to seduce their consumers will be able to increase the value added they offer and achieve high levels of customer retention and loyalty.

This chapter attempts to explore the trend of the tourism demand by providing a framework of analysis. It is argued that the traditional tourism products will no longer be adequate for the recreation of the new generation of tourists emerging. Instead, a more individualised product is expected to dominate demand in the near future. Tourism demand trends can be illustrated in a framework of five new S's, namely sophistication-specialisation-segmentation-satisfaction-seduction.

Emerging tourism products need to be sophisticated in order to delight the new, experienced, and demanding consumer. Moreover, a certain degree of specialisation is required in order to cater for the individual needs and wants.

This can only be achieved by detailed segmentation of the market where all cluster segments are identified and offered tailor-made products. The ultimate aim should be the total customer satisfaction before, during and after the consumption of the tourist product, which is underlined by both ethical and business motives.

Tourism organisations and destinations which achieve the above will 'seduce' their clientele and achieve sustainable competitive advantages. A thorough understanding of this transformation framework as well as the utilisation of marketing and information technology tools will be essential for all players involved in the tourism industry. Enterprises and destinations which fail to appreciate these developments and modernise their offerings will be marginalised in this century.

Chapter 6

Global Policies and the Tourism Industry

In the last decade, global environmental policies have made substantial progress in institutional development, international cooperation, public participation and private sector action. National governments and the private sector have developed stronger legal frameworks, market-based environmental incentive instruments, environmentally sound technologies, and cleaner production processes. Consequently, several countries report significant progress in controlling environmental pollution and slowing the rate of resource degradation as well as reducing the intensity of resource use (UNEP 1997).

The tourism industry, arguably the world's largest, bears a great responsibility in the effort to move towards sustainable development. The economic importance of tourism is undeniable. A study sponsored by the World Travel & Tourism Council (WTTC) and conducted by Wharton Econometric Forecasting Associates (WEFA) found that the tourism industry generates 11.7 per cent of global gross domestic product (GDP) and nearly 200 million jobs worldwide.

These figures are forecast to total 11.7 per cent global GDP and 255 million jobs in 2010 (United Nations Economic and Social Council 1999). While the economic development potential of tourism is substantial, there is also strong evidence of the negative environmental impact of tourism development. Nevertheless, tourism may be a more sustainable option for economic development because, unlike other natural resource based industries, it is based on enjoyment and appreciation of local culture, built heritage, and the natural environment which provides a powerful economic incentive to conserve these valuable assets (United Nations Economic and Social Council 1999).

The potential for tourism development to be a sustainable - that is for it to *meet the needs of the present without compromising the ability of future generations to meet their own needs* - has resulted in support for environmentally sustainable tourism development from both the public and private sectors at the national and international levels.The United Nations and its associated organisations, the World Bank, and regional development banks are attempting to 'green' their loan programmes and assistance mechanisms.

They are also supporting the development of environmentally sustainable tourism directly and indirectly through a variety of means, including sustainable tourism product identification, infrastructure development, environmentally sound hotel financing, and ecotourism development in protected areas.

The Commission on Sustainable Development (CSD) - an intergovernmental forum to coordinate and monitor the progress of Agenda 21's implementation - has produced a number of policy recommendations for stakeholders involved in the sustainable tourism development following their annual meetings in 1999.

These recommendations were broken down into private sector, public sector, non-governmental organisation, and international community policy challenges. The following section summarises these recommendations (United Nations Economic and Social Council 1999).

PRIVATE SECTOR POLICY CHALLENGES

The key challenges facing the tourism industry are to:

- Promote wider implementation of environmental management, particularly in the many small and medium enterprises that form the backbone of the tourism industry, and spread initiatives to all sectors of the tourism industry;

- Use more widely environmentally sound technologies, in particular to reduce emissions of CO and other greenhouse gases and ozone-depleting substances, as set out in two international agreements;
- Address the key issues of siting and more eco-efficient design of tourism facilities;
- Raise the awareness of tourism clients of the environment and social implications of their holidays, and of opportunities for their responsible behaviour;
- Develop a better dialogue with the local communities in travel destinations, and promote the involvement of local stakeholders in tourism ventures;
- Work with governments and other stakeholders to improve the overall environmental quality of destinations; and
- Report publicly on environmental performance.

Public sector policy challenges:

Governments need to further develop and implement the legislative and policy frameworks for sustainable development. In particular, they need to:

- Ratify, if they have not already done so, and work towards the effective implementation of, international and regional environmental conventions;
- Integrate more fully tourism development into the overall plans for sustainable development and develop participatory approaches;
- Develop more widely land use planning, and protect the coastline through building restrictions (for example, legislation in France, Spain, Denmark and Egypt forbids building within a defined distance from the coast);
- Identify and adopt the most appropriate mix of regulation and economic instruments, and, in many cases develop economic instruments to address environmental issues; and
- Work towards the effective enforcement of regulations and standards.

Governments need to raise awareness, build capacity and promote effective action for sustainable tourism.

This requires that they strive to:

- Improve the understanding of the benefits and burdens of tourism in environmental, social and economic terms, for the areas under their jurisdiction;
- Strengthen capacity for the management and control of tourism in their sphere of responsibility, and establish and maintain procedures for cooperation and coordination with neighbouring authorities, and with relevant state authorities;
- Provide support through pilot projects and capacity development programmes, including capacity development at the local government level;
- Ensure the participation of all stakeholders affected by or involved in tourism and its development, especially indigenous and local communities;
- Ensure that tourism makes a positive contribution to economic development, and that the economic benefits of tourism are equitably shared;
- Encourage and catalyse industry initiatives for sustainable tourism across all sectors of tourism, including accommodation, land, air and sea transportation, tour operators, travel agents, attractions sectors, etc.; and
- Promote changes in consumer behaviour in both tourist-originating countries and destinations towards more sustainable forms of tourism.

Governments will also need to develop monitoring of progress towards sustainable tourism. It is important to develop activities to monitor, control and mitigate adverse effects that may arise from tourism activities and development.

NON-GOVERNMENTAL ORGANISATIONS POLICY CHALLENGES

The key environmental policy challenges that face non-governmental organisations are to:

- More specifically voice their views in tourism policies and strategies;
- Contribute to the development and implementation of environmental standards for tourism;
- Develop or participate in raising awareness and education activities for sensitising tourists towards improving guest consumption patterns; and
- Assist in monitoring tourism activities and development and progress towards more sustainable tourism.

INTERNATIONAL COMMUNITY POLICY CHALLENGES

The key challenges facing the international community are to:

- Assist and support governments in the development of national strategies or master plans for the sustainable development of tourism, and of environmental land use and building regulations and standards for tourism;
- Raise awareness and build capacity of all stakeholders by providing information on best practices for sustainable tourism;
- Encourage the private sector to develop and apply codes and guidelines, and environmental management systems, and promote the development of the use of environmental reporting by companies in the various branches of the tourism sector;
- Assist in assessing the environmental effectiveness of existing voluntary initiatives in the various branches of the tourism sector, and make recommendations accordingly;
- Promote the transfer of environmentally sound technologies (ESTs), practices and management tools adapted for the tourism sector, and disseminate information on ESTs to governments and the tourism industry;
- Work with other stakeholders to establish and disseminate lessons from best practices projects on sustainable tourism;

- Provide support through provision of information and capacity development programmes, particularly on the costs and benefits of tourism development, the use of economic incentives to promote sustainable tourism, and on destination management; and
- Assist in the establishment of monitoring of progress towards sustainable tourism.

THE ROLE OF THE INTERNATIONAL COMMUNITY AND GLOBAL ENVIRONMENTAL INITIATIVES

Some other notable international environmental institutions that support sustainable tourism initiatives include:

The world bank group: Despite its formal distancing from the tourism sector in the 1970s, the Bank's focus on economic development and its private sector capacity, particularly in the International Finance Corporation, makes it technically well placed to address the pressures of a global tourism industry. Its now strong environmental capacity also makes it well placed to address the impacts of the tourism sector on biodiversity.

The united nations development programme (UNDP): A United Nations organisation whose mission is to help countries in their efforts to achieve sustainable human development by assisting them to build their capacity to design and carry out development programmes in poverty eradication, employment creation and sustainable livelihoods, the empowerment of women and the protection and regeneration of the environment, giving first priority to poverty eradication.

The united nations environmental programme (UNEP): The environmental voice of the United Nations, responsible for environmental policy development, scientific analysis, monitoring, and assessment.

The global environment facility (GEF): A financial mechanism that addresses the incremental costs that developing countries face in responding to selected global environmental problems. The World Bank, UNEP and UNDP implement GEF projects.

New international environmental conventions and agreements are being adopted, older treaties are being improved, and new approaches to international policy are being developed and implemented. Four important international environmental conventions and treaties that are particularly relevant to the tourism industry include the following:

RIO DECLARATION ON ENVIRONMENT AND DEVELOPMENT (AGENDA 21)

The plan of action adopted by governments in 1992 in Rio de Janeiro provides the global consensus on the road map towards sustainable development. Agenda 21 is grouped around a series of themes - comprising 40 chapters and 115 separate programme areas, each of which represents an important component in the overall strategy towards global sustainable development. The Agenda identifies three core tools to be used in achieving sustainable development goals:

1. Introduction of new, or strengthening of existing, regulations to ensure the protection of human health and the environment.
2. Use of free market mechanisms through which the prices of goods and services will reflect the environmental costs of resource inputs and process outputs.
3. Industry-led voluntary programmes that deliver environmentally responsible products and services.

In 1996, WTTC, the World Tourism Organisation and the Earth Council joined together to launch 'Agenda 21 for the Travel & Tourism Industry: Towards Environmentally Sustainable Development', making the tourism industry the first industrial sector to develop an industry specific action plan based on Agenda 21. WTTC has now introduced an addition to this programme - The Alliance for Sustainable Tourism - which invites public and private sector tourism organisations to record their Agenda 21 based activities on a central Internet site and encourage cooperation with other local partners.

THE CONVENTION ON INTERNATIONAL TRADE IN ENDANGERED SPECIES OF WILD FAUNA AND FLORA (CITES)

CITES is an international convention banning commercial international trade in an agreed list of endangered species and by regulating and monitoring trade in others that might become endangered. The international wildlife trade, worth billions of dollars annually, has caused massive declines in the numbers of many species of animals and plants.

The scale of overexploitation for trade aroused such concern for the survival of species that an international treaty was drawn up in 1973 to protect wildlife against such over-exploitation and to prevent international trade from threatening species with extinction (World Conservation Monitoring 1998).

THE UNITED NATIONS FRAMEWORK CONVENTION ON CLIMATE CHANGE

In the 1992 United Nations Framework Convention on Climate Change (UNFCCC), finalised for the Earth Summit in Rio de Janeiro, Brazil, the world's nations agreed on voluntary actions to reduce greenhouse gas emissions. Negotiations on the Kyoto Protocol to the UNFCCC were completed on 11 December 1997, committing the industrialised nations to specified legally binding reductions in emissions of six 'greenhouse gases'.

During negotiations that preceded the December 1997 meeting in Kyoto, Japan, little progress was made, and the most difficult issues were not resolved until the final days - and hours - of the Conference. There was wide disparity among key players especially on three items:

- The amount of binding reductions in greenhouse gases to be required, and the gases to be included in these requirements.
- Whether developing countries should be part of the requirements for greenhouse gas limitations.
- Whether to allow emissions trading and joint implementation, which allow credit to be given for

emissions reductions to a country that provides funding or investments in other countries that bring about the actual reductions in those other countries or locations where they may be cheaper to attain.

The convention on biological diversity:

A convention adopted as part of the 1992 UN Conference on the Environment and Development with the goals of:

- maintaining biodiversity;
- using its elements sustainably; and
- sharing in a balanced and fair way the advantages springing from the exploitation of genetic resources.

The Convention on Biological Diversity (CBD) is the major and most visionary global biodiversity agreement. Now ratified by almost all the countries in the world - with the notable exception of the United States, the CBD is attempting to develop a global framework for the management of biodiversity.

It is striving to meet the trinity of biodiversity objectives - conservation, sustainable use and equitable benefit sharing - through globally agreed policies and procedures for managing biodiversity. These policies and procedures are also intended to support the overall goal of sustainable development and the corollary objective of poverty alleviation. But given the tradition of biodiversity management, the CBD has understandably yet to address the pressures of globalise commerce directly.

There is, however, an increasing recognition that the private sector must be an active player in managing biodiversity, but this recognition has yet to be articulated into clear roles and responsibilities for the private sector and global market processes.

CRITICAL WEAKNESSES IN THE GLOBAL ENVIRONMENTAL POLICY STRUCTURE

While global policy structures and international environmental solidarity are growing in strength, they remain too weak to make significant progress a worldwide reality. As a result, the gap between what has been done thus far and what is needed is widening. From a global perspective, the environment has continued to degrade during the past decade, significant environmental problems remain, and the outlook is, unfortunately, pessimistic.

Internationally and nationally, the funds and political situation are not sufficient to halt continuing global environmental degradation or address the most pressing environmental issues, even though the technologies and knowledge are available to do so. The recognition of environmental issues as necessarily long-term and cumulative, with serious global and security implications, exists but the will to act remains limited. The continued preoccupation with immediate local and national issues and a general lack of sustained interest in global and long-term environmental issues remain major impediments to environmental progress internationally.

According to the CSD's report on:Tourism and the Environment, there are several important emerging issues with regard to tourism and environmental protection that must be addressed in order to overcome these impediments. These include:

Developing partnership: For sustainable tourism, the involvement and commitment of all stakeholders is essential. However, public, private and academic sector partnerships are still underdeveloped and therefore need to be encouraged.

Involvement of the banking and insurance sectors: Banks and insurance companies could greatly expedite the progress of sustainable tourism by incorporating environmental and social criteria into assessment procedures for loans, investments, and insurance. They could help to finance environmentally sound technologies and provide incentives for sustainable tourism. This approach has worked well in other contexts. Widespread involvement of the banking and insurance sectors should be sought.

Use of economic instruments: The tourism industry consumes increasingly scarce natural resources. The costing of energy and water in particular could expedite greatly eco-efficiency in the tourism industry and raise revenue for the improved management of those resources. Governments should consider the development and widespread use of economic instruments for sustainable tourism.

Involvement of tourism boards: Often, marketing strategies and messages are not in line with the principles of sustainable tourism. There is a need to better involve tourism boards in sustainable tourism efforts.

Capacity-building of local government: In many countries, local governments have important responsibilities regarding tourism development. Capacity-building programmes should be implemented to help them understand those responsibilities, develop integrated and participatory approaches, and define and implement policies for sustainable tourism.

Greater focus on transport: There is a continued development of long-haul travel. Economic, technological and management approaches should be developed to reduce emissions, waste and pollution resulting from tourism transportation. Changing consumption patterns should also be considered.

Emerging types of tourism: Tourism is rapidly diversifying. Emerging forms of tourism should also develop according to sustainability criteria. The increase of cruises and the current trend towards mega-ships necessitate that the cruise ship industry develop a socially and environmentally responsible approach.

Improve monitoring: Careful monitoring of impacts and results, as well as the adoption of corrective measures, are conditions for sustainable tourism. All stakeholders at all levels should thus develop monitoring programmes. As previously stated, the private sector should develop monitoring and public reporting of its activities. Local and central governments should develop monitoring tools, such as indicators, and should incorporate the results into their decision-making process.

Where appropriate, participatory approaches should be used. Monitoring is currently uncommon and that should be made a priority (United Nations Economic and Social Council 1999).

SUSTAINABLE TOURISM AT THE NATIONAL AND REGIONAL LEVEL

While the global policies and international donor organisation priorities discussed above are important because they tend to act as positive drivers toward environmental sustainability, particularly in the developing world, it is the national and regional policies within individual countries that are the key to sustainable tourism development strategies.

ENVIRONMENTAL MANAGEMENT SYSTEMS AND THE TOURISM INDUSTRY

Within the last two decades the concept of quality management systems emerged in an effort to gain consistent performance in meeting specified standards (initially in military equipment procurement and operations). The best-known QMS in the commercial world is the ISO 9000 standards of the International Standards Organisation. The implementation of a QMS is intended to provide consumers with an assurance that a company's products and services will be of consistent quality.

As the importance of environmentally-friendly private sector operations grew (as reflected generally in the industry sponsored sustainable development principles described previously), the conceptual model of QMS was applied to industry operations that impacted on the environment. (An EMS can be defined as a management system that incorporates management commitment, organisational structure, operational practices and procedures, and resources into a documented and implemented environmental policy.)

The implementation of an EMS represents the basis by which an organisation can exercise control over its impact on the environment by systematically gathering and coordinating knowledge about those impacts. Implementing an EMS demonstrates a strong commitment to Agenda 21 principles.

Typically, a private sector EMS most often conforms with the International Standards Organisation ISO 14001 standard, although the European Union's Eco-Management and Audit

Scheme (EMAS) is a valuable reference because of its rigorous parameters. It is important to note that all of the preceding material regarding QMS/EMS and ISO14001 is actually intended for use by private businesses or perhaps certain public sector agencies.

It is not designed for use with a tourism destination that comprises many different types of organisations from the public and private sector; but it does lay a foundation of terminology and processes that will be used in discussing EMS for tourism destinations.

The application of the EMS process to tourism destinations is an emerging area of interest, and while there is not yet a substantial amount of direct anecdotal or documentary evidence to examine we can look to recent work by groups like the World Travel & Tourism Council's Green Globe Alliance and others for case studies that illustrate the potentials and pitfalls of the destination-based EMS process. The rationale behind applying the EMS process to tourism destinations is simple and logical.

The natural environment is an extremely valuable resource for most tourism destinations and the aggregate impact from many different sectors of the travel and tourism industry - transportation, accommodations, and tour operations - tends to have a negative environmental effect. Coupled with this assumption is the fact that the public sector is responsible for many functions that should minimise negative environmental impacts - waste management, land use planning, transportation infrastructure, biodiversity conservation, etc. - but often fails to meet this challenge adequately.

Proponents of the destination-based EMS believe that truly sustainable destination management requires a public/ private sector partnership in the form of a cooperative management structure that deals proactively with environmental issues. With this in mind, we will be looking closely at methodologies and processes that can be used in the creation of a strategically designed EMS with broad public/ private stakeholder support.

The benefits of such an EMS will include:

- Providing a systematic framework for public and private sector cooperation on environmental issues;
- Improving compliance with regulatory requirements and industry codes of conduct;
- Reducing public and private sector operation costs as greater energy/resource savings are achieved;
- Increasing competitive advantage in the market for 'green' tourism destinations; and
- Creating a practical mechanism for pursuing the Agenda 21 principles of sustainable development.

PROPERTY-BASED ENVIRONMENTAL MANAGEMENT SYSTEMS

The creation of property-based EMSs to guide site audits and monitoring processes and in which to anchor certification processes is a new phenomenon in the hospitality industry and, to date, one without a defined standard. This is generating a mounting confusion within the industry over what environmental standards, which criteria, and whose certification programme to use.

The advent of EMSs into tourism is based on the success of EMS operations in other industries, the perceived market benefits of independent certification of environmental standards for individual tourism enterprises, and a demonstrated growth in demand for environmentally friendly or 'green' tourism destinations in major outbound markets. EMSs are desirable because their adoption can reduce operation costs through energy and resource savings, improve internal management methods, reduce liability/risk from environmental deterioration, improve a property's image in the area of environmental performance and compliance with regulatory requirements, and open opportunities for profit in the emerging market for 'green' tourism destinations.

The overall benefit of a properly designed and administered EMS, then, is its ability to provide credible and objective assurance to inbound markets that the environmental conditions in a particular property or destination are of a higher quality than those of competing locations.

THE GROWTH OF ECO-LABELS IN THE TOURISM INDUSTRY

The creation of environmental management systems for the tourism industry is a new phenomenon that is looking to build on three important trends:

- The success of EMS operations in other industries.
- The perceived potential market benefits of independent certification of environmental standards for individual tourism business.
- The demonstrated growth in demand for environmentally friendly or 'green' tourism destinations in major outbound markets.

A number of organisations are currently certifying tourism providers as 'environmentally friendly', including Green Globe, Green Seal and HVS Ecotel. The primary benefit, to date, of conforming with the various EMS standards developed for the tourism industry is the cost savings achieved through various operational efficiencies. It is anticipated, however, that as awareness of environmental certification within the tourism industry is raised, there will be an increased competitive advantage to being independently certified as environmentally friendly.

The hope is that as consumer consciousness of environmental issues increases, more people will choose tourism service providers and, indeed, destinations, based on their environmental performance. As indicated previously, though, there is not yet quantitative evidence to indicate that consumers make these types of choices based on their perception of environmental factors.

While there is not currently a defined standard for an EMS that deals with a destination as a whole, organisations like Green Globe, Green Seal and others are examining the best method to institute such a standard. Destinations are looking into adopting an EMS system for many of the same reasons individual businesses choose to create an EMS:

- Reduction in operation costs as greater energy/ resource savings are achieved;
- Improved internal management methods;
- Reduction in liability/risk from environmental deterioration;
- Improvement of a destination's image in the area of environmental performance; and compliance with regulatory requirements; and
- Desire to profit in the market for 'green' tourism destinations.

ECOLABELLING AND CERTIFICATION PROGRAMMES

The tourism industry is dependent on the environment for its sustainability and makes extensive use of the natural and cultural resources in its area of operation. The industry's prosperity is thus dependent on the conservation and responsible use of the environment.

Several organisations, including government organisations, not-for-profit industry organisations and non-governmental organisations, have addressed the issue pertaining to environmental conservation and best practices within the tourism industry by introducing ecolabelling and green certification schemes.

Each certification programme defines criteria and standards that enhance efficiency and reduce overuse and wastage. Each scheme is unique in that the certification period varies and may range from one to three years. Some schemes such as the PATA Green Leaf require the industry operator to merely sign the PATA Code, whereas others have more detailed application procedures. Evaluation methods also vary from scheme to scheme.

Though there is abundant information on the criteria required to participate in these schemes, there is a shortage of information on the evaluation mechanisms and duration period of each scheme. The following section discusses the individual certification programmes in greater detail. The majority of this information was obtained through personal communication or taken from the United Nations Environment Programme (UNEP) report entitled 'Ecolabels in the Tourism Industry'.

PATA GREEN LEAF (ASIA PACIFIC)

This is a green certification scheme developed by the Pacific Asia Travel Association, which is an industry association. It was launched in 1995 and requires that participants officially accept and abide by the PATA principles of conduct listed below. The PATA Code urges Association and Chapter members and their industry partners to:

Adopt the necessary practices to conserve the environment, including the use of renewable resources in a sustainable manner and the conservation of non-renewable resources.

Contribute to the conservation of any habitat of flora and fauna, and of any site whether natural or cultural, which may be affected by tourism.

Encourage relevant authorities to identify areas worthy of conservation and to determine the level of development, if any, which would ensure those areas are conserved.

Ensure that community attitudes, cultural values and concerns, including local customs and beliefs, are taken into account in the planning of all tourism-related projects.

Ensure that assessment procedures recognise the cumulative as well as the individual affects of all developments on the environment.

Comply with all international conventions in relation to the environment.

Comply with all national, state and local environmental laws.

Encourage those involved in tourism to comply with local, regional and national planning policies and to participate in the planning process.

Provide the opportunity for the wider community to take part in discussions and consultations on tourism planning issues insofar as they affect the tourism industry and the community.

Acknowledge responsibility for the environmental impacts

of all tourism-related projects and activities and undertake all necessary changes to those practices.

Foster environmentally responsible practices including waste management, recycling and energy use.

Foster in both management and staff, of all tourism-related projects and activities, an awareness of environmental and conservation principles.

Support the inclusion of professional conservation principles in tourism education, training and planning.

Encourage an understanding by all those involved in tourism of each community's customs, cultural values, beliefs and traditions and how they are related to the environment;

Enhance the appreciation and understanding by tourists of the environment through the provision of accurate information and appropriate interpretation; and *establish* detailed environmental policies and/or guidelines for the various sectors of the tourism industry.

TYROLEAN ENVIRONMENTAL SEAL OF QUALITY (AUSTRIA AND ITALY)

Tirol Werbung and Suditirol - public authorities operating in the area of accommodation and catering - promote this scheme. It was launched in 1994 and sets mandatory criteria pertaining to waste prevention, waste utilisation, energy, soil and transportation for businesses operating in the lodging industry. These include the hotel trade, the catering trade, private lodgings and farm holidays, camping sites and alpine refuges. The standards include but are not limited to the following:

WASTE PREVENTION

No portion packages in the catering and sanitary areas; no sales of beverage cans; refundable deposits instead of dispensers with disposable containers; no dispensers for beverages in disposable containers; no disposable tableware or cutlery; use of recycled paper or chlorine-free paper in the office, advertising and sanitary areas; drawing up of refuse concept guidelines.

TRANSPORT

Providing, hiring or arranging for guest bicycles (where terrain permits); advising visitors of best public transport connections (rail and bus) for arrival and departures; transfer service for guests arriving by public transport; facilities for storing winter sports equipment over the summer or between holidays.

GREEN GLOBE (INTERNATIONAL)

The World Travel and Tourism Council, which is an industry association, promote the Green Globe certification programme, which focuses on all industries within the tourism sector.

It was launched in 1994 and requires that the participating agents comply with the Green Globe minimum standard requirements, which are as follows:

WASTE MINIMISATION, REUSE AND RECYCLING

The company shall undertake a detailed assessment of the source and content of the waste produced.

The company shall ensure that all treatment of all waste is conducted in accordance with best industry practice and according to legislative requirements.

The company shall identify opportunities to reduce, reuse and recycle waste, and develop an action plan for implementing appropriate action.

ENERGY EFFICIENCY, CONSERVATION AND MANAGEMENT

The company shall undertake a detailed assessment of energy use throughout the company, establish the type of energy required for all activities, and monitor and review use on a regular basis. The company shall set targets for reducing energy use throughout the company.

The company shall ensure that energy efficiency is a key consideration in the purchasing of new or replacement equipment and in the design of new buildings or facilities.

The company shall encourage energy efficiency among

staff, residents, guests and business partners. The company shall research alternative, environmentally benign methods of energy generation, such as solar, wind or biomass power.

MANAGEMENT OF FRESHWATER RESOURCES

The company shall undertake a detailed assessment of water use throughout the company and monitor water use on a regular basis, installing sub-meters where necessary. The company shall set targets for reducing water consumption and ensure that its water requirements do not adversely affect the water supplies for nearby communities.

The company shall identify opportunities to reduce and reuse water and take action accordingly. The company shall minimise the wastage of water by undertaking regular maintenance checks. The company shall where possible, install water saving devices in new and existing buildings. The company shall ensure that water efficiency is a key consideration when purchasing new and replacement equipment, and is built into the design of new buildings and facilities.

WASTEWATER MANAGEMENT

The company shall dispose of waste water responsibly, by ensuring that all effluent is treated to match existing minimum standards for the area. The company shall establish emergency procedures to ensure that the aquatic environment is protected from disasters within the facility.

The company shall avoid products containing potentially hazardous substances that may eventually find their way into the water system.

Traditional 'command and control' governmental approaches are not currently capable of developing the greatest value from investments in sustainable tourism. A special report by the World Tourism Organisation (WTO) emphasised the importance of the changing government role in tourism and the need to reexamine traditional activities undertaken by the public sector. These changes have been particularly evident in Europe and North America where government owned assets have been divested and privatised. Governments have also created public-private partnerships to market their countries as international travel destinations.

Successful sustainable tourism initiatives require the active and concerted involvement of the public and private sectors. This involvement can and must occur at a variety of levels. At the most general level, we observe that the core resources that attract tourists are national patrimony - the cultural and resources that make a country, region or people distinctive or even unique.

As national patrimony, these resources tend to be owned and managed (or at least directed) by the government. Tourism also requires the active participation of private sector entrepreneurs to develop services that make enjoyment of those assets possible (such as hotels, restaurants, tour companies, transportation providers). However, these services are largely meaningless if there is no infrastructure to permit tourists to enter an area or support the entrepreneurs. Airports, roads, potable water and other basic services are generally provided by the public sector.

At a more operational level, public-private partnerships can take many forms: such as concessions or outsourcing contracts to manage public assets; joint ventures to develop tourism attractions; agreements to develop and operate paid infrastructure such as roads, ports and water systems; user fee systems to support common objectives such as resource protection; and other simpler forms of cooperation such as agreements between governments and the private sector to support shared objectives with human and financial resources.

The principal objective of these mechanisms is to leverage investment capital. The governments provide the core assets, necessary investment conditions and the 'licence' to invest in activities that have a much greater impact than the government alone is capable of achieving.

For example, these mechanisms are used to help advance tourism development in local areas near major protected areas. Declining government budgets and other financial difficulties have led to weak governmental mechanisms to care for national parks. Local governments are requesting the private sector and non-governmental organisations to assume management responsibility for most of the nation's parks.

This form of public-private partnership allows for greater management agility, lowers government budget obligations and provides the parks with more flexibility to enter into agreements with donors, tour operators and the local hospitality sectors. However, the only thing public about the parks is the land itself; the public sector is not necessarily participating in the management of these areas. In many countries, government rules greatly restrict the options for generating park revenue and entering into alliances with the private sector. While not necessarily the ideal long-term strategy, the current arrangement offers numerous advantages over a purely public park system.

Additional public-private cooperation will be needed to protect the natural and cultural assets that attract visitors. National governments will need to work with the private sector to identify common objectives and opportunities for producing revenue to protect the parks and protected areas of the region, ensuring the sustainability of these core attractions into the future. User fees, room taxes, environmental performance bonds for new tourism development and a variety of other mechanisms could be considered.

In addition to providing revenue, these types of mechanisms provide assurances to tourists that the destination is serious about the quality of its attractions.

Effective public-private partnerships can accomplish other desirable sustainable development goals, such as providing greater opportunities for smaller enterprises to participate in tourism development, and reducing 'leakage' of tourism revenues out of the country. Overall, tourism development decision-making could be improved by enhanced collaboration of the private sector in land use planning and environmental impact assessment and more transparent use of permitting and zoning.

Chapter 7

'Hosts' and Destinations

In 1963, Katherine Whitehorn in the UK *Guardian* wrote: 'The only unspoilt village is the one no outsider has ever visited, not even you.' While this is extreme in its denial of the dynamic element and benefits of social integration and acculturation, it makes the point about the effect of visitors and tourists on local communities.

Nearly forty years on, there is a vast body of work that demonstrates that local communities in Third World countries reap few benefits from tourism because they have little control over the ways in which the industry is developed, they cannot match the financial resources available to external investors and their views are rarely heard.

This chapter focuses on these local communities which receive tourists and looks at their levels of power, control and ownership of tourism.

In the chapter title the word 'hosts' is in inverted commas. This draws attention to the implication that there is a willingness on the part of those who receive guests and possibly even an assumption that they have a degree of control over tourist developments in their community.

As already discussed and as is well-documented elsewhere, it is not often the case that local people derive benefit sufficient to outweigh the disbenefits of their community receiving tourists. Particularly, illustrated the uneven and unequal relationships of power within local communities.

The terms 'destination community' and 'visited population' are used interchangeably rather than the word 'host', but 'hosts' is used in the title because, as will be seen in this chapter, there are examples of communities managing to take a degree of control of, and to exercise power over, the developments of tourism in their localities.

Also throughout the chapter the term 'local community' is used somewhat loosely, reflecting its common usage which fails to acknowledge that the term is often contested, between different groups within the community for instance, and is often assumed to represent a homogeneous population. As we shall see, this assumption is questionable and fails to acknowledge the heterogeneity and different interest groups within what are commonly referred to as 'local communities'.

The body of this chapter examines the different levels at which local communities participate in tourism and the levels of ownership and control that they, and others, hold over the resources of the tourism industry.

The relationships of power between local populations and the tourists, the governments, the industry, the NGOs and the supranational institutions produce effects which reflect and promote the unequal development of visited populations and these other players in the activities of tourism. The differences in the approaches taken in pursuit of community control and government control are also outlined.

The word 'destinations' is used in the chapter title because all too often the local communities visited by tourists are viewed precisely as that - places, to be collected, as if the people who live there are either irrelevant or at best incidental to the place.

Alternatively, where 'experiencing the local culture' is considered to be important as part of the tourist experience, then the local people may be considered as objects or commodities. In no instances is this more so than in the case of organised tours to visit tribal peoples, a feature of the industry which is also discussed in this chapter. Pratt's notion of transculturation and the ways in which cultural domination is transmitted from one group (the tourists) to another (the visited population) are then discussed. Throughout the chapter, we examine the demands made upon the visited populations that they be 'authentic'.

LOCAL PARTICIPATION IN DECISION-MAKING

The two words, 'local' and 'participation', are regularly used together to emphasise the need to include and involve local people; and it is this juxtaposition of the two words which implies, paradoxically, that it is local people who have so often been left out of the planning, decision-making and operation of tourist schemes. At various points in the 'age of development', however, participation and people-focused approaches have become axiomatic with development.

One of the criteria often agreed as essential to the conditions of sustainability and development in any 'new' tourist scheme is the participation of local people. For the most part there has been an overwhelming benevolence towards the process of participation and a once marginal activity has become mainstreamed in the work of many INGOs, multilateral and bilateral agencies.

Indeed, the 1990s was the decade of participatory development. As Henkel and Stirrat argue, 'It is now difficult to find a development project that does not ... claim to adopt a "participatory" approach involving "bottom-up" planning, acknowledging the importance of "indigenous" knowledge and claiming to "empower" local people'. And as Jules Pretty points out:

In recent years, there have been an increasing number of comparative studies of development projects showing that 'participation' is one of the critical components of success ... As a result, the terms 'people participation' and 'popular participation' are now part of the normal language of many development agencies, including non-governmental organisations, government departments and banks. It is such a fashion that almost everyone says that participation is part of their work.

Moreover, Survival International has noted that 'it has become fashionable for conservationists to talk about "consulting" local people ... This looks good on paper, but

[is] hardly an adequate substitute for land ownership rights and self-determination' (1996).

Through the evolution and development of Local Agenda 21, participation has become part of the apparatus of development, an inseparable process. The association of participation with 'empowerment' and 'sustainability' and the multi-beneficial direct and indirect impacts identified as arising from it has tended to place it on a pedestal.

Participation is not, however, without its critics. Cooke and Kothari (2001), for example, refer to participation as the 'new tyranny', a critical attack on much development practice some would argue, but also a critique which seeks to expose and understand the sanctity in which participation is held, and the manner in which there are at times 'evangelical promises of salvation'; and there is a whiff of spiritualism in participatory practices that mirrors the discourses of travel.

As a powerful discourse, participation, it is argued, must be subjected to a critique and must be alive to the possibility that participation has 'the potential for an unjustified exercise of power'. Thus, phrases such as 'targeting local people' and 'eliciting community-based participation', and sentiments such as 'environmentally sustainable development ... rests on gaining local support for the project', and 'projects must provide direct benefits to local peoples' come from the perspective of the project planner, usually from the First World, as are all these examples.

The planners are often associated with a major INGO (such as WWF, Conservation International and TIES as in these cases) or a supranational institution such as the World Bank (as in two of these cases) and all seek their own form of sustainability through their appropriate projects.

It is not so much the good intentions or ethical and theoretical value that lie behind participation that are open to question, but rather, the often uncritical manner in which participation is conceptualised and practised that has drawn increasing attention. Commentators have pointed to the manner in which participatory exercises have been conducted and the way in which it has been subsumed into contemporary developmental practice - codified and 'manualised' as part of a technical activity.

Cleaver argues that a new faith in participation arises from three key tenets: that participation is inherently good, that good techniques can ensure success, and that considerations of structures of power (and politics) should be avoided. Before turning more directly to its application to tourism, we consider these points in turn.

Commentators have already referenced the 'spiritual whiff of righteousness' in elements of the development discourse and participation is no different in this respect. Participation has been regarded as an inherently positive force for change and development. Henkel and Stirrat, for example, refer to Chambers's 'theology of development' requiring practitioners to undergo an experience 'akin to that St Paul underwent on the road to Damascus', with Cleaver positing participation as an 'act of faith in development'.

But far from the exercise of a value-free (perhaps 'ecumenical') approach Henkel and Stirrat suggest that what the 'new orthodoxy boldly calls "empowerment"' has special resonance in what Michel Foucault (1980) calls 'subjection', where the technical framework, approach and means of participation in participatory rural appraisal is preordained and fixed. Ultimately, critics argue, this form of participation drives participants to seeing and representing their world within the context of the PRA 'expert's' vision. Or perhaps, local people are simply pragmatic and are able to off-load local knowledge into predetermined structures, but with the view to realising opportunities and resources from external programmes.

Second, and leading on from the inherently positive nature of participation, there has been an overwhelming belief that problems exist only in terms of the methods and techniques employed. But a number of critics have questioned the underlying methodology - that is, the philosophy of methods. Kothari (2001) argues that there is a number of tropes in participatory discourse expressed as dualisms that favour the South, the local community and participation over the

North, the global community, government, and non-participation; the former are imbued with morality, the latter immorality. There is an underlying assumption that participation is a trip-switch to development. But as Cleaver questions, 'Are we in danger of swinging from one untenable position (we know best) to an equally untenable and damaging one (they know best)?'

There is also an interesting parrellel to be drawn from the application of Goffman's (1997) writings on the presentation of self in everyday life, to the staged authenticity thesis in tourism and the application of participation processes through techniques such as PRA. Kothari argues that PRA represents an act with participants performing distinct, 'contrived' roles and practitioners or facilitators acting as 'stage managers or directors who guide, and attempt to delimit' the performance of participants. In this way only partial or distorted representations of everyday lives are offered up or participants provide the information they believe is required to secure support and manipulate interpretations to serve their interests; as Cooke suggests 'participatory processes may lead a group to say what it is they think you and everyone else want to hear, rather than what they truly believe'.

A further point of criticism is the degree to which participation manages to challenge the traditional top-down and mechanistic approach to development practice. As Mosse argues, rather than 'local knowledge' structuring and modifying development projects, formulaic project frameworks (such as widely used logical frameworks) relying on participatory planning techniques, in effect structure and articulate the local knowledge (2001:24). As such there is increasing evidence that development practice is increasingly influenced by western managerialist thinking, especially human resource management.

Third, and as Cleaver forcefully argues, an emphasis on perfecting method has inevitably resulted in a belief in problem solving through participation 'rather than problematization, critical engagement and class' (2001:53); and this belief in problem solving through participation fails to acknowledge the structures of power, both within so-called 'communities' and between these communities and outsiders conducting participatory exercises. This neutralisation of power structures and political priorities is also a noted limitation of the sustainable livelihood approach to development, of which participation is a critical element. This aspect is especially significant within the overall context of this book, with its emphasis on uneven and unequal structures and relations of power.

The problems start with the notion of *a* community as *the* '"natural" social entity' and identifiable reality, and the manner in which the heterogeneity and unequal access to power is assumed away. There exists a further assumption that members of a community are willing and able to participate equally.

This has been an enduring debate and problem within community development studies. The emphasis on solidarity in communities together with a closed and bounded conceptualisation of place, culture and community leads to the relegation and cognisance of conflict and exclusion in communities, and a failure to understand social and power structures that greatly influence the conduct and outcome of participatory processes.

As suggested above, however, a consideration of relationships of power and the discourse of participatory development also necessitates 'an investigation of the motives and ideology of the "experts" who advocate such an approach' (Hailey, 2001:98), for as Hailey argues, 'There is a suspicion that those "experts" who advocate participatory approaches to development appear to sit on some moral high ground and as such are immune to criticism' (2001:97).

Most critically some commentators have argued that participatory discourse and practices must be understood within the broader context. Attempts 'to obscure the relations of power and influence between elite interest and less powerful groups such as the "beneficiaries" of development projects in local communities in developing countries' are indicators that this broader context is being ignored.

In Taylor's view, participation is simply not working, because it has been promoted by the powerful, and is largely cosmetic, but most ominously because 'it is used as a "hegemonic" device to secure compliance to, and control by, existing power structures'. As such then, participation simultaneously veils and legitimises existing structures of power.

While participation is a fundamental means of interaction and 'development', it is certainly not a panacea and does not automatically or necessarily lead to a change in the underlying structures of power.

There are many well-documented examples of the relative lack of power held by local people in tourism developments in their locality - Brandon cites over fifty schemes, 'many of [which] had initiated nature tourism activities, but few of the benefits went to local people'.

This exclusion of local people from involvement and decision-making in the operation and benefits of tourism can be seen in some of the examples cited in this chapter and elsewhere in this book.

PRETTY'S TYPOLOGY OF PARTICIPATION

The principle of local participation may be easy to promote; the practice is more complex, and clearly participation may be implemented in a number of different ways. Pretty has identified and described different types of participation, which offers a critique of each type.

Local circumstances, the unequal distribution of power between local and other interest groups, and differing interpretations of the term 'participation' are reflected in Pretty's typology of participation, which is just as applicable to the idea of 'partnerships', another mantra of the current phase of development, as it is to the idea of participation.

Pretty's typology is especially helpful in developing an understanding of the factors which affect the development of tourism schemes in local communities, and the case studies illustrated in this chapter are referred to the typology.

The six types of participation range from *passive*

participation, in which virtually all the power and control over the development or proposal lie with people or groups outside

Table: Pretty's Typology of Participation.

Typology	Characteristics of each type
1. Passive participation	People participate by being told what has been decided or has already happened. Information being shared belongs only to external professionals
2. Participation by consultation	People participate by being consulted or by answering questions. Process does not concede any share in decision-making, and professionals are under no obligation to take on board people's views
3. Bought participation	People participate in return for food, cash or other material incentives. Local people have no stake in prolonging technologies or practices when the incentives end
4. Functional participation	Participation seen by external agencies as a means to achieve their goals, especially reduced costs. People participate by forming groups to meet predetermined objectives
5. Interactive participation	People participate in joint analysis, development of action plans and formation or strengthening of local groups or institutions. Learning methodologies used to seek multiple perspectives and groups determine how available resources are used
6. Self-mobilisation and connectedness	People participate by taking initiatives independently of external institutions to change systems. They develop contacts with external institutions for resources and technical advice they need, but retain control over resource use

the local community, to *self-mobilisation*, in which the power and control over all aspects of the development rest squarely with the local community. The latter type does not rule out the involvement of external bodies or assistants or consultants, but they are present only as enablers rather than as directors and controllers of the development. The range of types allows for differing degrees of external involvement and local control, and reflects the power relationships between them. For local people, involvement in the decision-making process is a feature of only the *interactive participation* and *self-mobilisation* types, while in the *functional participation* type most of the major decisions have been made before they are taken to the local community.

The only forms of local participation that are likely to break the existing patterns of power and unequal development are those which originate from within the local communities themselves. This chapter provides a few such examples, but even these illustrate the fact that local circumstances always manage to complicate the best of intentions.

It would be easy here to make the prescriptive assumption that the greater the degree of local participation, the better (by whatever definition) the project. There are those, however, who might disagree with this assumption, especially, but not exclusively, those who represent a vested interest in a particular development project - the development agencies, governments, supranational institutions, or operators for instance. In these cases, some of the lesser types of participation might be considered preferable. It is precisely this point which emphasises the importance of the power relationships involved in any (tourist) development project, and the fact that Pretty's typology reflects this underlines its value.

At this point, it is worth contrasting a number of examples of local participation in tourism developments in order to illustrate the manifestations and effects of different levels of involvement. We have attempted simply to describe the situations of each case study in the appropriate box and in the text to relate it to Pretty's typology, which allows us to make a consideration of the power vested in each interest group and their relation to the local community.

It is described in Mundo Maya publicity material as 'a ground-breaking tourism and regional development initiative ... [which] seeks to improve the lot of area inhabitants with low-impact projects which give visitors the opportunity to explore the area'. In 1991 the project initially received US$1 million from the European Commission to promote three kinds of tourism in each country: cultural tourism, coastal tourism and eco/adventure tourism. The project promotes infrastructural improvements, new hotel construction, archaeological projects and extensive international marketing through glossy brochures, in-flight magazines and travel trade shows.

As the editor of *Tourism Link* (a journal of the Belize Tourism Industry Association) explained 'full decision making powers for all Mundo Maya affairs lie in the hands of only five persons - basically the top public sector tourism officials of each country' (1992:4). The fact that this statement came as part of an article of complaint by private sector representatives about public sector control of the project underlines the irrelevance of local communities in this contest for power. According to Pretty's typology, this example might be classified as *passive participation*.

Although there has been a degree of external assistance in this case, the idea for the scheme arose from within the community itself and all the tourists' activities are under the direct control of the community. Moreover, it is one of the advantages of this type of tourist scheme that money for services rendered goes direct to those who render them without being 'creamed off' or cut down to a minimum by middlemen and agents. Although the community received considerable assistance in its early years, its tourism venture has been largely unassisted, which classifies this scheme as *self-mobilisation* in terms of Pretty's typology.

MARKETING MEN PUT CURSE OF TOURISM INDUSTRY ON MAYAS

Order a prawn cocktail in a hotel in Chetumal, south-east Mexico, and it will probably come smothered in 'Mayan sauce'. A trivial example, but one that shows how the tourist industry, helped by Latin American governments, is turning a great pre-Columbian civilisation and its present-day descendants into a marketing concept.

But critics, including Mayan organisations, claim that archaeological sites and indian villages face being turned into a giant theme park, and that the millions of indigenous inhabitants have no part in decision-making. 'The bottom line is that they are just exploiting the resources of our people', says Greg Cho'c of the Kekchi council of Belize. 'Mayan people are not involved and cannot influence the project.'

The aims of the Mayan World scheme ... include improving the quality of life of local residents, protecting the environment, and safeguarding historical and cultural heritage.

But the Mexican government's own archaeological and cultural institute, the INAH, is sceptical. 'They have no awareness of what ecology is', says the director of the local INAH office, Adriana Velásquez. 'If they put up a palm-thatched hut they think it's "ecological".'

She cites the once-unspoilt Xcaret ruins, which have been turned into a park for day-trippers from the up-market resort of Cancún. The entrance fee is about £13, out of the reach of local people ...

Rolando Pérez, a Quiché Maya, is one of about 30,000 Guatemalan refugees living in south-east Mexico ... Mr. Pérez ... believes white and mixed-race people want to eliminate the indians. 'They see us as an obstacle to development,' he says. 'They just want to build big hotels for the tourists. They're the ones that benefit, not us.'

Local initiatives, such as a village guesthouse scheme started by Mayan villagers in Belize, have been ignored, says Stewart Krohn, managing director of Channel 5 television in Belize ... 'If you go to a meeting of the Mundo Maya you won't find a Maya there, except maybe serving dinner,' Mr. Krohn says. 'The Mayan people are just being used as low-cost labour. If I was a Maya, I'd put sugar in their gas tank.'

These two examples come from Central America, but later examples in this chapter are from Africa and the Himalayas, as well as Latin America. You might also find it useful to refer other case studies presented elsewhere in this book to Pretty's typology.

PARTICIPATORY APPRAISAL AND INQUIRY TECHNIQUES

In their efforts to involve local populations in the planning, decision-making and operating of tourist schemes, planners and academics have developed a range of techniques. Some of these techniques were listed and briefly mentioned in 'The tools of sustainability in tourism'. As was pointed out, techniques which allow for consultation and participation are still young in their development and suffer various shortcomings.

It is debatable whether any of the relatively sophisticated techniques that have become available recently are able to improve on the traditional and well-used technique of the meeting. Local communities the world over traditionally use both formal and informal meetings to debate the courses of development and issues which may affect them. Of course meetings are not always all-inclusive; for example, women and children are excluded from many but by no means all such meetings.

The Longo Maï movement, based in France, aims to give war refugees a positive and productive home and work environment rather than a temporary and transient camp. In 1978 the movement helped a group of Nicaraguan refugees fleeing Somoza's terror to form a small community in southern Costa Rica. After Somoza's overthrow in 1979 they returned to Nicaragua but were soon replaced by Salvadoran refugees fleeing the same type of state terror.

The community is now called Finca Sonador and has a population of around 300, mostly Salvadorans with a few Costa Rican campesino families, refugees from poverty and landlessness in their own country. The Finca is a relatively self-sufficient agricultural village which produces coffee and a few other products for sale beyond the village. In low income months their traditional survival agriculture is based on corn, beans, rice and yucca.

Since 1992, the Finca has attempted to diversify its economic activities by attracting a few visitors. A few families are willing to accommodate visitors and have the space to do so, although in some cases visitors may find themselves sharing a room with children.

Prices for meals and accommodation are negotiated with the family, although there is a non-binding guidelist of tariffs. By the standard of the northern professionals who form the majority of visitors, prices are ridiculously low. Other activities offered in the village include horseriding, guided tours, involvement in farming and general inclusion in fiestas. These ensure that the tourist money is distributed further afield within the community. Advertising for the scheme is largely by word-of-mouth, although a publicity sheet is posted in the Quaker lodging house in San José.

The small scale of the scheme would seem to be an essential feature both for the tourist and the host. For the visitor it is important that the experience has its air of exclusivity in the sense that this is not the usual tourist experience. For the host, it earns a little extra income with little extra cost and does not disrupt the community's or the family's way of life.

More sophisticated survey techniques, public attitude surveys, stated preference techniques and contingent valuation methods all suffer the disadvantage of being conducted, administered, promoted and publicised by persons outside the local community affected by a tourism development. They are tools used by professionals administering the surveys on local communities, who by definition do not therefore enjoy control over it.

Both inputs and results are often open to dispute. In terms of Pretty's typology such techniques may help to improve the level of participation, but they are unlikely to attain a high level unless they focus on the degree of decision-making devolved to the local community as well as its active involvement in the operation of the scheme. There is little doubt, however, that with their systemic and structured learning processes they can increase the likelihood of sustained success of schemes. A number of the examples given in this chapter illustrate this.

These techniques represent recent attempts to involve local people in research, policy appraisal and implementation themselves. But in reviewing the origins of participatory appraisal, Chambers notes that rural appraisal techniques can be traced to the late 1970s and early 1980s as a reaction to the 'biased perceptions derived from rural development tourism (the brief rural visit by the urban based professional) and the many defects and high costs of large-scale questionnaire surveys'.

Accompanying the general fashion for 'local participation' discussed above, recent years have seen the development of a trend for participatory approaches to enquiry and research. Participatory action research (PAR), participatory research methodology (PRM), participatory rural appraisal (PRA), rapid appraisal (RA), rapid assessment procedures (RAP), rapid assessment techniques (RAT), rapid ethnographic assessment (REA), rapid rural appraisal (RRA) and a bewildering array of other acronyms and initials have entered into use.

Although they are often formally stated to involve many steps in the process, essentially they all follow the three-step procedure of participatory enquiry, collective analysis and action in the locality. (For a more detailed outline of the general procedure, see the work of the International Institute for Environment and Development (IIED).)

The principle of local participation underlies all these techniques, but they involve differing degrees of participation often in different stages of the appraisal, and the same technique may be interpreted and implemented in different ways by different people. A specific example is given which includes extracts from a 1996 advertisement (on the internet) for members of a team to conduct a PRA in Ecuador.

While the request for support or assistance in this case came from the community, through the Ecuadorean NGO EcoCiencia, to Jon Kohl at Yale University, there is an implication that it is the 'outside tecnicos' and professionals who, out of largesse, will solve the problems of the local community. The leader has a clear preference for the establishment of an environmental interpretation centre, and it is uncertain whether the idea for this arose from within the community and/or is what the local people had in mind. Nevertheless, it is likely that this example would be classified as *functional* or *interactive participation* by Pretty's typology.

A little more precision in the classification may be possible with more information regarding the number and kind of major decisions which were made before the process began to involve the local community.

RECRUITING A PRA TEAM FOR ECUADOR

This summer I will be working with an Ecuadorean NGO called EcoCiencia and will be leading a Participatory Rural Appraisal (PRA) in a small peasant community located in Pululahua Geobotanical Reserve, a 30-minute bus ride north of Quito. EcoCiencia has held some successful campamentos with kids and parents but now sees potential and has interest in establishing a more permanent environmental education programme with complete local participation. They suggested possibly a small andean zoo.

I'm taking the zoo suggestion one step further by doing a PRA and thus figuring out with the residents what are their biggest problems and what are suggested solutions, some of which might be addressed by an interpretation centre of some kind ...

For those who are unfamiliar with PRA methodology, in short, it's a workshop of 2-3 weeks on site where a team of outside tecnicos works with a local community team to investigate the site, discuss problems and solutions, and present them to the entire community who then discuss and prioritise them. A document results, done in part by the people and it is designed to promote autosuggestion on the part of the locals to use action plans and start their own development process.

In my case I will also be using the PRA results as a feasibility study for the establishment of an environmental interpretation centre which would provide economic, educational, and any number of other benefits.

PRA is an impressive methodology catching on in Latin America (while it is mainstay in India and Asia) which really puts into practice the principle of local participation that many talk about and few do. I am currently recruiting tecnicos for the interdisciplinary team ... Requirements are proficiency in Spanish, some experience working with rural or local people, disciplinary skills that complement the yet unformed team, and a desire to work hard during the short stay. The offer is open to all students and professionals. I welcome recommendations of other people, especially latinos, as well.

While the techniques of local appraisal are well-intentioned by those who lead and conduct them, the critical questions concerning the balance of power are who leads them and to what ends. In general they are led, or at least significantly advised, by First World professionals, and the idea that a group of outsiders visiting for a short period of time can appreciate, let alone solve, the problems experienced by local communities is rather pretentious and patronising, and suggestive of neo-colonialist attitudes.

It is no doubt exciting, and a little 'ramboesque', for the First World professional to be whisked off to help a community somewhere in Latin America, Oceania, South East Asia or Africa, and will certainly add kudos to their curriculum vitae. But such approaches may not be appropriate for addressing the structural and long-term problems of community development. This is not to say that collaboration between First World professionals and local communities is not possible or desirable.

But a crucial element in such collaboration might be to redress existing imbalances of power so that the outcome of the exercise represents the interests of local people rather than the interests and values of the 'outside tecnicos'. To this end, Heeks (1999) suggests that there are specifically several questions to be asked where participation is being considered: what are the political and cultural contexts? who wants to introduce participation? and why? who is participation sought from? do they want to, and can they, participate?

OTHER PARTICIPATORY TECHNIQUES

Another related technique which attempts to involve the

notion of participation in the making of decisions is the Delphi technique, which is used to set threshold values or critical levels or standards of specific aspects of a development (such as pollution levels or maximum visitor numbers) or to identify positive and/or negative impacts of a development. It is a judgemental technique involving the subjective assessments of those who take part, although it is often seen 'as a means of collecting expert or informed opinion and of working towards consensus between experts on a given issue'.

The technique uses responses of the participants to an initial questionnaire about the issue under study. The second stage compiles these responses and informs participants of the results (that is, the total responses). The third stage repeats the first but participants have the benefit of knowing all other responses. The stages can be repeated numerous times if a consensus is not close enough.

Although meetings between its participants can take place as part of the process, one of the advantages of the technique is that it provides anonymity, or at least separation, for each individual participant, thereby reducing peer pressure in the formation of opinions and permitting more honest responses. Meetings and/or collection and dissemination of responses form an important part of the attempt to reach a consensus from all individual responses.

It highlights the general limitations on the depth of participation attained by the technique and the consequent suspicion with which its results may be treated by local people. Despite this, there is no doubt that such techniques may be useful in the field of tourism planning. It is not possible to be precise in a classification of this scheme according to Pretty's typology, largely because of the limited amount of information available. One important issue concerns the adequacy of the representation of the local village population by the mayor - some groups may feel inadequately represented. On present information, however, its classification could range from Pretty's *passive participation* to *functional participation*.

Disadvantages of the Delphi technique include its method of selection of participants, the possibility of the dominant influence of particular personalities, its design by professional planners rather than those most affected by the plans, and the arbitrariness of the selection of its values. The selection of participants is normally made either by the professional planners or by the interested party who wishes to see the proposal go ahead; and is most unlikely to be made by those affected adversely by the plans.

The anonymity of participants does not necessarily preclude the inordinate influence of a dominant personality over the outcome of the technique as a result of the power relationships between the participants. As with any subjective assessment technique, it is feasible that the same group could produce a different outcome at a different time and a different group could produce a different outcome at the same time. Moreover, it has the potential to be used as a means of ensuring that control stays with the 'experts' and out of the hands of the local people.

AN ILLUSTRATION OF THE DELPHI TECHNIQUE

A landowner intends to lease an area of land close to the rim of an active volcano to a building consortium which has plans to develop the site for a hotel and tourist observation post. The hotel will incorporate a restaurant which will be open to non-residents. The site is in a National Park area and is adjacent to a small wildlife reserve within the park.

Apart from the crater itself, which has little vegetation other than a few mosses, the area outside the crater rim is covered by cloud forest and has all the rich and varied wildlife and plant life associated with that vegetation type. At present, there is only a rough track, just suitable for four-wheel drive vehicles. The scheme will necessitate the construction of a surfaced road. The park authorities are seeking agreement from all interested parties about several factors concerning the development.

These are:

- The width of the road;
- The capacity of the hotel;
- The height of the hotel;

- The numbers of tourists allowed into the reserve;
- The training and management of the tourist guides;
- A possible minibus system from a village 3 km away to the observation post;
- The possible need for a car park next to the observation post. The people to be consulted are:
- The managing director of the building consortium;
- The landowner;
- The national park director;
- The mayor of the nearby village;
- A biologist who works at the research station in the wildlife refuge;
- A vulcanologist (who works at the same place);
- The director of a tour company interested in running tours to the volcano;
- A conservationist from a leading environmental organisation concerned particularly with tourism.

All these people are to be asked to answer the following questions as part of a Delphi process of approaching a consensus:

- What should be the maximum height of the hotel?
- How should sewage from the hotel be dealt with?
- Should there be a maximum capacity fixed for the hotel?
- What should be the maximum width of the road?
- Who should pay for the road?
- The hotel will have a car park for its residents' cars. Should a car park be constructed next to the observation post for other members of the public? Or should the public be encouraged to use a minibus service? (It is possible to prevent cars, other than those of the hotel users, from using the road.)
- As very few people visit the crater at present, there has been no need to restrict the numbers of people on the trails in the wildlife refuge. But many more visitors are expected once the hotel is built. What should be the maximum carrying capacity of a trail in the wildlife refuge?

- Guides will be needed in the refuge. Who should train them?

effective carrying capacities of a trail in the Guayabo National Monument in Costa Rica, each of these measures refers to some tangible and physical factor pertaining to the area under study. Clark (1990), however, outlines the need to add a further dimension to these calculations by incorporating the social carrying capacity to measure the level at which tourist activity becomes a cause of social unrest and/or tourist discomfort.

Clark expands the number of factors under consideration and the number of output measures or results, and makes it clear that he does not see carrying capacity purely as a negative idea which results in restriction, but relates it instead to the notion of sustainable development. Despite acknowledging difficulties in measurement and definition, he does however assume that a scientifically rational balance can be reached between all these factors, resulting in an 'objective' measure.

Watson and Kopachevsky, however, argue that the result of carrying capacity measurements will always depend on the context of the situation being measured and that this context will vary not just with the physical and social environments, but also with the values of those asking the questions and establishing the conditions for measurement: 'carrying capacities cannot be determined in the absence of value judgements that specify the type of experience a given area is attempting to provide ... the establishment of target levels is fundamentally an exercise in human value judgement' (1996:175).

They identify different types of carrying capacity and are adamant in their belief that values 'influence all phases and elements of social research' and 'play a critical role in the choice and application of science'. Referring to the work of Thomas Kuhn (1962), they state that 'conceptual frameworks and paradigms rise and fall ... as much on political grounds as on scientific ones'.

In other words, human judgement will always be required

in assessing appropriate threshold levels for a given activity, in this case tourism.

It is also clear that carrying capacities may vary with time, a point made by the Belize Centre for Environmental Studies (BCES): 'the physical carrying capacity of a road may decrease at night when visibility is less, or the environmental carrying capacity of Half Moon Caye, in terms of visitor numbers, may decrease when the boobies are nesting' (1994:1).

The way in which visitor carrying capacity has had to be recalculated over time as visitor numbers have increased to the Galápagos Islands also illustrates the point about calculation changes with both time and perceptions or values. Jonathan Croall reports that the Galápagos Islands' 'sustainable' capacity of 12,000 visitors per annum set by the Ecuadorean government was soon increased to 50,000 for economic reasons (1995:61).

This growing realisation, that the setting of limits is a normative process which cannot be divorced from the objectives of the exercise or from the values of those who set them, has led to enquiry into the techniques of setting limits of acceptable change (LACs), which are to some extent developing out of the work on carrying capacity.

One essential element that has been built into the development of LACs has been the involvement of different interest groups in the technique, on the grounds that the setting of limits based on value judgements would be more acceptable to users if they were involved in setting them. As Sidaway says, 'In LAC, the entire process involves the interest groups from the outset' (1994:1).

Sidaway identifies the features which distinguish the LAC approach from carrying capacity and other management planning systems as 'its attempts to identify measurable aspects of quality, to monitor whether environmental quality is maintained and the degree of interest group involvement throughout the process' (1994:3).

The first two of these features show a similarity with another recent development in planning systems, that of sustainability indicators; and in its degree of interest group participation it resembles the Delphi technique discussed earlier.

TYPES OF TOURIST CARRYING CAPACITY

The level of tourist development or recreational activity beyond which the environment as previously experienced is degraded or compromised.

PHYSICAL-FACILITY CAPACITY

The level of tourist development or recreational activity beyond which facilities are 'saturated'; or physical deterioration of the environment occurs through overuse by tourists or inadequate infrastructural network.

SOCIAL-PERCEPTUAL CAPACITY

The level reached when local residents of an area no longer want tourists because they are destroying the environment, damaging the local culture or crowding them out of local activities.

ECONOMIC CARRYING CAPACITY

The ability to absorb tourist functions without squeezing out desirable activities. Assumes that any limit to capacity can be overcome, even if at a cost - ecological, social, cultural or even political.

PSYCHOLOGICAL CAPACITY

This is exceeded when tourists are no longer comfortable in the destination area, for reasons that can include perceived negative attitudes of the locals, crowding of the area (traffic jams) or deterioration of the physical environment.

Despite the recognition of LACs that the universal standards implied by carrying capacity calculations are not compatible with temporal and spatial variations and that the definition of standards of quality varies with time, space, interest group and value, the technique still attempts to define maximum or optimum thresholds applicable to a given situation. But as Munt asserts about carrying capacity, LACs also tend to provide 'both the ecological and social justification for forms of exclusionism - an objective carefully nurtured by a growing corps of eco-missionaries and ego-travellers in Third World countries' (1992:213).

GOVERNMENT CONTROL/COMMUNITY CONTROL

In tourist-speak, suitable destinations are just as likely to be countries as they are to be specific small-scale resorts, towns or settlements. In fact a browse through the brochures of new forms of tourism shows that most are organised by country or even by groups of countries rather than by resort or community. But the countries that tour operators speak of are nation states and are run by governments which often represent different interests and have different priorities from those of local communities.

The Malaysian government, for instance, promoted 1990 as 'Visit Malaysia Year' with advertisements featuring images of indigenous peoples in colourful traditional dress while at the same time imprisoning members of these same groups for protesting against the logging of their land. Burma is a similar case, and there exist many other examples of government marketing policies being at odds with the same government's treatment of indigenous and other communities.

This raises the question of what is a community. Gujit and Shah (1998), cited in Cooke and Kothari (2001), argue that: simplistic understandings of 'communities' see them as homogeneous, static and harmonious units within which people share common interests and needs. This articulation of the notion of 'community', they argue, conceals power relations within 'communities' and further masks biases in interests and needs based on, for example, age, class, caste, ethnicity, religion and gender.

Although a community can be defined by scale, sector, interest, level of power and by numerous other features which express its diversity and heterogeneity, it is taken here as an amorphous term over which there is considerable debate. For the purpose of discussion, community is not regarded here as a homogeneous construct; rather, it is seen as something locational within which there are divisions of differing degrees of contrast according to many criteria. The formation and influence of local elites as a result of these divisions are discussed later. The definition of the community, then, differs according to the case study under question, and where divisions between sectors or groups within the community are significant these are pointed out and discussed if necessary and appropriate.

Gerardo Budowski has posed 'the possibility of a mass ecotourism towards natural areas' (1995) and asks whether this will affect the development of ecotourism. He further asks whether the development of 'megahotels' will operate in opposition to the small rural and rustic hotels noted for the low impact of the tourism they promote. It is this last question which highlights the different courses of action available to national governments.

On the one hand, they can promote relatively small-scale, locally owned, community-based tourism facilities (small hotels, pensions, restaurants and other facilities which form an integral part of the community in which they are located). On the other hand, they can attract transnational investment into the country in the form of large-scale, luxury hotels with all associated facilities integral to the hotel.

The former approach to tourism development offers more chance that the economic benefits of the exchange will remain in the hands of local people, although the government is still able to extract indirect revenue from taxes and from tourist contributions such as park entry fees, transport tariffs, banking charges and other enterprises which the tourists make use of and which the government either taxes or manages.

The latter form of tourism development concentrates the economic benefits with the government, although it would be contested by the supporters of this approach that the employment deriving from such schemes would also ensure some trickle-down of benefits to local workforces. Of course there are more than two approaches available to national governments and local communities. There are numerous ways in which revenue can be shared, both indirectly (through taxes) and directly (through allocation of a proportion of profits or takings), and there are combinations of these.

The examples of Belize and Costa Rica have been cited in a number of places throughout this book, partly because they have both built international reputations as destinations for new forms of tourism. They have also both publicised themselves as pursuing community-based tourism development. In 1994, Henry Young, then Belizean Minister of Tourism and the Environment, for instance, delivered a speech entitled 'Community-based tourism development in Belize: government policies and plans in support of community initiatives' in which he outlined plans 'to direct tourist dollars to ... flow into and stay in local communities' (1994:21). We give further details of how the Belizean government has used the language and rhetoric of sustainable tourism and its stated promotion of community-based tourism to further its international reputation and attractiveness.

It is noteworthy that the quotation above from Henry Young is found in a booklet funded by USAID and jointly published by the Ministry of Tourism and Environment and the Belize Enterprise for Sustained Technology (BEST). The parts played by BEST, USAID and the Belizean government in supposedly promoting community-based tourism development but actually undermining it in the region of Toledo are outlined below.

In 1991 the Toledo Ecotourism Association (TEA) initiated the construction of guesthouses in six indigenous villages (Kekchi, Mayan and Garífuna) in the district of Toledo in the south of Belize. Each guesthouse sleeps eight visitors, and is built in traditional style, using local materials. As extras, concrete floors, water tanks, screened windows and private shared bathroom facilities are also included. In early 1996 there was a temporary lapse in activity in all but two of the villages because of the need to upgrade the facilities, but there are now thirteen villages involved in the scheme.

From the start the scheme encountered a number of difficulties. Local businesses, hotels and lodging houses in Punta Gorda, the district capital, opposed the scheme in the belief that it would take clients away from them. Cement for the construction was not easily obtained. Money and support from the government of Belize was slow in coming. Rivalries and local political squabbles between villages within the TEA hampered the smooth operation of the programme.

Time has helped overcome some of the local political squabbles and the government's suspicion of a scheme over which it did not have control. Recently, however, another problem has presented itself in the form of competition in a number of the villages.

In a misguided attempt to improve an environmentally and socially tarnished image in the region, USAID is promoting the development of village-based and community-controlled tourism on condition that these developments also promote the benefits of competition. Through the organisation BEST, the Agency funded the construction of a new guesthouse at Laguna village. The BEST guesthouse is in competition for tourists with the TEA guesthouse.

In practice such developments are likely to cause rifts and rivalries between and within families in these villages, and this case was no different in that respect. The villages are small and, despite individual effort, enterprise and family-based cultural development, many of the practices, customs and norms of village life have depended strongly on cooperation and community action rather than on the spirit of competition.

Additionally, the BEST promotion works directly against the aims of the TEA. The need to coordinate and plan the programme and to rotate visitors to different villages to ensure a fair distribution of the benefits has been at the heart of the efforts of the TEA. In one move, the USAID created untold difficulties for the TEA and all the villagers who take part in its programme.

And, as if not to be outdone, the United Kingdom's Overseas Development Administration (as it was then) also funded the construction of a new guesthouse in a village which already has a TEA guesthouse. The suitability of this type of promotion can be considered to be flawed. In the words of Chet Schmidt, an adviser to the TEA:

These agencies showed what I consider to be no cultural sensitivity at all, not an overall idea of planning, nor an holistic view of the whole development process here ... All the ugly things that happen with uncontrolled tourism begin with this kind of thing - and it was done by foreign aid.

The USAID and BEST efforts in this case would appear to be highly selective in their participation and somewhat arrogant in their willingness to override already existing community structures. On Pretty's typology their exercise could well classify as *manipulative participation*.

A further example from Central America also helps to illustrate some of the problems and limitations of the processes of participation and development. In the Cosiguina Peninsula of Nicaragua a local NGO has devised and initiated an ecotourism development programme whose ultimate aim is the improvement of the quality of life of the residents of the region.

To Mowforth, who carried out the feasibility study outlined there is no doubt that the scheme will benefit a small minority of people in the Cosiguina Peninsula of Nicaragua. But it is difficult to envisage the alleviation of the poverty suffered by the majority of the area's population through the trickle-down effect. Five hundred years of resource extraction for the sake of satisfying the consumption patterns of other societies have not yet managed to reach them. Indeed, it is debatable whether in relative terms the area's level of poverty is any lower now than it was five hundred years ago.

Certainly neoliberalism imposes market and financial disadvantages on the campesino sector which it never experienced before the latest round of globalised development. Throughout the most recent decade of IMF structural adjustment policies imposed on Nicaragua, UN sources have consistently reported poverty rates at over 50 per cent of the population, those living in extreme poverty at over 40 per cent, and the country as a whole as being one of the three poorest in the hemisphere (UNDP Human Development Report, annual).

Nearly 40 per cent of the population has no access to clean

drinking water. All these statistics are worse in the rural areas such as the Cosiguina Peninsula. SELVA's tourism programme offers a genuine chance to improve their quality of life to a small number of people in the Cosiguina Peninsula of Nicaragua. For all that, its proponents will admit that there is little chance of the programme, if successful, affecting any generalised indicators of poverty, economic well-being or sustainability in the region.

The list of beneficiaries from the successful conduct of the programme is not particularly long. It includes the members of the local NGO, SELVA, who are responsible for its operations and who will benefit financially through salaries, those few people who are employed by SELVA in the establishment and the day-to-day functioning of the activity (service providers), and of course the visitors.

If the programme achieves its long-term goal of involving ten villages in the peninsula as well as SELVA's own centre in the town of El Viejo, then a few persons in each village will also benefit. Doubtless, there will also be a multiplier effect on the economic activities carried out by others in the villages, such as fishermen who might offer boat trips, farmers who might hire out horses and storeholders whose stores may be patronised by the visitors. Even counting the whole population of each village in the total number of beneficiaries

It has been very difficult for us to write what is happening here, probably because it is hard for us to understand ...

With organised groups in 13 communities we have been told the TEA [Toledo Ecotourism Association] is the largest indigenous ecotourism conservation association in the western hemisphere ...

The unfortunate fact is that even with this overwhelming evidence of the TEA's ability to help the local people to unite, to plan, operate, control and directly benefit from ecotourism in their areas, the major sources of funding in the country for conservation, sustainable national resource management and ecotourism development have refused to assist the TEA ...

More difficult for us to understand is the fact that they are, on the other hand, helping to organise and are funding other independent individual groups to be involved with tourism in direct competition to the TEA groups ...

These competing groups have divided our people and seriously threatened to weaken and destroy the unity the TEA has painstakingly developed over the years. This unity represents the only realistic hope and chance the rural and urban people of Toledo have to continue to control and benefit from responsible ecotourism.

We have been told that this is happening because there are other national and foreign interests who are not from our villages who want to take advantage of the opportunities for tourism and other developments ...

The indigenous and other poor people know what this is all about. Before the coming of the TEA, 95 per cent of all tourism in Toledo was controlled by a small group of foreigners and wealthy Belizeans ...

Many of them still resent and resist what they consider to be a loss of their exclusive political and economic powers. Those who oppose the real empowerment of the ... people of Toledo are falling back on the old colonial system of divide and conquer. They have influenced the major funding agencies to use the money ... earmarked to strengthen local community-based organisations for ecotourism and conservation development, to weaken the most successful association established for this purpose - the TEA.

...what about the major ecotourism organisations in the world and our government leaders who have endorsed this programme? It appears that they have been intimidated by the wealthy people ...

Our only hope now lies with individual citizens abroad, who will write to the large conservation and ecotourism organisations to which they contribute ... They could demand to know why the TEA has been consistently denied this assistance, and to write to the Belizean Prime Minister and Minister of Tourism and the Environment to encourage them to continue to stand up for and encourage aid for the TEA.

In 1998 the Methodist Relief and Development Fund (MRDF) financed a feasibility study of an ecotourism development programme for ten small communities in the Cosiguina Peninsula of Nicaragua. The programme was devised by SELVA, a local environmental organisation.

The study concluded that, despite the problems of this rural area - the lack of potable water, the lack of a sewage system outside the only town of El Viejo, the lack of electricity in most of the area's 130 villages, the poor road system, lack of social infrastructure and the widespread and evident poverty of the area - there were also significant potential attractors to backpackers, adventurers and nature tourists.

These include the Cosiguina Volcano, accessible by foot or horse, thermal waters, artesanal fishing, boat trips into the Gulf of Fonseca, a still relatively diverse wildlife despite deforestation, and completely unused beaches and cliff shorelines. It also concluded that the development of tourist facilities should progress slowly in order to integrate local people into the programme as genuine beneficiaries and to avoid the creation of divisions between those involved in the programme and those not involved.

The Cosiguina Peninsula is an area not normally visited by tourists, other than Nicaraguans (mostly from the local area) during the Christmas and Easter holidays. There are no facilities in the area to cater for foreign tourists.

Two years later the MRDF funded a two year programme for the construction of the necessary facilities on a small area of land owned by SELVA in the town of El Viejo, which would serve as the point of entry into the peninsula for any future visitors. At the time of writing this programme is drawing to a close and the facilities now include a visitor centre offering accommodation for up to 16 people, an adjacent dining room and bar with all the appropriate equipment, and a toilet and shower block.

All these facilities are built in the local rancho style with palm-thatched roofs and cane walls lined with tule matting. The photograph shows the visitor rancho with the San Cristobal Volcano behind.

The effect may be significant in individual terms or to a family, but as with many small-scale NGO-inspired schemes, it gives no significant widespread response to the problem of poverty, even on the scale of a small region such as the Cosiguina Peninsula with a total population of about 80,000. Yet poverty alleviation is one of its principal stated aims.

In more than one of the selected villages, SELVA personnel have experienced difficulty in explaining to their contacts that the benefits of the scheme and involvement in it should extend beyond the immediate family and friends of the SELVA contact. In one particular village, the local 'cacique' or village head assumed that all persons involved should be members of his family and all others should be excluded.

In another village, SELVA risked losing goodwill and interest by alienating a local village head who did not take kindly to the idea that as many villagers as possible should be involved. If the programme begins to show some signs of success, SELVA also risk converting themselves into a local elite, whom others will approach with deference. This is not their aim and to their credit it can be said that they are aware of the problem.

Another group of potential beneficiaries exists: that is, the national tour operators. Currently, they show only the vaguest signs of interest in SELVA's programme, but if SELVA show any degree of success in their efforts to attract visitors to the area, then it has already been suggested by one of the most prominent Nicaraguan eco-tour operators that they would be interested in considering a deal with SELVA to provide ecotourists to use SELVA's facilities. In such an eventuality, the new beneficiaries will be both the operators and SELVA, with a little more trickle-down to those already benefiting in this way.

The question then would be whether the proportion of financial gains made by the operator(s) would be greater than the extra income created by the extra business brought in by the operators. At this stage and with the deliberately slow development of this programme, that question will remain unanswered for some years to come.

SELVA now faces the following issues and problems: How to attract visitors? How to promote the centre's use as a springboard for visiting other points of interest and the ten villages in the peninsula? How to involve the local people in the centre's use? (Local people were employed in its construction.) How and whether to turn themselves into a small-scale tourism micro-enterprise? How to ensure that the economic benefits of the activity can be used to improve the general quality of life in the area and to alleviate poverty?

The slow development of the programme is not accidental. SELVA wish to maintain control over their programme and to be in a position to monitor progress and to spot problems. In this way, the worst aspects of cultural intrusion and colonialism by the visiting culture can be avoided and changes can be incorporated gradually and sensitively. In the sense that SELVA is a local NGO, clearly the scheme can be said to be in local hands.

As a NGO, however, it does not have the power of a local municipality nor the finances associated with some national and international NGOs. In truth, the slow development of the programme has to some extent been due to the lack of finance, which is another factor which might qualify the project for funding under a First World governmental pro-poor tourism initiative.

Another question for SELVA to face in the future might well concern this speed of development should substantial finance suddenly become available for the programme whether from INGOs or from private tour operators. And a corollary of this will concern the extent to which they can maintain control over the management policy of the programme as other organisations and/or companies invest in the scheme.

This case study illustrates the difficulties facing local communities attempting to enter the western capitalist economy by diversifying their sources of income, a strategy conventionally considered as wise, and in this case widely considered necessary because of the failure of traditional agricultural production to provide an adequate living. Paradoxically, earlier advice from IFIs for areas such as this concerned the concentration of production on those crops for which the area has a natural advantage - following the neoliberal theoretical plank of comparative advantage.

This still remains a part of the dogma we hear from IFIs despite its abject failure to meet the needs of both the local producers and local consumers. It is tempting to ask whether the advice was always meant to reflect the desires of the First World rather than the needs of the Third World, and further to ask if the advice to develop tourism reflects the same.

Because of the roles of TNCs and supranational institutions, the case of the Costa Rican government's promotion of both community-based, sustainable tourism at one moment and large-scale tourist condominia at another is presented later. It is no less relevant to the discussion here, however, and the gulf between the two policies is clearly demonstrated by the case.

The arguments of those supporting community control of the development of tourism are aired regularly in the pages and letters' columns of the Costa Rican daily and weekly newspapers, and with tourism being the single most important foreign exchange earner in Costa Rica the debate is high on the political agenda and in the forefront of general discussion. Despite the international renown it has achieved through its earlier promotion of small-scale, community-based ecotourism projects, however, the 1990s saw the government's approval of a number of large-scale, foreign-owned tourism development projects.

In the same region, the policy divergence between small-scale, community-based tourism and large-scale, mass tourism is emphasised for Honduras by Ron Mader over the internet:

There are two strategies Honduras is pursuing simultaneously - though from different quarters. A World Bank consultant and officials from the Institute of Tourism tout the development of a handful of luxurious five-star hotels near various 'ecotourism' destinations - Cusuco, Tela, La Tigra, Celaque and Copán. ... Another approach promotes community-based efforts.

USAID has sponsored the creation of an ecotourism association - APROECOH - which has trained dozens of

Hondurans. This type of grassroots, community development should be more successful (in my view).

These examples highlight a number of points about this divergence. First, it is obvious that both governments and communities face a range of options and courses of action between the two extremes of government-inspired mega-projects and community-inspired local projects. While it is important that ideas for and control of tourism developments should come from within the community, it is also important that local communities can make use of and benefit from the assistance of national government resources to help establish and coordinate their ideas and schemes.

This is especially so where management of protected areas is pertinent to the scheme and where the advice of specialist professionals may be helpful. It can also be crucial in enabling communities to gain access to the tourists themselves. Indeed, channels of communication and information should be an intrinsic part of the tourist system so that local communities can seek assistance when they deem that they require it.

Second, the examples discussed here draw attention to the division between the rhetoric of national politicians and their actions. Governments which in public espouse the language of the sustainable and ethical high ground of local community tourism development may be subject to external pressures (from supranational lending agencies for example) which dictate a policy of economic liberalisation and foreign exchange maximisation.

Such pressures and circumstances are more likely to lead them into the development of mega-projects which at best ignore and at worst trample on local communities, regardless of their rhetoric and stated aims.

Third, local communities may lack the base of resources, skills and finances required without assistance from a higher-tier authority such as provincial or central government. Hence, a partnership arrangement may often be more suitable than a community attempting to do everything entirely from within its own human, physical and financial resources. Partnerships do not necessarily have to include government departments or ministries, and indeed may be best advised to exclude them if they are perceived by the local community to be corrupt or likely to pervert the aims of the development. Industry or the academic community can also be involved in partnerships, especially where the tour operator's access to tourists is required or where survey or research work is required as part of the process of tourism development. Where the resources required are financial, however, then the assistance of governmental or international bodies may be necessary. But it needs to be stressed that partnerships are subject to the same types of manipulation and power-brokering as is the idea of participation.

A number of aspects of partnerships are illustrated, which outlines one community's development of the Campfire scheme (Communal Areas Management Programme for Indigenous Resources) in Zimbabwe. The Campfire initiative is designed to help rural communities manage their wildlife and natural resources for the benefit of the community as a whole, and treats wildlife as a resource rather than a threat and a problem.

The CAMPFIRE scheme is heavily cited in tourism's academic literature, and more general details can be found in McIvor (1994), IIED (1994), Child (1996) and Murphree (1996). In all the CAMPFIRE examples and in others where partnerships may be more complex, there is a clear need for ultimate control to rest with the local community.

A PHOTO-TOURISM PARTNERSHIP IN THE CAMPFIRE SCHEME

The safari hunting contract provided the initial impetus for the programme, and still produces the bulk of the income. However, further schemes for generating revenue are now being developed. In 1993 a contract was set up with a photo-tourism safari operator, to run walking safaris from a tented camp.

From the beginning, the local people were more involved in setting this up than they had been with the hunting contract, which was done purely at Council level. Still the business belongs to the operator, so the risks and responsibility lie with him - the joint venture is purely a financial one.

In 1994 a further step was taken in devolution, when one community began building their own small tourism camp. Limited funding was obtained from an outside donor, so that the local WWC [Ward Wildlife Committee] had to budget and plan the project properly. They have been the decision-making body at every stage ... When it is completed it will be staffed and managed by the WWC ...

The money-making potential is not large, since the project is very modest, aimed at the budget traveller or weekenders from the city, but it has been, and will continue to be, an enormous learning experience for the people involved, as well as being a source of pride within the community. Having worked through this project, I can see the need for a centralised training facility to serve all such ventures ... [and] provide a forum for sharing ideas and experiences, so that each District can learn from the activities of others. This would require outside funding to set up and run ...

The connection between the hunting, photo-tourism and small-scale projects is community participation and responsibility.

Fourth, despite the need for partnership arrangements with outside bodies, there is also a need to balance the advice of the 'experts' or professionals with the advice of the community, where the term community is as all-inclusive as practice allows. Experts and professionals are as subject to values and the sway of competing interests as are local people.

They may have greater knowledge of a particular field, they may have greater funds of money, they may have greater access to particular market sectors, but they all represent interests of some kind, whether it be market forces, a political interest, a requirement for more research funding, or an ego; and it is important to balance the nature of their advice and expertise against the local interest.

LOCAL ELITES

Notwithstanding the potential problems created by

outside bodies, Krippendorf noted that: 'Some locals do, unquestionably, make a nice profit out of tourism, but they are usually a very small minority belonging to the propertied classes. It goes without saying that they are staunch advocates of a further development of tourism' (1987:54-5). It should be acknowledged, then, that the local community itself is not immune to the divisions which may come from within its own number and which may expose either the influence of a dominant local elite or the need to balance the demands and wishes of different sectors of the community. Again, an analysis of the distribution of power, in this case within the local community, is essential for an understanding of the dynamics and effects of tourism developments.

The example of the Kuna indians of Panama illustrates this point. In the main group of the San Blas Archipelago of islands on which the Kuna live (off the Caribbean coast of Panama) there are only three hotels, one of which, the Hotel San Blas. It is generally perceived by the Kuna, for a number of reasons, as being in their own interests to keep it this way in order to prevent too great a number of tourists visiting their islands and in their attempts to prevent foreign involvement in their islands' tourism industry.

But many of the Kuna manage to derive financial benefit from the tourists by selling their appliqué cloths (*molas*). The greatest profits from tourism, however, undoubtedly accrue to the owners of the hotels and their families. Doubtless also these families gain respect from this position and in turn derive more than average influence in the development of their islands. In the case of the Kuna, this is not an influence which is generally begrudged on account of the general benefit derived from tourism and the decision-making systems in the community. Regardless of how this power and influence is used, however, the case serves to illustrate how local elites may be formed.

The case of the TEA discussed earlier illustrates the potential dangers of tourism benefits being divided among only a few. As the case makes clear, one of the essential objectives of the TEA is to distribute tourism benefits widely between and within the associated villages. In villages of up to 500 and 600 population, however, it is not possible for all families to participate in the activity of catering for tourists - not that all families would wish to do so. But inevitably, there is space for the rise of favouritism within the allocation of tourists to households for meals, for instance. In the TEA villages

CRUISING ROUND THE CHOCO AND KUNA

To visit the Choco tribe in the Darién jungle, we stepped off the ship into *cayucos* at 4 am and made the first two hours of our journey in these dug-out canoes in total darkness. We were amazed to see at first light the intricate palisades of mangrove on either side ...

We powered upriver for another two hours in a convoy of eight vessels to ... their little riparian village, about 40 houses on stilts built along a broad avenue that features centrally a basketball pitch ... Beyond are some clearings of light cultivation, but mainly they are hunters of meat, though their small stocky build suggests that over the centuries protein has been hard to come by.

They were waiting for us all along their riverside avenue, behind platforms and logs spread with the goods they had fashioned for sale, and were being continually reinforced by others who'd been alerted by messages in Coca-Cola bottles dropped from a plane by a dynamic American Mr. Fixit who has lived in Panamá for 40 years.

The men make music; the women sell. They are the advance guard of a 'nation' of about 6,000 people. They carve beautifully in rosewood, imaginative little ornaments and earrings from ivory nut. The women make the dyes and the baskets. They used to make them large, but they've learned that tourists can only handle small ones. Their goods sold on merit too - 'Who would imagine that I'd get up at 3 am to do my Christmas shopping in the jungle?' said my schoolteacher friend - and I estimate that we spent $5,000. Our cruise director takes along a float of $3,000 to bankroll those who run out.

We left more like $10,000 with the Kuna on Acuatupu in

the San Blas Islands. The Kuna is a larger nation, about 50,000, with a much greater exposure to tourists. They are not as good-looking as the Chocos, their features are sharper, but they're more together commercially. ... for the past 25 years they've had the rights and control for domestic purposes of the archipelago.

They don't carve, but they make brilliant 'molas' (a word for clothes that now means specifically their appliqué designs on squares which people have been known to buy for $10 and sell for $60 at Nieman Marcus) ... The garment of one was overprinted, *'500 años de resistencia indígena.'*

And they make a dead set at the photographers, offering not only their own images but carefully contrived little tableaux. For instance, a little girl with an umbrella sitting on a bench, smoking a pipe and affecting to launder a brightly coloured shirt ...

As the Kuna see the trade flagging, they rapidly pack up and jump into dug-outs, pulling plastic covers over themselves and their goods for the choppy journey ... to a secondary outlet, the large cruise ship *Radisson Diamond*. I remarked to our ship's official photographer that we'd just been looking at what the anthropologists call 'staged authenticity'. He was shocked by this comment, and replied that that was surely an oxymoron. 'That's what they like about it', I said.

This has occurred in the past, but it is to the credit of the structure and operation of the TEA system of tourist allocation that the problem has thus far always been detected and corrected, in one case with the suspension of one family's involvement in the scheme. In the case of the TEA, though, the competing scheme promoted by USAID and BEST is likely to create divisions within the village which could lead to the formation of a local elite, especially as this competing scheme has access to far more funding opportunities than does the TEA.

Finally, it is worth pointing out that elitism may not relate solely to the financial aspect of tourism. Local district councils may develop an elitism of influence and decision-making without necessarily benefiting financially from it. In such cases a social distance and a communication gap may develop between the decision-makers and those they represent. Some district councils in the frequently acclaimed CAMPFIRE scheme in Zimbabwe during the 1980s, for example, have been described by McIvor as 'almost as remote as the central government in the minds of the people'.

In such circumstances, representatives of local communities may take decisions on behalf of interests other than those of the people they represent. This is alluded to by O'Riordan, who states that 'participation on a mass scale is an idealistic dream. In a representative democracy, it is impractical and unnecessary; in a political culture with a tradition of elitism, it is out of the question'. In the prevailing economic and political system, arguably, nothing else should be expected.

DISPLACEMENT AND RESETTLEMENT

Of all the problems experienced by local communities facing tourism development schemes, the most harrowing involve accounts of people being displaced. Such events normally reflect the distribution of power around the activity of tourism and highlight the powerlessness of many local communities. And it seems to be rare that displacement and subsequent resettlement of displaced people result in a more even and equal development.

In the literature most case studies of displacement and resettlement illustrate a deteriorating situation for those displaced. This has been especially well documented in cases where the development promotes mass forms of tourism, as in Guatemala, where three hundred campesino families were evicted in June 1996 from land they claimed belonged to the state - police burned down their homes and arrested several of them - to make way for a Spanish businessman's plans to build a tourist complex.

But the UK Tourism Concern's *In Focus* magazine (2002b) makes clear that displacement, often by violently enforced eviction, is also a feature of a surprising number of eco-tourism projects in many parts of the world. The example of the forced relocation of the Padaung communities in Burma for the development of tourist complexes and the creation of tourist attractions - a kind of mass eco-tourism or eco-voyeurism - and details of the displacement of groups in eastern Africa are documented in this section.

Around Third World countries, the list of such stories is endless and is charted regularly in the newsletters and publications of tourism campaigning groups, such as Tourism Concern, and human rights groups. One would assume, however, that the supposed ethical base of new forms of tourism would avoid such pitfalls. Unfortunately, much evidence appears to contradict this assumption, and displacement and resettlement have become frequent outcomes of policies aimed at conservation and protection.

Two examples are cited here, both from Africa, together with others elsewhere in the book, in order to illustrate the ways in which the goals of tourist money, conservation and 'sustainable' development policies may be linked together in the dispossession of local communities and indigenous groups from their land. Neither example here, however, is entirely pessimistic nor both include an element or two of a positive nature for local communities.

THE MAASAI IN KENYA AND TANZANIA

It makes clear that the displacement was not a single move, a one-off event; rather, it has been a prolonged and systematic persecution of the Maasai by the Tanzanian and Kenyan authorities, although it should be stressed that these authorities were guided in their actions by First World conservationists and operated not only in their own interests but also in those of developers in the tourism industry.

It is clear that after the Second World War, all the policies of exclusion and resettlement in this case have been pursued in the name of conservation, especially the conservation of wildlife. The mechanism for doing this has been the creation of national parks and wildlife reserves, and the impetus for creating them came largely from First World conservationists and scientists who suspected that pastoralism was responsible for environmental degradation and decreases in wildlife numbers. George Monbiot accuses some scientists of having 'maintained that local people have always been a threat to wildlife: that they hunt the game with destructive methods and over-graze the land. These arguments have been well-rehearsed among conservationists, and are known to many of the tourists visiting Kenya' (1995:11). Monbiot argues that the Maasai's activities did not threaten the wildlife and that the work of earlier scientists was clouded by 'colonial disdain' and 'genuine misunderstandings about savannah biology'. He summarises:

What is incontestable is that a fantastic abundance of wild game continued to exist alongside the herds of the Maasai and other nomads up to and beyond the arrival of the British in East Africa. It was indeed because the Maasai had not destroyed the populations of game that the Europeans wanted to conserve their lands.

Today, it is difficult to escape the realisation that wildlife and the pastoral activities of the Maasai have managed to co-exist in the region for many centuries, and that the landscape (at least until recently) was the product of their grazing and burning practices. To Deihl, it seems 'ironic ... that one of the first steps in establishing a national park is to rid the region of its original caretakers' (1985:37).

As the Maasai have been excluded, so the tourists have been allowed access. Despite the exclusion of the Maasai from the crater areas within the Ngorongoro Conservation

DISPLACEMENT OF THE MAASAI

Early 1900s	European hunters eliminated some wildlife species and decimated others which had survived over 2,000 years of contact with Africans and their livestock.
Second World War 1959	Hundreds of thousands of wild animals killed to feed British troops.
	Serengeti National Park in northern Tanzania divided into the Ngorongoro

	Conservation Area (NCA) and smaller Serengeti National Park. The Maasai who lived in the latter (and had done so for over 200 years) were moved into the NCA so that the Serengeti would become a game park with no human interference. In the NCA, 'should there be any conflict between these interests, those of the latter [the game animals] must take precedence' (Governor of Tanganyika, 27 August 1959).
1960	Establishment of the Maasai Mara Game Reserve in Kenya, adjoining the Serengeti in Tanzania, further restricted the movements of the Maasai.
1974	Maasai forced to evacuate the two crater areas within the NCA on the grounds that their presence was detrimental to the wildlife and landscape.
1975	All cultivation within the NCA prohibited.
1976	Maasai prohibited from entering the Olduvai Gorge on the grounds that their 'livestock were detrimental to the archaeological value of the site' (Olerokonga, 1992:6).
1980	Collection of resin, a source of cash for the Maasai, stopped. Burning grasses in the highland areas also restricted.
1987	Anti-cultivation operation mounted by the authorities against the Maasai, who were farming small plots: 666 people arrested; 9 jailed for six months; 549 fined (Olerokonga, 1992:6).
1994	Allegations of torture, false imprisonment, theft and corruption by the Kenya Wildlife Service against the Maasai (corroboration by Paul Ntiati, an African Wildlife Foundation representative, cited in Monbiot, 1994:93).

Area (NCA), for example, there are several camp sites for tourists on the crater floor, although casual camping is no longer allowed. Tracks and roads have been created to allow tourist vehicles easy access to wildlife, thereby destroying natural vegetation.

Although the Maasai have been excluded from the Olduvai Gorge, many tourists enter it every day, some even removing stones as souvenirs.

Tourists also gain access in hot air balloons, gliding low over herds of wildlife, stampeding and disorienting them, although there is no recognition of this problem in Abercrombie and Kent's 2002 brochure in which they advertise 'Ballooning over the Masai Mara can be an unforgettable experience. Sail over the endless game-filled plains, drifting to a gentle landing before a lavish bush breakfast'.

In 1991, Perez Olindo of the African Wildlife Foundation in Kenya and formerly director of the Kenya Wildlife Department outlined several of the plans of the Kenya Wildlife Service (KWS) which were aimed at addressing the tourism and conservation problems in the game reserves and national parks.

These included road construction, a ban on the development of new tourist accommodation and on casual camping, minimum flight levels for balloons, and the promotion of ecological sensitivity in the tourists.

There is no mention there of the guardians of the original environment, the Maasai, neither in terms of their land and grazing rights nor in terms of an acknowledgement that tourism and conservation have been largely responsible for their dispossession and displacement.

Although seen by some as the best disciplined conservation management force in Africa, Monbiot describes the KWS as a 'para-military sustainable tourism-conservation organisation' and Fernandes says it 'has implemented sustainable market driven model growth strategies which deserve to be condemned'.

Moreover, it is clear that much of what is done in the name of conservation is actually done to protect the profits from tourism: 'Several times I was told by (tourism) conservation officials that the Maasai had to be kept out because the tourists did not want to see them there'. And Olerokonga (1992) makes it clear that the tourist and the Maasai are currently alienated from each other.

Fernandes (1994) maintains that such strategies owe much to the Brundtland-inspired sustainable development approaches. It is the action plans and agendas which have emerged from this generalised approach which Adams (1990) claims are 'firmly anchored with the existing economic paradigms of the industrialised North. This might be called the approach of "green growth"'.

The implication is clear: the power exercised here derives from the First World, is expressed by conservationists, acted upon by a powerful local elite, benefits First World tourists, and serves to increase the inequality of development by, first, preventing the local communities from conducting their traditional ways of life and, second, excluding them from the benefits of the activity of wildlife tourism. As Olerokonga explains:

Since the mid-eighties many stand along the main road to Serengeti and the Ngorongoro Crater waiting for tourists and hoping that they will pay to take pictures of them ... For both, their only interest is to profit as much as possible from each other - the tourists by taking pictures of the Maasai, the Maasai by getting money from the tourist. They don't see each other as dignified human beings.

In the first half of the 1990s, then, conservation in East Africa was still largely a matter of separating land from its traditional human inhabitants. New approaches are currently being explored, however, with the aim of attaining some redress of dignity and power.

In 1996, for example, a small group of the Maasai opened the Kimana Community Wildlife Sanctuary covering over 6,500 acres in Kenya, having negotiated a deal with a British tour operator to construct a luxury lodge, from which a proportion of the tourist payments (approximately US$12 out of each US$80-100 paid per tourist per night) are made to them.

Having calculated their takings before the deal was signed, they developed plans for a school and clinic for their community. In November 1996, the British Guild of Travel Writers recognised the significance of this deal by the Kimana community with one of their annual awards.

By the year 2002, the school and clinic had not materialised and the benefits had not been as widely distributed as originally intended, which detracted from the significance of the scheme. Nevertheless, this was still an important step for one group of the Maasai - in the past such deals directed benefits into the hands of a single individual or a single family rather than a whole group.

Other examples, perhaps more successful than the Kimana Community scheme, exist. The Eselenkei Community Wildlife Sanctuary in Kenya, for example, is owned by a Maasai community in which the financial benefits of the wildlife tours in the sanctuary are reported to be widely distributed and appreciated throughout the community.

For the Maasai, these cases may not make good their displacement, nor retrieve their former lifestyles, nor compensate them for all the losses and betrayals they have suffered in the past.

But now for some groups of the Maasai at least such schemes offer a hope of improvement, even if they can hardly be said to threaten the dominant model of development which has been at least in part responsible for the displacement. Such mild 'success' as this highlights a deep division among the Maasai over the wisdom of involvement in these kinds of tourism projects. The views of the Kimana community proponents of the sanctuary and lodge contrast sharply with the views expressed in the following statement from one of the Maasai:

We know there is money to be made from tourism. We already have tourists staying on our lands in tented camps. And, yes, they bring us an income. We don't need the Kenya Wildlife Service to tell us that. But you can tell Dr Leakey this. We don't want to be dependent on these tourists. We are Maasai and we want to herd cattle. If we stopped keeping cattle and depended on tourists, we would be ruined when the tourists stopped coming.

MOUNTAIN GORILLA CONSERVATION IN UGANDA, RWANDA AND ZAIRE

The case of the international conservation agencies' attempts to save the remaining mountain gorillas from extinction in Uganda, Rwanda and Zaire illustrates an example of wildlife conservation that has had some success, although the onset of genocidal inter-ethnic strife in the region in the early 1990s has led to uncertainty about the long-term prospects for mountain gorillas. The case is included here because publicity about the success of the wildlife conservation and tourism revenue attraction measures has over-shadowed the human displacement which these measures caused.

Between 1960 and 1973 evidence showed that the mountain gorilla population in the area of the Virunga volcanoes had declined from 450 to 260, mainly through poaching. The gorillas were under pressure not just from poachers but also from local farmers who required more land to provide food for a growing population.

As a result of this pressure, the Mountain Gorilla Project (MGP) was established in Rwanda in the late 1970s. The project had the linked goals of promoting ecologically sensitive tourism, improving park security and spreading conservation awareness. The ecologically sensitive tourism essentially took the form of gorilla watching similar to that described in Uganda's Mgahinga National Park by Melinda Ham:

Holding their breath, the four tourists crouch in the grass, their long-lens cameras at the ready. Less than five metres away, their prey gently breaks off a piece of bamboo as thick as a human arm, tears off strips with his teeth and chews the soft green core. The silver-backed gorilla stands proud. Beside him a female grooms her neighbour while a baby gorilla somersaults playfully beside her.

They take little notice of the human presence ... The tourists have spent nearly two hours climbing up through the dense, muddy bamboo forest, accompanied by two trackers and a Uganda National Parks (UNP) ranger. The trackers carry machetes to cut a narrow path through the forest. The ranger carries an AK47 assault rifle in case of a chance encounter with armed poachers. Under the strict rules governing gorilla-tracking tourism in Uganda the tourists can spend only one hour with the gorillas once the trackers find them.

For Rwanda's Parc National des Volcans, Lindberg and Huber (1993) show that the revenue from tourist fees to see the gorillas rose from US$7,000 in 1976 to US$1 million in 1989, a sum which far outweighed the cost of running the park (approximately US$200,000 in 1989). Demand was high and only 24 visitors per day were permitted entry. This allowed the fixing of a high individual fee - almost US$200 per person for a one hour visit which, as Sherman and Dixon (1991) suggest, was around the highest charged anywhere in the world and may have been near the upper limit that visitors were willing to pay. Moreover, it has been estimated that an extra US$3-5 million annually was paid into the national economy by foreign tourists.

The high fees have drawn charges of economic elitism, but the scheme was widely deemed to be successful. From the late 1970s to 1989, the gorilla population in this area rose from 260 to 320, which was due, according to William Weber, a specialist in primate conservation at the New York Zoological Society, to tourism revenues paying for more forest guards and in turn reducing gorilla poaching. Since 1994, when genocide in Rwanda took up to a million lives, the popularity of gorilla watching declined from almost 7,000 people per annum in 1993 to just over 2,000 in 2001.

In Uganda a similar success in terms of wildlife conservation was achieved only after the displacement of over 1,300 people. Despite the success in Rwanda, it was clear that very considerable threats - civil unrest, poaching and loss of habitat to cultivation - still loomed over the primate population. Accordingly, in 1990 several international conservation agencies led by WWF formed the International Gorilla Conservation Programme (IGCP) in cooperation with the Ugandan, Rwandan and Zairean governments. Under the

Global Environment Facility the World Bank provided US$4 million to fund gorilla conservation projects in Bwindi and Mgahinga National Parks in Uganda.

Uganda has only begun to realise and exploit the potential tourist revenue from its gorillas since the creation of the IGCP. The Mgahinga National Park covers only 33 square kilometres in the Ugandan part of the Virunga Mountains and shares the gorillas with Rwanda and Zaire. Ten square kilometres of this bamboo forest had been cleared illegally by over 1,300 peasant farmers who planted peas, potatoes and wheat on terraced plots.

Apart from the food grown by these families, the land was also used to provide timber and bamboo for construction, and plants, barks and fibres for medicinal purposes. They also used the forest for their beehives and their water supply came from streams in the reserve. Every year the gorillas were pushed further up the slopes of the volcanoes and across the border into Zaire and Rwanda. Melinda Ham explains the official response to these actions:

Originally Mgahinga ... was only a forest reserve. But in 1992, the IGCP encouraged efforts to turn it into a protected National Park ... In mid-1992 the UNP [Uganda National Parks] evicted the peasants from their illegal plots. However, after a year of bitter hostility between National Park authorities and the community, the villagers were compensated with funds provided by the US Agency for International Development ... Didas Mutabazi, one of Mgahinga's six park rangers, says: 'Even though the villagers have received money, they are still very angry about losing their land' ... Only two farmers were offered employment in the new national park as trackers. Both refuse to talk about the loss of their land.

Melinda Ham also points out that Mgahinga was already 'being eyed by major tourism companies for investment'. Such displacement, resettlement and later compensation certainly qualifies the success of the conservation measures. Ham describes the Mgahinga case as an 'ideological battle between international and local conservationists' and cites Jaap Schoorl, a Uganda National Parks adviser seconded from the international aid agency CARE, as saying 'We have learned that if you don't get the cooperation of the local people you can forget about gorilla conservation altogether. People have to see the benefits of having a national park on their doorstep'.

After the eviction in 1993 the Ugandan government established an advisory committee for the region which included representatives from the local community.

The committee decided that the whole community could still have access to the park, to collect water, gather plants or place their beehives in the forest. But access would be limited and subject to detailed agreement between all groups. The committee also agreed that the community would receive ten per cent of the revenue generated from the park entry fees paid by tourists.

This example shows up the potential conflicts between wildlife conservation and human survival strategies and serves to highlight the importance of tourist revenue in these conflicts. Tourism and conservation can be the cause of displacement and are factors which serve to increase the unevenness and inequality of development. But potentially they also offer a partial solution to some of the problems which they create in the first place.

The Ugandan example further highlights the gap between two opposing conservationist views widely discussed - *parquismo*, as Lorenzo Cardenal calls it, and an integrated approach. The former is the policy of excluding humans from the area to be protected and conserved (the *parque*), and the latter refers to the integration of human activity with flora and fauna conservation.

In the case of the Mgahinga National Park, the difference is emphasised by the words of Jaap Schoorl above. Jean Carriere of CEDLA (Centro de Estudios y Documentación Latinoamericano) also highlights the former approach in his description of US-influenced environmental institutions as tending 'to see environmental protection in isolation from the social context, and [would] soon convert Costa Rica's forests into fenced-off green museums surrounded by starving peasant families'.

Colchester (1994) has pointed out that conservation NGOs have generally derived their funding from the establishment and have attempted to use the power of the state to impose their visions and goals. In search of funding for their conservation programmes, international conservation organisations tend to form alliances with supranational organisations such as the World Bank, First World governments, or even transnational corporations.

In so doing they find their programmes becoming geared to the kind of economic justifications - hence, the need to raise tourist revenue - which fit with the dominant economic paradigm promoted by these organisations. With such justifications, and with the moral high ground of ecological sustainability on the side of the conservationists, it is relatively easy to treat local people and communities as inconvenient and to confirm the need to displace them.

VISITOR AND HOST ATTITUDES

Tourism is widely touted as a beneficial cultural exchange for all parties involved, as having contributed to the general well-being of peoples around the world, as having stimulated economic development and as 'promoting better understanding between races, religions and human beings worldwide'. With such descriptors one might be forgiven for believing that the relationships between tourists and local people in the visited destination areas are always rosy.

Many friendships are indeed made between the visitors and visited. But the relationships between visitors and hosts give rise to a range of other outcomes. In the following pages we discuss three possible outcomes of the relationships created by tourism to Third World destinations.

TRANSCULTURATION

One of the most protracted criticisms of tourism in the Third World has concerned its impacts on indigenous cultures. Critics have consistently rounded upon cultural 'bastardisation', 'trinketisation', the destruction of indigenous cultures, and so on. Tourism, they contend, is a process of acculturation through which Third World cultures are assimilated into materialistic First World lifestyles.

In the first part of this book, it was suggested that advocacy of the need to protect cultures finds strong resonance in colonialism and romanticism of the past, an approach that has the potential for institutional racism that celebrates primitiveness. As Robins describes, in a process of unequal cultural encounter, 'foreign' populations 'have been compelled to be the subjects and subalterns of western empire, while, no less significantly, the west has come face-to-face with the "alien" and "exotic" culture of its "Other"' (1991).

Similarly, in discussing travel writing, Pratt refers to 'contact zones', 'social spaces where disparate cultures meet, clash, and grapple with each other, often in highly asymmetrical relations of domination and subordination - like colonialism, slavery, or their aftermaths as they are lived out across the globe today' (1992:4). Contemporary tourism, and particularly new tourism in the Third World, is staged in these so-called contact zones, which serve to emphasise that tourism is experienced in sharply differentiated ways by visitor and host. Pratt continues:

A 'contact' perspective emphasizes how subjects are constituted in and by their relations to each other. It treats the relations among colonisers and colonised, or travellers and 'travelees', not in terms of separateness or apartheid, but in terms of co-presence, interaction, interlocking understandings and practices, often within radically asymmetrical relations of power.

However, this asymmetry of power between host and guest tells only half the story. First, this has been encapsulated in the ideas of Edward Said in *Orientalism*. More often than not, it is charities, social movements and tourists that talk about the rights, cultural practices and uniqueness of Third World cultures, as if these people do not have a voice (which of course many do not) and are unable to represent their own views. Hence, Said's satirical 'quotation' of Marx: 'They cannot represent themselves; they must be represented.'

Second, through a process termed transculturation, Pratt

(1992) attempts to encapsulate the way in which marginalised or subordinated groups select and invent from materials transmitted to them by dominant 'metropolitan' cultures. Hall (1995) refers to this as a 'cultural strategy' which operates between previously sharply differentiated cultures which are forced to interact. It is this process of change that those engaged in the promotion and undertaking of new tourism find difficult to accept.

It is a feeling that we are somehow being cheated of 'authentic experiences', that this is no longer the real thing. This search for authenticity lies at the heart of much new tourism activity, where it was suggested that authenticity might be understood as a part of the desire for (cultural) sustainability. It is an aspect of new tourism that is sharply reflected in trekking, an activity about solitude and distance from other tourists, but also about contact with 'real' cultures.

Trekking is the visiting of off-the-beaten-track locations and involves walking, often but not always in organised parties accompanied by a number of porters. The names of some of the small independent tour operators which organise trekking tours testify to the rugged mountainous areas often visited by trekking parties and individual trekkers, but gentler highland areas such as Thailand, Kenya and Tanzania are also favourite trekking destinations.

The phenomenal growth of trekking in South-East Asia, Latin America and Africa (Brockelmann and Dearden, 1990; and as testified by the brochures of the 'new', specialised tour operators) underlines its importance in new middle-class travel. In Nepal the number of trekking permits issued rose from 8 in 1966 to approximately 13,000 in 1976, 47,000 in 1987 and 61,000 in 1988. The Annapurna area attracts over 38,000 trekkers annually, roughly equivalent to the area's year-round population; the Khumbu (Everest) region, home to around 4,000 people, receives 8,000 trekkers a year.

The environmental effects of trekking in the Himalayas are documented in many papers and articles. Nepal's forest area is believed to be decreasing at a rate of 3 per cent per year with higher rates in lowland areas and heavily trekked routes in the hills. One hectare of cleared forest loses 30-75 tons of soil annually. Also regularly cited is the problem of litter, with a special topic of interest appearing to be the ugly and unhygienic streamers of used toilet paper, which are the exclusive contribution of western trekkers.

In Nepal trekking also provides an estimated 24,000 full-time jobs with as many as 70,000 people employed as porters on a freelance basis. 'Porters are poor people, and the majority work without proper insurance, without proper clothing and for very low wages. They get next to nothing if they are injured or disabled while working, and they receive no proper training' (Agha Iqrar Haroon, President of the Ecotourism Society Pakistan, quoted in Tourism Concern, 2002a).

As Tourism Concern make clear, the cultural impacts of trekking are almost impossible to quantify, gives anecdotal evidence of some of the subtle cultural

THE CULTURAL EFFECTS OF TREKKING

We wait on a path in the Hinku Valley as another weather-battered group creaks towards us from Mera, one of Nepal's 20,000 feet trekking mountains. Their strained, peeling faces contrast with their porters' clear complexions and bored expressions. One scabby Lancastrian in hi-tech gear gasps through wind-cracked lips, 'It's amazing. But now I'm shattered; I'm emotionally and physically drained.'

Twenty over-burdened, under-clad porters rush past, anxious that nothing should interrupt their journey home to the comfort of a wood fire. It is just as well they hurried away, as they might not have cared for the parting words of one of our number ... 'They have to learn,' he said 'They can't keep chopping down trees.'

His remarks epitomised one of the chief ambiguities in what has come to be known as 'sustainable tourism'.

After he [Sir Edmund Hillary] had climbed and succeeded, he was so grateful to the Sherpas because without them he couldn't have done it. He wanted to do something ... and decided that what these people needed were schools. After the school had been built, as elsewhere in Nepal, governmental authorities took over. They wanted to use the schools to homogenise the country's diverse ethnic communities. So they're using the Hillary schools to teach the Sherpa children Hindu ways and Nepali, and English and Mathematics as well, so that they can serve the tourists and bring tourist currency to the country.

In these schools they teach nothing about the Sherpa-Tibetan culture - and nothing about their own 1,200 year old written language, which is classical Tibetan, of course. Most of the Sherpa children growing up in Kathmandu ... do not learn a word of Sherpa. If you get off the aeroplane at Lukla, ... you are met by a whole group of youngsters who speak 'Hillary School English' to serve you. Over the years they have been completely incorporated into the tourist economy. Most of the younger inhabitants of this area don't know how to run their farm any more.

Younger Sherpa men, of all Nepalis, are the most 'hip'. They dress in expensive jeans, tracksuits, baseball caps. They have Walkmans, tend to speak good English and smoke designer cigarettes. The women, however, have on the whole kept up the traditional - and hard - way of life ...

Western influence, which followed expeditions to Everest ... has greatly affected the Sherpas' way of life. Schools, hospitals and clinics, postal services, air transport and radio communication changed a semi-nomadic life to one much more dependent on tourism, trekking and expeditions.

On the basis of his observations of trekking in Thailand (1974 and 1989), Erik Cohen modified the idea of *staged authenticity* identified by MacCannell into the idea of *communicative staging*. Central to this debate has been the way in which local populations adapt to tourism. The last example particularly reflects the notion of transculturation in its description of those manifestations of First World influence which have been 'selected' for use by the younger Sherpa men.

One advantage of the concept of transculturation is that it allows us to explore possibilities that lie beyond the often repeated, even slavish, charge that tourism distorts, disrupts and bastardises Third World cultures. In some instances this is, of course, exactly what happens, especially where the power of the tourism industry is intense, as described in the next few pages. Indeed, these problems are also common features of trekking, as illustrated in the UK Tourism Concern's campaign entitled *Trekking wrongs: porters' rights* (2002a). But it is a view that debars us from considering how the visited actually adapt and borrow from cultural practices and in turn modify their own cultural practices or ways of making a living, even in circumstances where their power is differentially distributed.

TRIBAL PEOPLES AND ZOOIFICATION

Survival International, an INGO which supports indigenous groups, has in recent years adopted the term 'tribal peoples', reflecting their representation of people who live by tribal norms, customs and practices rather than those of mainstream society. The term indigenous groups includes tribal peoples, while the term tribal peoples excludes members of indigenous groups who live by the norms and practices of mainstream society. In the tourism industry not all host communities are tribal peoples but tribal peoples which have had contact with the 'civilisation' of the First World are potential host communities.

This chapter has already cited a number of examples of tribal peoples and their interaction with the tourist industry: the Maya, the Choco and Kuna, the Sherpas, and the Maasai. This section highlights one particular point about their experience as 'hosts' in the tourism industry: namely, their treatment as objects to be viewed, a process which 'forces Indigenous Peoples to become showcases and "human museum exhibits"' and which might be called the 'zooification' of tribal peoples.

The nineteenth-century and earlier christian fundamentalist and explorer's view of tribal peoples as savages whose souls needed saving may not be as pervasive a public viewpoint now as it used to be in the early part of the twentieth century. But it helped to shape the common perception of tribal peoples as 'noble savages'. The characteristic of nobility owes something to the development of this early First World view by conservationists and environmentalists in their interpretation of wilderness as inclusive of the peoples who are indigenous to it. '[T]hese images [of godless, natural, wild and blameless savages] are retained to this day and lie behind conservationist policies of "enforced primitivism", whereby indigenous people are accommodated in protected areas so long as they conform to the stereotype and do not adopt modern practices'.

The build-up of area protection policies and an associated conservation ethic have clearly been important in the promotion of the common perception of tribal peoples as natural and wild. It is this perception which, in some cases, dominates the relationship and exchange between tourists and tribal peoples and which confirms and strengthens the already prevailing prejudices and can, at times, lead to the process of zooification.

Visiting tribal peoples' settlements is an activity especially associated with new forms of tourism. Such visits are advertised as small group tours, implying low impact; tribal communities are described as 'almost untouched' or 'totally unchanged', implying an authentic experience; conditions are referred to as 'primitive', implying an experience with a difference, thereby conferring status on the tourist; and some tours to tribal settlements mention the possibilities for artefact purchases, implying that the exchange will assist in the development of the settlements and peoples visited.

In general, 'small group tours' is an accurate description, but these can hardly be claimed to be low in impact. Even the lone traveller can have an insidious and disruptive effect on local culture, especially if the host community has had little contact with mainstream society.

Description of the supposedly primitive nature of tribal peoples by tour operators is used to emphasise the 'otherness' of the experience. Again, examples have been cited where this cultural authenticity is often falsely enacted, such as the divesting of T-shirts solely for the sake of the visiting tourists. The economic exchange involved can of course be significant, as the Choco and Kuna cases illustrate. Equally, however, it can contribute to the 'trinketisation' of a culture and can lead to conditions of near-slave labour, as in the case of the Yagua in Peru where traders or middlemen take all the profit.

TOURISTS AND TRIBAL PEOPLES

The scene is a Bushman camp in a remote part of Botswana. In the distance a plume of dust shows the arrival of a jeep. The people drop whatever they are doing, quickly pull off their T-shirts, trousers and cotton dresses, and begin to dance. In the Himalayas, fields lie uncultivated. The men who once farmed them have become porters to climbing expeditions.

In the Peruvian Amazon, women of the Yagua tribe make bags, hammocks and jewelry for the tourists. They work hastily because they are being paid almost nothing. The traders make all the profits. Decoration is crude, the finish careless - 'Well,' the women say, 'these people don't know any better.'

In Tuareg camps around Tamanrasset in Algeria, the tents of the drought-stricken refugees are normally covered with plastic sheets - only when the tourists arrive are the old coverings of animal hide brought out.

After an Amazon trip, Mick Jagger told an interviewer: 'What the tour guides do is take all the Indians' clothes off and put their little skirts on them, hand them a spear which they hand back at the end. The Indians dance a little around you.'

A Survival member writes to us in disgust: 'In the Mulu National Park (Sarawak) I realised how the Penan are being treated like animals in a zoo. Almost every tourist group that visits the park is taken there to walk around and look at the Penan "way of life". A longhouse is now in the process of being built for them, which as you know is not the way the Penan live. The atmosphere is one of despair.'

Another Survival member describes how her party were taken to stay in a village of the Meo tribe in the hills of Thailand. She paints a picture of the tragic gap in understanding that remained between the hill people and their well-intentioned visitors, who were quite unprepared for the 'primitive' conditions they found. A young German, looking bewildered, asked where the toilet was. Our guide laughed, and exclaimed 'Everywhere!' As the initial exhilaration of our adventure gave way to fatigue, relations with the villagers became strained and our interaction with them was reduced to stares and picture taking. Occasionally, as an inadequate response to our own guilt and to demonstrate our gratitude we made them gifts of whatever we had. A soap box or a second hand toothbrush.

The authenticity of the tourist experience is put into question by many of the examples cited in this chapter. Even in those cases where control of the visit is in the hands of the tribal people, the nature of their ceremonies or products is altered for the sake of the visiting tourists. The Kuna, for instance, carry out rehearsals of dances and songs on the night before a cruise ship is due to arrive.

One example actually refers to the treatment of the Penan (in Sarawak) as being 'like animals in a zoo', but most of the other examples also hint at this kind of treatment. Knowledge of the fact that the tourist experience is staged often fails to deter the tourist from wanting to experience it, a reflection perhaps of the new tourist's need to collect cultural capital.

The zooification process involves turning tribal peoples into one of the 'sights' of a rainforest expedition or a trek, giving rise to Rigoberta Menchú's statement that 'our costumes are considered beautiful, but it's as if the person wearing it didn't exist'. As a 1995 Survival Background Sheet says, 'All too often tour operators treat tribal peoples as exotic objects to be enjoyed as part of the scenery.' But the following example, from the Green Travel internet bulletin board, shows that this attitude is just as likely to come from professionals such as archaeologists and anthropologists as it is from tour operators.

There is a group of archaeologists and anthropologists who are travelling the jungles of Mexico, Belize, Guatemala and Honduras totally self-contained on X-country bikes. They are uploading journals and graphics via a satellite linkage of their adventures for all to see on a World Wide web site ...

The purpose of the expedition is to explore remote and nearly inaccessible Mayan pre-Columbian ruins and to study the present day Mayas in their native habitat. These travellers are all young people ... and their adventures make ... interesting reading for anyone.

The process of zooifying tribal peoples leads inevitably to a position of powerlessness for them as well as a complete loss of human dignity. The key to avoiding such situations is control of and participation in the tourism activity, which do not necessarily mean simply a greater share of the financial profits. As Pretty's typology suggests, it also implies control over all the conditions of the tourism development. Again, as was noted in the discussion on local participation, one of the most important elements in the success of a tourism scheme is that the idea and impetus for it should come from within the community itself.

It is of course too simplistic to demand a single-minded, blanket policy of total control to the tribal groups involved in any tourist development. There are dangers, as Colchester points out, in making 'an assumption that once an area is under indigenous ownership and control the problem is solved ... This is patently not the case' (1994:57). Notwithstanding these dangers, it can be argued that the community has to own and control the development if it is to avoid the pitfalls associated with external control.

DOXEY'S LEVELS OF HOST IRRITATION

Broadening out the analysis of relationships between hosts and visitors to include local communities from the Third World rather than just tribal peoples, it is a helpful starting-point to use Doxey's index of irritation, first put forward in 1975.

The Irridex is a causal model of the effects of tourism developments on the social relationships between visitors and the visited. Beginning with a state of very little tourism development and only the occasional passing visitor, the model's four stages describe different states of tourism development and the ways in which tourists and local people perceive each other in these stages. Its final stage is that of antagonism in which the stresses and tensions between the visitors and visited, resulting from high levels of development for the tourists, are at a peak and are likely to lead to a deterioration in the reputation of the destination.

Clearly, this is a highly generalised model, and its sequence and relevance will be subject to a wide variety of factors which differ with time and space. Its original application was in a First World, mass tourism context, but it is feasible that the relationships between Third World communities and the new tourists who visit them will follow a similar sequence to that of the relationships in First World resorts. (Tourist motivations may be somewhat different, but tourism effects are not likely to be dissimilar.)

Community control of the developments from the outset may go some way towards breaking what may appear from the Irridex to be the inevitability of the sequence of worsening social relationships. The Irridex relates the type of social relationship (euphoria, apathy, annoyance, antagonism) directly to the level of development of tourist facilities and infrastructure. The last two stages indicate that a level of change to local lifestyles above what is considered acceptable by local people has been reached, and especially in the final stage has been surpassed. This may come about as a result of dimensional changes, such as overcrowding (in which case planning and visitor management techniques may be able to provide solutions) or structural changes (such as the outside influence of foreign investors or national politicians pursuing goals different from those of the local community).

The latter cause especially implies that local control of development may act as a solution, and it is interesting to speculate on the association between Doxey's levels of irritation and the degree of local control. This association may be a pointer for worthwhile future research, a starting-point for which we have provided by extending to include speculation on the power relationships implied by the level of irritation as well as the social relationships.

It should be stressed that the Irridex is offered here only as a loose framework for considering the relationships between visitor and visited. It should be noted that its applicability will be compromised by circumstance. It should also be noted that Doxey's is not the only attempt to characterise the different stages and features of these social relationships. Butler (1975) and Murphy (1983), for instance, offer more detailed models and descriptors of social interaction that make explicit allowance for a number of variable factors.

Both acknowledge that communities can adjust their lifestyles in order to overcome stresses caused by uneasy social relationships between visitors and visited. But perhaps rather than looking for remedial action to counter the inequalities and unevenness of tourism developments, it might be more suitable for local communities to control developments from the start, as has been emphasised throughout this chapter.

The relationships of power, one of the book's key themes, are central to a consideration of the role of local communities in tourism. In this chapter these relationships have formed a background to a consideration of local participation in tourism developments. Although widely seen as a wholly benevolent feature of tourism planning that is associated with the notion of sustainable development, there is evidence to suggest that participation is becoming something of a buzzword, a *sine qua non* for development project proposals, to such an extent that its role may even be seen as tyrannical, in itself a determining force for project proposals. Our examination of issues of participation has used Pretty's six-point typology of participation to describe differing degrees of involvement and control by local people over (tourism) developments in their communities.

The case studies presented in this chapter have been related to this typology and it is suggested that reference to the scale of participation is something that could profitably happen at the outset of all tourism development schemes. Likewise, techniques for assessing the degree of local participation in schemes need themselves to be subjected to a consideration of who is doing the assessing and for what purpose. A note of caution needs to be sounded, however, for the general assumption that the greater the degree of local control and participation the greater the scheme's supposed sustainability and the wider the distribution of benefits within the community does not always hold true.

First, as has already been well established, sustainability differs according to the interests of those who are defining it, and the interests of the local community will not necessarily coincide with those of others; nor is it likely that the interests of the local community will be the same for all within the community.

Second, local power relationships within the community can be as factional as those which include players on a broader stage such as national governments, INGOs and supranational institutions. Thus, the emergence of local elites is as likely to produce inequalities within the community, just as these other players produce disparities of benefits at a different level.

At its worst, tourism and the conservation measures which have been used to support it have been responsible for the displacement and resettlement of local communities. The case studies from eastern Africa used to illustrate these phenomena are disturbing, but it is noteworthy that they are not entirely negative examples. A number of other case studies highlight the important point that only where the impetus for tourism development comes from within the community is the prevailing inequality of development likely to be challenged.

The notion of transculturation, the process by which local communities adapt themselves to the cultural mores and habits of those with whom they interact, was used to demonstrate that this interaction is not purely a case of the imposition of one set of cultural values upon another, as it is often represented in tourism analyses.

The term 'zooification' was introduced, however, to illustrate that in the cases of some tribal peoples this dehumanisation of local peoples does indeed take place, leaving them no power or dignity. Less extreme cases of First World new tourist - Third World local community interaction may be appropriately analysed according to Doxey's Irridex, which can be extended to describe the relationships of power as well as the social relationships between the visitors and the visited.

Chapter 8

Accessibility in International Travel and Tourism

Enormous increases in international travel by public sector employees and others, along with incidents of terrorism, accidents, and disease, raise a variety of ethical issues not normally covered in the training of public personnel administrators or in the standard administrative ethics course. Issues of accessibility for individuals with disabilities may be familiar to personnel administrators and students of ethics, but take on vast new dimensions when those individuals travel abroad.

Travel-related ethics issues involved in health, safety, and accessibility may include identification of individual and institutional responsibilities, informed consent, contingency planning, emergency response mechanisms, fairness, and equal treatment.

This study provides an overview of trends and issues, explores their ethical dimensions, and identifies relevant strategies to prepare public administrators to deal appropriately with these concerns. The study treats both tourist and educational travel abroad, and considers risks to host societies as well as to travelers.

Governmental agencies, professional associations, and other institutions have sought to develop effective responses to health, safety, and accessibility challenges arising from rapidly-expanding international travel. The U.S. State Department, the Centers for Disease Control, and the World Health Organization are valuable sources of public safety information, but political considerations sometimes undermine accuracy and credibility. Health and safety guidelines, vulnerability assessments, and other ethics strategies will help institutions and administrators to deal with future challenges, but the key task is for administrators at all levels to become more aware of the issues surrounding this, the world's largest industry.

Public personnel both in the U.S. and abroad are faced with an ethical crisis they scarcely recognize: what to do about international tourism. In 1998, more than 600 million people traveled internationally, a figure that is expected to soar to 1.6 billion by 2020. That kind of growth will put intense pressures on governmental personnel to cope with a wide range of health, security, and accessibility issues. This article explores the ethical dimensions of challenges facing the public sector at all levels, not the least of which is the very reluctance of public officials to acknowledge negative problems from tourism.

Most nations consider domestic and international tourism to be an important part of their economies with pro-growth efforts expected to be supported by both the public and private sector. Even the United States, which makes a virtue out of the private sector and often a scapegoat out of the public sector, by 1985 had 43 federal agencies dealing in some way with tourism. Every state and all major cities along with hundreds of smaller communities are making elaborate efforts to boost economic growth through tourism. Indeed, tourism is one of the few public sector areas that has not been downsized.

Public sector employees not only boost, manage, budget, monitor, and administer tourist attractions, but they also administer the licensing, taxing, and zoning through which tourism is developed and maintained. Those same employees are also tourists themselves—dependent at home and abroad on the policies that support their health and safety. Terrorism, accidents, disease, and accessibility problems may be increasing with tourism growth, but not all these threats are borne by the tourists.

Balancing visitor and community needs grows more and

more difficult. Host populations, local health, transport, and criminal justice facilities may also be taxed by the health-related issues exacerbated by tourism.

What is needed? A new level of coordination and commitment by public bodies ranging from the local level to the World Health Organization are essential for meeting the challenge. Yet, there is little evidence of the necessary political will to confront the problems associated with the rapid expansion of tourism. No one builds a career squelching tourism; little credit is given to exposing new problems so that they might be prevented.

Still, it is critical that students of public administration and government employees learn to recognize and confront the host of ethical issues not typically covered in the training of public administrators or in the standard ethics course. In the U.S., for example, issues of accessibility for individuals with disabilities are covered in training about the Americans with Disabilities Act, but not considered generally are U.S. government personnel, tourists, or other travelers going abroad.

Ethical issues involved in health, safety, and accessibility for travelers include: identification of individual and institutional responsibilities, informed consent, contingency planning, emergency response mechanisms, issues of fairness, and what constitutes equal treatment.

In Part I of this article the range of issues and trends confronting public personnel will be addressed, while in Part II specific ethical dimensions of these issues will be examined. In Part III the evolving efforts to deal with these issues are discussed and recommendations made about how to improve the protection of the traveller and the host destination.

International travel is not a new phenomenon. The arrival of wide-bodied jets in the 1960s democratized travel by making it more affordable. The decolonization of Asia and Africa plus the Cold War also meant increasing numbers of embassies, consulates, and transnational corporations that governments needed to keep secure. Thus, what was once the Grand Tour for the select few became a mass movement of government personnel, business people, tourists, and students—all of concern to their home and host countries.

Health and safety issues are also not new issues in travel. Within a week of the 1912 sinking of the Titanic, policies were passed around the world mandating adequate lifeboats on ocean liners and calling for international monitoring of icebergs. The international community can make ethical judgments to save lives when the attention of the world is clearly focused on the problem.

The 1917-1918 influenza epidemic also served as a cautionary tale of how the movement of travelers B in this case primarily soldiers B could unleash deadly terror on civilian populations and their unprepared governments. Between 20 and 30 million people died, far more than from World War I fighting.

Accessibility for people with disabilities is a relatively new issue and, except in a few nations, has been scarcely addressed. These issues are certain to become more serious and will raise increasingly difficult ethical dilemmas. Whereas travel was once considered a private decision, it is now ringed by government policies on access, promotion, safety, immigration, customs, disease control, and even foreign policy. Tourism trends will dramatically accelerate ethical issues for public administrators in all these policy areas.

The first concern is the enormous growth in travel, for which public administrators and policy makers are simply not prepared. More than a 300 per cent increase in international travel is expected by 2020. Already over two million people cross international boundaries every day. Domestic tourism will be several times that amount! Crowding exacerbates a desire to get away from it all; so, at the same time tourism is becoming more urban, it is also radically changing once remote settings.

The U.S. national parks are an example. Parking rather than the park itself is becoming the preoccupation of park service personnel. Is this simply a changing role to which personnel must adapt as they encourage access and participation in the once wild parks? Or should employees resist by banning cars or rationing access as a way to protect the larger public interest in preserving a national resource and keeping the quality of the experience special? Cost-benefit analysis does not prepare the administrator adequately for protecting either the long-term integrity of the resource or measuring the quality of the experience unlimited access provides. What other values need to be weighed?

A second concern is the global booming senior market. "...according to the UN, the number of senior citizens in the year 2025 will be 1,100,000,000 B almost double the number estimated for the year 2000 and five times the 1950 figure.... Throughout the world we are witnessing 'double demographic aging'...a phenomenon in which a longer life span, together with the record decline in birth rates, produces demographic growth rates very close to zero, and in some cases, negative growth..."

In the U.S. seniors are 25 per cent of the population but control 70 per cent of the wealth. They also have disproportionate political clout. Yet their propensity to travel creates extra safety and health concerns, especially when they venture abroad. These concerns are beginning to impact global decision-making bodies. The United Nations declared 1994 the International Year of the Elderly.

There is a growing awareness that "a central requirement of any social programme is the principle of the right to useful and worthwhile activity for all. This means that government must draft and implement active policies for training, leisure, and social integration." Currently, little if anything is being done to prepare public sector personnel for participating in tourism development that targets the special needs — particularly health needs—of this group.

Deregulation, privatization, increased industry competitiveness, and the speed of world travel have encouraged pressures to cut corners on safety, especially in terms of food preparation and sanitation. Today, food poisoning and medical emergencies are a far greater threat than crime or terrorism. A study done by the British Consumers Association revealed that 15 per cent of their members had been sick on vacation. Sixty to 75 per cent experienced illness when visiting developing nations. These percentages are probably similar for other travelers.

The pillows or blankets on planes often harbor lice, mosquitos, fungi, viruses, and germs as the plane moves through airport after airport before getting a thorough cleaning. Dengue fever, TB, hantavirus, malaria, and other diseases are carried around the globe in hours.

Public officials are often faced with increasingly lax policy standards at a time of reduced vigilance by the private sector. Public pressures may also reduce safety: Immigration, agricultural inspectors, and customs officials are sometimes upbraided by U.S. Department of Commerce personnel and members of Congress for their slow handling of inbound planes and ships. The critics remind employees that they must facilitate tourism to boost it. The visitor or returning citizen must not be harassed or delayed. The conscientious employee may be urged to lighten up.

Many ships and planes simply register in countries where restrictions are looser. Allowing the whistle on potential hazards for the traveling public or the host destination is often not an option. Increasingly, concerns are voiced even in the tourist industry press. The World Health Organization, criticized for timidity in the face of member resistance, is also beginning to act. Increasingly, the link between a potential for bioterrorism or even accidental spread of infectious disease has gradually encouraged greater global NGO and public sector cooperation.

These trends have highlighted a growing awareness that tourism B once and still promoted as a boon to one's health and the salvation of many a community's tax base B may be a mixed blessing at best.

ETHICAL DIMENSIONS

In this section the ethical dilemmas public officials face vis a vis these tourism trends are explored. One has already been alluded to: the political pressure to facilitate tourism in the name of economic development over "red tape" that may include protection of both tourist and non-tourist. Just as community, state, and national officials are loath to assess the politically useful industry in terms of its costs rather than merely its tax receipts, they also oftentimes lack the political will or the contingency planning effort needed to prevent major problems.

Often the "rational" decision for local bureaucrats is to acquiesce to local demand, though they may foresee a larger, long-term threat to the public interest. Cost-benefit analysis tends to discount the future threat over the present advantage.

The importance of tourism economically and politically has shifted the bureaucrat's constituency to a few economic interests and favors the tourist over the general citizenry. For example, tourist resorts may lack adequate sewage facilities. In the short run, the tourist may be spared dysentery by drinking bottled water. In the long run, however, the communities and villages surrounding the resort may experience polluted wells, unsafe beaches, and a decline in the local fishing industry.

If the public sector seeks to enforce tough standards in the design phase, its inspectors may be bribed or the dangers belittled and the advantages of economic development oversold. Later the resort or attraction may have its own local clout sufficient to control planning.

Even when a major health hazard exists as with the medical waste washed up on New Jersey's beaches a few years ago or even where disease and political instability threaten, public officials generally do not dissuade tourists from coming. One of the few exceptions, and that possible only because of the government's authoritarian control, occurred when Marshall Tito, President of Yugoslavia, closed his country's borders in 1975 and forbade travel among towns, successfully "burning out" a smallpox epidemic.

More commonly, public sector tourism organizations promote tourism as being good for the health and a "stressbuster." Some even wink at prostitution by advertising "a fresh peach on every beach" and "Try a Virgin...island." Even where prostitution is prosecuted, which is far from every place it is illegal, there is usually a double standard that leads to prosecution of the prostitute but not the one buying the sexual services. In an era dominated by the AIDS epidemic, such public sector marketing is a disgrace.

Nor are children adequately protected from pedophiles B some of whom actually tour as groups exploiting children. This is a serious problem in many countries, but it is particularly difficult to control in developing countries where low civil service salaries encourage bribery.

A second ethical problem is the distribution of police and judicial services. Affluent travelers are often afforded more protection than non-tourists. Some cities have special patrols in the tourist belt. Sentences may be harsher for crimes against tourists. Is this consistent with equal justice? Many would argue it isn't. "Those who have less in life should have more in law," argued former Philippine President, Ramon Magsaysay.

Others, however, note the special vulnerability of tourists, often unfamiliar with the destination, its language, signage, money, traffic patterns, or customs. Moreover, on vacation people are more apt to be careless or behave more recklessly than at home.

All of these behaviors set them up for criminals. Hawaii and several other states have taken special efforts to fly tourists back to their state in order to testify against alleged criminals. Enforcement officials say this is necessary to protect tourism and keep tourists from being targeted because they are transients. The motives may not be altogether altruistic, but they might fit John Rawls' dictum on justice, which includes treating everyone equally, except in those instances where the most vulnerable would benefit from unequal treatment.

A third ethical issue for public sector personnel has both domestic and international dimensions. National, state, and local officials seldom if ever warn in-bound tourists of health, safety, or accessibility issues. Though an extraordinarily violent nation with extremely expensive health care, the U.S. and its communities are careful only to accentuate the positive. Nor is this practice unusual. The Philippines still includes in its brochures information about areas the unwary would discover were in the midst of a civil war. It is left to the Internet and private guidebooks to provide cautionary advice to the domestic or international tourist. As an example, Fielding's Guide to Dangerous Places found that Florida was far more dangerous for Europeans (42 per cent affected) than North Africa, Turkey, California, and Kenya, combined.

On the other hand, governments are not nearly so loath to warn about other countries. Keeping tourism at home obviously supports a nation's balance of payments, but it is more than that. Developed nations, especially the U.S., Japan and the U.K., are quick to note areas of risk, often with a range of foreign office bulletins ranging from advisories to "don't go" to absolute prohibitions on travel.

The latter are sometimes more political than strictly cautionary. This leads to the dilemma: Should travelers' health and security advisories serve foreign and economic policy? Or does a lack of candor sacrifice government credibility on future, perhaps more important, issues? For those who read the warnings and don't go abroad, credibility may be the issue. But for those who go to places where genuine risks are not acknowledged, tourist safety is jeopardized. Isn't government's first responsibility—to protect its citizens — being overshadowed by political convenience? Or does the larger national interest dictate that health and security threats from friendly nations be treated differently from those from unfriendly ones?

For example, some countries with good records on tourist health and safety like Iran and Libya are nations to which U.S. travel is either forbidden or called "extremely dangerous." Meanwhile, Guatemala—where rapes of students in broad daylight and banditry are frequent—has only a mild U.S. advisory. Critics have charged that the U.S. —having brokered the Guatemalan civil war truce and being lobbied by investors who have massively increased holdings—did not want to protect tourists as much as the Guatemalan economy. Similar considerations appear to have influenced the "watering down" of advisories about Egypt, one of the three top recipients of

U.S. aid, and about Mexico, whose bailout needed tourism for repayment. In general, however, most experts concede that the warnings are generally warranted. Now posted by U.S. Consular Affairs on the Internet as well as available from the State Department, the advisories have a global impact.

Japan has been historically even more protective of its traveling citizens. The national economy of some nations has been hurt by a simple announcement from the Japanese government detailing some health or security threat abroad. Japanese citizens respecting the credibility of the government advisories followed the recommendations immediately.

Public sector employees need training in thinking through their responsibility to their profession, to the institutions involved in making health and security advisories, and to the larger public interest. Pressures from superiors and constituents may pull the employee in different directions. Few important issues are clearcut. Here, Albert Hirschman's classic Exit, Voice and Loyalty may be helpful in suggesting options and consequences. Institutionalized channels like the U.S. Department of State's dissent channel, offer opportunity for responsible and confidential debate.

A fourth ethical dilemma concerns both tourist and non-tourist health and safety. Is it ethical to be reducing health requirements world-wide in the name of facilitating tourism at a time of increased vulnerability to infectious disease?

For example, the few nations now barring visitors who test positive for HIV are in violation of World Health Organization (WHO) guidelines, which require less and less scrutiny of incoming tourists. How does WHO come to be in such a sorry state...? WHO does not operate according to its own definition of health. WHO is slavishly in thrall to its member states. Appropriate respect for rational sovereignty has been overtaken by blind obeisance...e.g., the desire to avoid embarrassment that an epidemic is underway.

Accidents are another major source of injuries and fatalities for travelers. The July 1999 canyoning deaths of 19 adventurers in the Alps, and the numerous fatalities that have accompanied the commercialization of Mt. Everest treks have raised additional ethical questions. Should there be tighter controls on popular but potentially dangerous activities? If so, how much of the burden of filling in the details of such policy will fall to civil servants?

Inadequate signage is another significant contributor to accidents. The use of international signage that communicates through pictures rather than a specific language is widespread in Europe, Australia, and New Zealand, but more scarce in the United States B where foreign visitors have far more accidents in the U.S. than citizens B and rare in developing countries. The World Travel Organization (WTO) has urged member nations to increase international signage.

The whole literature on bureaucratic discretion details the scope for and the extreme care public employees need to take in making "street level" decisions. Requiring more safety measures to be taken or insisting on more experience from those participating on so-called "adventure tours" is a possible approach, but others may argue that the doctrine of caveat emptor relieves the government of responsibility for their safety. Becoming more proactive on behalf of tourist and non-tourist health and safety, however, is fraught with controversy whether at the local public health office or at the international level. Many people have a visceral distrust of government. Also, there are often legitimate needs to go slow, to build consensus, to protect investments, and to avoid "crying wolf" and thereby destroying citizen confidence.

But, we are in a more litigious political environment in many countries. Thus, even if the population is unenthusiastic about some expenditure for health, safety, and accessibility, that same public may expect government to fulfill its core role of keeping them safe. Public sector training that emphasizes thinking through long and short term considerations, doing contingency planning and generally seeking to put in place cooperative internal and international mechanisms to deal with such crises is vital.

INTERNATIONAL EDUCATIONAL TRAVEL

Individual tourism is governed by consumer law and

government policies, but public educational institutions have additional ethical issues surrounding their international student services and study abroad programs for their own citizens. Such situations are only beginning to be addressed. International educational travel is complicated by the fact that the students are typically 18-22 —at the prime time in their lives for risk-taking behaviour. They may be going to countries with unfamiliar laws and customs. Sexual freedom varies markedly around the world. The prospect of running afoul of drug, drinking, or other laws needs to be addressed as the laws differ greatly in severity.

Because international students often bring financial as well as educational and cultural benefits, universities in many countries are increasingly involved in recruitment of such students. International study opportunities are seen as an important dimension of a student's career. Exchanges, study tours, international internships and community service projects abroad are some ways in which universities structure college credit and travel—sometimes with established procedures and appropriate supervision, sometimes merely with eager faculty and a tour company.

Some recent statistics illustrate the magnitude of the issue. Over the past decade the numbers of Americans studying abroad have doubled, from 48,483 in 1985-86 to 99,448 in 1996-97. Most of that growth has occurred in the 1990s. Such students are only about a fifth of the 480,000 foreign students to the United States, but American interest is mushrooming. From the mid 1980s to the mid 1990s, foreign enrollments in the United States increased by about 40 per cent, while American students abroad increased by 105 per cent.

American student travel abroad has also become much more diverse. In the mid 1980s nearly 80 per cent of all travel was to Europe; by 1996-97 that percentage had dropped to 64 per cent. Travel to Latin America had more than doubled and other, predominantly developing nations were increasing their share. In many cases, the geographic diversification has left students exposed to greater risks and their supervisors unprepared for coping with the sheer variety of threats to health and safety. Economic competition, recruiting, and a genuine belief in the educational value of such opportunities keep educators committed to their expansion.

The United States is not the only country dealing with these issues. In Australia, New Zealand, and throughout Europe, the practice of student travel is well ahead of the U.S. pace. In many of these societies, vacations are longer and government policies subsidize the travel of youth and workers. Still, consideration of ethical and legal issues of such travel has been slow to keep pace.

The first key issue is quality control. In many places, there is no litmus test or set of neither standards for the myriad of existing programs nor set requirements for the faculty leading tours. Is the emphasis on increasing numbers coming at the expense of adequate preparation of those traveling internationally? This may be in terms of language preparation or more basic screening. On what basis are students and faculty refused the right to participate? What are the criteria, the processes, and the responsibilities by which specific individuals are given institutional authorization to lead groups abroad?

Are there any screening requirements in addition to academic criteria that can assess the mental health or emotional maturity of participants? If not, shouldn't there be? Some students and faculty are subject to crippling depression when put in entirely new surroundings even without language and customs barriers.

Secondly, this raises the dilemma of privacy versus the institution's need to know. To what extent is obtaining information on a student's or faculty member's mental and physical condition itself an invasion of privacy? What legal information is appropriate? A third issue has to do with the nature and type of orientation, if any, offered to or required of those going abroad. Are students made aware of the health and safety risks of excess drinking abroad, accidents in unfamiliar settings, the penalties for illicit drugs, restrictions on women and the political situation into which they are going?

Finally, should national or institutional policies acknowledge or explicitly waive responsibility for warning travelers of health and security risks? How can institutions protect themselves, their students and their faculty?

ACCESSIBILITY ISSUES

Reasonable accommodations for the handicapped constitute still another set of ethical issues for government personnel serving outside the country and students seeking an international study or work experience. The United States has gone further than any other nation in providing access to transport, accommodations, and attractions to the handicapped thanks to the Americans with Disabilities Act. Yet issues of fairness remain.

Should special needs students have separate but comparable opportunities or is there a value for the handicapped and non-handicapped to travel together? Should all trips enjoying official government or university sponsorship be accessible to the handicapped even if it means that groups cannot go some places or that additional costs would be involved? Should individuals with disabilities be subsidized in order to equalize their opportunities? Or should a more utilitarian approach be adopted arguing for the greatest good for the greatest number? Should handicapped students pay the differential in travel costs for sign language, braille information, wheelchair accessible sites, or personal attendants?

Currently there is no clear legal standard for making such decisions. Rather individual universities are making decisions based on their own resources and notions of fairness. Two private universities, for example, responded to this issue in quite different ways. When Kalen Feeney, a deaf student, applied to go to London on one of Willamette University's study abroad programs, the university paid for an interpreter, even though that meant over $10,000 in additional university costs. The College of St. Scholastica opted not to provide a sign language interpreter for one of its students wanting to go to Ireland.

These and other cases raise several ethical questions of fairness and distributive justice, of utilitarian or Rawlsian notions of decision-making. There is also the question of whether administrators should pursue defensive or proactive strategies with respect to accessibility issues. While U.S. courts have not applied domestic ADA requirements to university study abroad programs, coordinators of the programme must still wrestle with their responsibilities to make such experiences available to all students. In other countries, the dialogue about these issues has scarcely begun.

And then there's the question of gender and sexual orientation. Should universities only establish international exchanges with countries having comparable non-discrimination policies? Or, does that defeat the advantage of study and research abroad which is to experience countries with different values? These issues by no means exhaust the travel-related ethical problems with which public sector personnel must grapple. However, they suggest the breadth of concerns with respect to health, safety, and accessibility that must be confronted. In Part III we will examine what is being done to address some of these issues.

FROM ISSUES TO INITIATIVES

In this article the authors have argued that there is an unusual but enormous threat to public health, security, and accessibility from the huge growth and multiple facets of travel and tourism. Deregulation, privatization, heightened competition for tourists of all types, and a sharp increase in the proclivity and ability to travel combine to make tourism and other forms of travel a stew of ethical problems for the public administrator.

These can be challenging for public sector training to address. Still, there are mechanisms that could potentially deal with these issues. At the most general level, there are Codes of Ethics. The International Personnel Management Association (IPMA), the American Society for Public Administration (ASPA), and the International City/County Management Association (ICMA) are but a few of the professional societies that address in their Codes of Ethics broad guidance that could be applicable to travel and tourism.

These Codes of Ethics include general advice on avoiding conflicts of interest, abusing the public trust, and serving the public fairly and compassionately. However, nowhere is the public sector employee charged with responsibility for recognizing and coping with the complexity of issues that surround tourism and the public interest. Too often, it is simply assumed that more tourism is desirable. If, as we have seen, health, safety, and accessibility issues are neglected, travel and tourism may threaten the public interest.

The tourism industry has begun to recognize this. Efforts are underway to develop a Global Code of Ethics for the industry. However, it is not clear whether the tourism sector will recognize that the various components of the world's largest industry must be partners with the public sector in not only creating sustainable tourism, but also in maintaining healthy, safe, and accessible destinations.

Several codes of ethics for travelers have been developed, which are excellent in encouraging responsible behaviour by tourists. These evidence concern for host peoples' customs, feelings, and economic condition, but they do not address health, security, and accessibility issues. Nor are there, to our knowledge, any codes by host destinations except perhaps in the area of consumer protection in terms of tours, accommodations, and purchases.

The World Health Organization's performance remains a critical gap in developing a coordinated strategy. It was founded at a time of very little international travel, much smaller global populations, and when many infectious diseases now plaguing the planet were unknown. Since 1976, over thirty new infectious diseases have been identified, but out-of-date monitoring and disclosure mechanisms at WHO failed to alert the member nations.

Approaching its half century, these challenges of organizational identity and continued relevance confront the World Health Organization. However, the key issue is not how WHO will respond but whether it will respond at all. The existing leadership of WHO has adopted a fortress mentality, fighting bitterly to sustain the status quo and meanwhile allowing good will and opportunities for revitalisation to slip away.

The Organization is demonstrably off-course—untrue to itself and consequently suffering from both a myriad of internal ailments and a loss of the intellectual coherence that is essential for global health leadership....

In 1999 new guidelines and information were released by WHO amidst signs that a health crisis looms, but it remains to be seen if member nations will act to avert a disaster. They failed to do so with the AIDS epidemic, which afforded much more time for coordinated responses than Ebola, Rift Fever, the Marburg Virus, and viral pneumonia will.

These emerging health threats are symptomatic of many of the new challenges raised by increased globalization, and they require comprehensive, sustained policy responses....

...A network of this sort need not be built entirely from scratch. For example, the WHO has recently established a global surveillance network, called WHONET, linking microbiology labs around the world to a central database...

The U.S. Centers for Disease Control and health counterparts throughout the world provide immense quantities of data, but each nation processes information through the prism of its own national interest. The traveling public and the host society are not necessarily protected in the process, since few nations have the political will to warn non-citizens and thereby risk decreasing tourism.

Moreover, in a federal system like the United States, linkages from the Centers for Disease Control down to local public health offices may be routine, but incomplete and underutilized. Enormous outbreaks of E.coli infections in the United States in the summer of 1999 were possible because of gaps between the Environmental Protection Agency and local jurisdictions in monitoring the water supply. In one case, more than a thousand people were sickened and several died from contaminated water at a state fair. Because the fair was not a permanent attraction, regulations did not require the kind of scrutiny that was obviously necessary. How many circuses, fairs, and exhibitions fall through the screening process in even a developed country? How many may die on pilgrimages throughout the world?

In developing nations, information, monitoring, and sanctions are even more erratic and problematic, because the public sector lacks the capacity to implement policies even if a consensus existed on what needed to be done. Such countries are particularly reluctant to work with bodies such as the WHO or international carriers by attempting to document outbreaks of infectious disease. Why raise fears the nation cannot address and at the same time discourage the tourism so vital for foreign exchange?

The World Bank has once more signaled an intention to get back into making loans for tourism development, largely halted in the 1980s. It will be important to see that new development provides a healthier and more accessible infrastructure for the host societies and not merely the tourism enclaves for the affluent outsider that too often characterized past World Bank tourism aid.

In the foreseeable future, the Internet and the private sector will provide the vast bulk of information about travel and tourism, albeit without any quality control for accuracy. There are, however, more encouraging consequences of the cyber-revolution. A large global e-mail network, The Programme to Monitor Emerging Diseases (PROMED), was initiated in 1993 by doctors who on their own are monitoring health conditions within their borders.

Today, there are more than 10,000 subscribers in 130 countries. There are also modest signs that protecting their citizens against the traveling public or lapses in security abroad is becoming an increased responsibility of governments. In September 1999, for example, the United States Department of State listed specific nations unlikely to be Y2K compliant by January 1, 2000, and while not urging travelers to avoid such countries, it served notice to the traveling public of anticipated problems. Other nations are expected to follow suit.

Sanitation scores on cruise ships, spraying of airplanes, and strict controls on agricultural products and animals are some of the current efforts being made to shield the travelers and the destinations from some of the effects of tourism. But even these modest steps are bitterly resisted by many in the tourist industry and among the general public.

Some of the most potentially effective efforts are underway at public universities, which have started to develop policies to cope with student and faculty travel. One of the first steps taken was to develop professional organizations for those charged with providing services to international students.

One of the earliest was the National Association of Foreign Student Advisors, now known as "NAFSA: Association of International Educators." Originally formed in the late 1940s to encourage ethical standards and professional conduct among educators providing foreign student advising, the association now encompasses study abroad advisors, admissions officers, and other international education officials as well, each within an organized section.

In the 1970s, however, as many institutions sought to develop university-wide coordination and oversight of their international programs, NAFSA opted not to create a section for all-university international administrators. A parallel organization was therefore established, the Association of International Education Administrators (AIEA). These are but two of several professional organizations formed to provide guidance and support in the broad field of international education. The responses of these and other associations to ethical challenges parallel those of public sector professional organizations, like IPMA, ASPA, and ICMA.

CODES AND GUIDELINES

One strategy for protecting the health, safety, and other interests of students learning outside their home countries, has been to develop codes and/or guidelines for their behaviour, their home institutions, and/or their host institutions. There are at least two recent examples:

In 1997, the American Association of Collegiate Registrars and Admissions Officers (AACRAO) developed a "Bill of Rights and Responsibilities for International Students and Institutions." Except for one brief reference to insurance (Article I, Section 8: "International Students have the right to services and information that support their unique needs as international students, such as counseling on immigration regulations, cultural adjustment, orientation to the host institution, and information on insurance and taxes."), there is no mention of health, safety, or accessibility or related issues.

In May 1997, NAFSA, AIEA, and the Council on International Educational Exchange (CIEE), formed a joint task force to formulate a set of health and safety guidelines for institutions that sponsor study abroad programs, and then to seek endorsement by major study abroad organizations and universities. The preliminary guidelines were revised, then reviewed at professional meetings in 1998. By early 1999, the discussion had moved from what should be in the guidelines to how they should be implemented.

The current document, "Responsible Study Abroad: Health and Safety Guidelines," has three substantive sections: (A) Guidelines for Programme Sponsors (listing 14 responsibilities of sponsors); (B) Responsibilities of Participants (12 items); and (C) Recommendations to Parents/Guardians/Families (6 items). Health and safety issues are central to this document. There is no mention of accessibility as a concern. This document seems to be having real impact; it remains a lively part of professional dialogue and the subject of serious implementation efforts at many universities and in study abroad organizations.

INFORMATION MANAGEMENT

A second ethical strategy pursued in international education might be identified as parallel to the openness or disclosure strategy familiar to public administrators. Many of the recommended ways of dealing with health, safety, and accessibility issues with respect to student travel involve providing participants and others with appropriate and accurate information. For example, the U.S. Department of State, in addition to its advisories and country background information, referred to earlier, has an excellent "Tips for Students" page that in turn provides linkages to several other valuable sites.

The "Bill of Rights and Responsibilities" identifies several types of information that individual international students and their institutions have a right to acquire and/or a responsibility to provide. Many of the study abroad health and safety guidelines focus on providing accurate and timely information.

Mobility International USA (MIUSA) has set up a network of several organizations and institutions to assist universities and individuals to locate and develop accessible study abroad opportunities. Under a 1995 grant from the U.S. Information Agency, USIA, Mobility International established a clearinghouse on Disability and Exchange, a collaborative effort involving itself, USIA and 16 other international exchange and disability-related organizations.

It is important to also communicate the limits of responsibility, i.e., to inform participants of those things which the institution or the sponsor cannot be expected to provide. Waivers, signed by the participants, are a common way of dealing with this, but programs should not simply see waivers as a way of protecting themselves and their institution from lawsuits.

ORGANIZATIONAL ASSESSMENT AND CONTINGENCY PLANNING

The first of the Guidelines for Programme Sponsors indicates that they should "Conduct periodic assessments of health and safety conditions for the programme, and develop and maintain emergency preparedness processes and a crisis response plan." Several of the other guidelines focus on specific areas of preparedness. This strategy echoes the "ethics inventories," "vulnerability assessments," and other mechanisms found in much of the administrative ethics literature. Individual universities have established emergency response teams and crisis guidelines specific to their own institutions and programs. The University of Georgia, for instance, has a web site with Y2K advice for students abroad.

TRAINING AND EDUCATION

Professional associations such as NAFSA and AIEA, and some universities, provide training for practitioners who deal with ethical challenges associated with international travel. Because of the rapid growth of travel and tourism as an area of public and private enterprise, however, and because of the tendency of many people not to regard travel and tourism as a serious subject of concern, there is a tremendous need for both pre-service and in-service ethics training for administrators.

As with the public sector in general, a major incentive for training administrators, offering orientation programs, and developing contingency planning has been the liability of the educational institutions. The last 25 years have seen a transition from the general immunity from lawsuits of public officials to qualified immunity to personal liability of public personnel in a variety of situations.

A duty of care is expected and required. Failure to fulfill one's obligations to provide such care may stem from inadequate hiring, training, supervision, retention or from a variety of situations that may endanger the traveller or others. The health, safety and accessibility issues touched on in this article represent areas of increased vulnerability for public employees.

Even in the absence of legal pressure, important strides have been taken with respect to accessibility. While it is important to acknowledge the progress being made, however, it is critical also to recognize how much needs to be done in training public sector employees generally to understand and deal with the ethical dimensions of travel-related health, safety, and accessibility concerns. As with most ethical issues, there is, unfortunately, no neat and tidy formula to apply. The law may be pegged too low or worded too loosely to protect the public interest.

Training employees in the anticipation of problems,

prevention of obvious sources of danger, orientation of travelers to their new environments, and better surveillance and monitoring between and across levels of governmental responsibility can help to establish a record of care and due diligence. But often inadequate staff and resources may force tough choices as to which clienteles— the tourists or the general public—to monitor most closely.

Failure to protect the public can lead to a backlash against such travel in general and toward outsiders in particular. Tourism is an incredibly easy industry to sabotage, for there are always alternative destinations. Public personnel attention to the ethics surrounding health, safety and accessibility issues in tourism can do much toward protecting the public and the "health" of this, the world's largest industry.

Chapter 9

Experiential Education as an Instructional Methodology for Travel and Tourism

Many of the curricula involved in travel and tourism on both national and international bases are constantly seeking new forms of instructional methodology to increase their effectiveness. Many of the travel and tourism programs are located in a variety of academic disciplines and units. This makes any discussion of instructional methodology more difficult because of the indigenous nature of the methodology of the discipline where the travel and tourism programme is housed.

Another common element of travel and tourism academic programs is that there is usually a practical base to most instructional methodologies. A common instructional methodology used is the case study. The case study and its effectiveness directly depends upon the quality of the text being used or the quality of the case study that has been developed by the instructor.

The most common type of instructional methodology is that where a text is used as a basic guideline and modified by the instructor. In a few incidents, several instructors have developed their own case studies but because of the time involved, this is the least common methodology. The primary advantage of the case study methodology is the active participation of the student in formulating and synthesizing a position and having a standard by which to compare their synthesized position to the ultimate solution of a particular problem raised by the case study.

An extension of the case study methodology is experiential education. In experiential education, the basic framework of the case study is used, but the classroom is abandoned for the real world laboratory. Most case studies have finite limitations because they are in a university laboratory setting and do not allow the complexity found in the real world. The advantage of experiential education is that the real world, in fact, brings many different types of variables into the mix. This introduces a complexity not able to be replicated in the university setting.

This complexity, even though it makes it very difficult as an instructional methodology, is dynamic. This type of dynamism helps to motivate the student because they can see the direct application of theory in the classroom to the real world. This motivation is the primary element because the excitement generates additional new ideas and calls for direct involvement of the student as well as the group in the problem-solving process.

Experiential education, to be effective, needs some type of structure, either qualitative or quantitative, to provide the guideposts to develop problem solving skills. Effective learning must begin with qualitative guideposts that provide intense discussion and allows the student to draw conclusions. The most effective is the quantitative guidepost that allows the student to discriminate various levels of action. In addition the student develops the discussion using levels of data analysis to make definitive conclusions which are effective in problem solving. These conclusions are related to various types of variables that can be used in experiential case studies to make definitive generalizations.

Experiential education process has to be built on a sound theoretical foundation. The student has to have a firm foundation in travel and tourism parent sciences in order to perform effectively in experiential education. This may require several foundation courses before experiential education can be effective. Experiential education may be more effective in graduate education because the foundations for content as well as the necessary quantification skills for the manipulation of data are part of the student's repertoire. Some programs are inductively based, and that the experiential methodologies are the first experiences of the travel and tourism student. What is being suggested is that the approach outline where the informational base is first in forms of foundation is probably the more effective of the methodologies.

When students are innately curious, the inductive approach may be the best method because it is a form of learning that stimulates the intellectually curious to new heights. There have been little data available on experiential education as an effective methodology in travel and tourism in order to examine its effectiveness and potential motivation. More data are needed to support theory to be related to the practical world so that competencies can be developed and be directly applied to real world problem solving.

The research by Skipper Charles (1995) is essential to understanding the nature of instructional methodologies and their application. His hypothesis is that each instructional methodology, if appropriately applied, can be effective in producing learning outcomes. The lecture and similar processes are appropriate for introductory experiences. Those methodologies that are more open are appropriate for higher level courses especially graduate education.

The lecture is associated with structured knowledge and the more open approach is related to higher cognitive functions such as, problem-solving and strategic planning. The introductory instructional methodologies provide less freedom while the more open methodologies provide freedom for student expression, input, and response.

PURPOSE

The purpose of this study is to examine experiential education as an instructional methodology for travel and tourism classes. This method is different from the usual classroom based and frequently used case study method. The students learn by doing. This methodology is categorized in the group of experiential methodologies. The disadvantage of textbook case studies is that the described studies are usually perfect examples. But in reality, experiential education cases are complex and dynamic. Usually in the real world there are weaknesses in certain areas of the cases. It is the purpose of experiential education to define these weaknesses.

The advantage of this methodology is that the students learn how to evaluate important tourism areas and to evaluate the quality of a tourist site or area. Students obtain a feeling for which questions to ask, how to interpret answers, how to get information on different areas, and how to solve problems, work in a team and develop strategic plans.

The primary purpose of this study is to examine experiential education and determine outcomes and success from this type of instruction. This study was conducted in two phases. Phase one was about the student's experience with different instructional methodologies, such as lecture, lab, field trip, experiential education, and case study. Phase two was performed to evaluate the used methodology, regarding motivation, prerequisites, outcome satisfaction, freedom, and involvement of the student.

A graduate course of study was selected because these individuals have a foundational competency in which to effectively participate in an experiential based instructional method. There are several critical elements to the effective examination of the experiential method and its potential outcomes: 1. students who have a knowledge of both content and process of travel and tourism, 2. a framework to examine the cases on the basis of a qualitative and quantitative approach, 3. an effective method of analysis and interpretation of data, 4. and a site that will lend itself to the instructional plan being executed.

There are two important dimensions to the evaluation of an experiential instructional methodology; one is the effectiveness or outcome for the student, and the other is the motivation level. Student outcome and motivation is measured through student feedback as to the degree to which the course compares to other traditional instructional methodologies. The primary form of data collection was the questionnaire of student input. Students are asked to compare learning outcomes as well as motivation to other traditional courses on a comparative basis as to the effectiveness of this instructional methodology, upon completion of the course.

The travel and tourism courses selected for study were two graduate courses: Foundations in Travel and Tourism and Strategic Planning in Travel and Tourism at Bowling Green State University. These courses were selected because for four years they had adopted an experiential approach to travel and tourism education. There was a consistent mode of instruction developed through the four year period. In the fifth year of instruction it was appropriate to evaluate this methodology and its effectiveness. Student evaluation for this course showed satisfaction consistently, therefore the quality of the instruction could be controlled as a variable.

The protocol for the study was two weeks of instruction on the foundations as well as the strategic planning process in travel and tourism. Students were involved in all the decision making processes for the course. During this time, a framework was isolated in which to examine experiences using an Importance-Performance (IP) analysis and evaluation of the strategic planning process.

The reasons these data analyses were used is because they are common in travel and tourism. Once these processes were established then a pilot study was used in the field to develop competency in the basic procedures that had been established. An extensive experiential education trip was taken to selected sites and data were collected on the sites and information tabulated for discussion to develop the strategic plan for future development.

This instructional sequence consisted of three steps:

- Data Collection (a content expert methodology, unobtrusive methods, a consensus approach, and a contextual approach)
  - Evaluation of the strategic planning process
  - Importance - Performance Analysis of the site/area/attraction

- Interpretation of the collected data:
  - Strategic planning profile of the organization
  - Strength/Weaknesses of Site/area/attraction
- Synthesis of results:
  - A strategic plan for further development is created as a result of the organization's profile and the IP analysis.

The type of data analysis used in this case study was a criterion clinical approach in which individual scores were compared with means and individual scores to develop criteria to describe trends in the data. The clinical criterion approach was used in order to allow treatment of the data on an individual basis. The trends that were described are based upon comparisons on a particular question, as well as comparisons on individual scores within a question sequence. In a clinical approach, reliability and validity are harder to determine.

The data were analyzed in this study by establishing means and analyzing individual score patterns to describe relationships in the data. The data are reported in two parts by: Part I, general questions about instructional methodologies and Part II, outcomes associated with the used experiential education.

All of the participants had experience with the instructional methodologies listed which were: lectures, labs, case studies, experiential education, and field trips. For the general experience with lectures, the average score was 4.1 and the distribution of scores indicated that the participants had had successful experience with lectures during their high school and college careers.

The findings indicated that for labs the average score was 4.0 and the individual scores indicated that all but one of the individuals had successful experience with labs. In regard to case studies, the average score was 4,0 and the individual patterns among the scores indicated that all/but one had had successful experience with case studies. In regard to experiential education, the average score was 4.7 and all of the participants but one had had successful experience with experiential education. With regard to field trips, the average score was 4.7 and all of the clients indicated that they had had successful experience with field trips. When the general patterns of comparison among the instructional techniques were examined by individual scores, there was one individual who was an aberration from the general trend. This individual had more success with lectures and field trips. Labs, case study, and experiential education were not effective methods of instruction.

The analysis of the second series of questions related to the motivation of each of the instructional methods based upon experience in college and high school. The mean for lectures was 2.9 and the individual patterns ranged from (very) low to (very) high and showed a diversity in terms of range of scores.

In regard to the lab and its ability to motivate, the mean was 3.9 and the range of scores was very high, with the exception of one individual. In regard to experiential education, the mean score was 4.6. When the individual scores were analyzed all of the scores were high, with the exception of one individual. The mean score for field trips was 4.7. All of the individual scores were high. General patterns in individual scores, when analyzed across the questions on an individual basis were either high on all the instructional forms or had a mixed pattern of high and low based on the instructional methodology.

The next question for analysis was on the efficiency of the instructional methodology. In regard to lecture, the mean score was 3.3 and there were three scores that indicated the lecture was not an effective method of instruction. In regard to labs, the mean score was 4.0 and there was only one low score in regard to lab effectiveness. The mean score of the case study was 3.9 and there were two scores that indicated low effectiveness in case study.

In regard to experiential education, the average score was 4.6 with only one score being low. The mean score for the field trips was 4.4 and all the scores were high. Patterns of the individual scores indicated all high effectiveness among several of the individuals on all of the instructional techniques.

There were three of the individuals who had all high scores in regard to the effectiveness of instructional technology and there were four individuals who had mixed patterns of the scores of some high and low based upon a particular instructional technique.

The participants were then asked to rank order the instructional techniques in regard to their effectiveness. Their mean ranking score of lectures was 4.1 with only one individual ranking lectures high. The mean ranking for the labs was 3.1 with four of the scores being of high ranking. In the case studies the mean ranking score was 3.6 with one of the scores being of high ranking. The mean score for the experiential education was 1.6 with only one of the scores being low.

The mean score for the field trips was 2.6 with three of the scores being high. Individual analysis with these questions was not completed because the data were in terms of rankings. In the lectures, there was only a ranking difference of one with the exception of one individual and it was a range of four. In the laboratory technique there was a general range of three ranking differences in position. In regard to case study there was also a range of three. In experiential education there was no deviation in ranking with the exception of one individual who had a low ranking.

In regard to field trips there was a range of one in the rankings. When the overall patterns were analyzed, there was one individual that had an aberration in scores among the experience, motivation, efficiency and the ranking of the most efficient method. This individual's pattern of scores seemed to be the reverse, or deviated from most of the other patterns in a reverse order with the lectures and the structured instructional methodologies having a higher ranking while the instructional methodologies that allow more freedom to the student being of the lower score.

The foundational knowledge was isolated as an important prerequisite for the use of instructional techniques in travel and tourism. It was found in the analysis of the question related to foundation of knowledge, that the individual who was more comfortable with the structured methodologies had a low foundational knowledge in regard to travel and tourism.

The next section of analysis is section II, and this analysis relates to the specific course where experiential education was used as the primary methodology. The first analysis was regarding the first use of the experiential education method and knowing what to do. The mean score was 2.7 for three individuals with not feeling comfortable the first time they used the experiential education methods. The mean score for the motivation of the experiential instructional technique was 4.4 and there were not any low scores. In regard to the importance of not learning the basics in the classroom, the mean score was 1.7 and all of the scores were low. In regard to being able to use this methodology without some type of introduction, the mean score was 1.4 with all scores being low.

The next question regarding feeling comfortable after using the method in a case study format, all the scores were high with the exception of one and the mean score was 4.3. After using the instructional methodology, all the scores indicated were high with the exception of one individual and the mean score was 4.6. In regard to the input of the student and involvement with the course, all of the scores were high with the exception of one individual who had a low score and the mean score was 4.4.

When the improvement of problem solving skills was analyzed the mean score was 4.4 and all of the scores were high. When team working skills were analyzed, all of the scores were high and the mean score was 4.3. In regard to the freedom of the student to work, the mean score was 4.9 and all the scores were high. When the overall satisfaction with the outcome of the course was evaluated, all of the scores were high and the mean score was 4.7. When the aberrations from the patterns were analyzed, it was found that the one aberration from the general mean pattern was the same student who had low foundational knowledges in regard to travel and tourism. The pattern of this individual's learning type score indicated that the freedom and the higher cognitive functioning skills were a problem.

There was also a chance for the student to comment on the course. The comments supported the results. Some of the comments were: Advantages: "Learning to work with a team. "Learning patience and compromise." "Learn more than with a lecture because have experienced it." "Was motivated and enthusiastic about learning." "Helped to focus on learning." "Was able to focus on details that normally would not be considered in the class." "Team building skills." "Small group helped to get individual attention and facilitated discussion among students." "A feeling of success and accomplishment." The primary disadvantages expressed were, that the higher cognitive types of skills were not detailed and explained enough in the classroom part of the course.

The results support the initial hypothesis developed by Skipper Charles who indicated that the more experience that an individual has, the greater the preference for instructional methodologies that have less structure and more freedom for the student. He also hypothesized that these types of instructional methodologies have greater motivational value. The first conclusion that is supported is that a foundational knowledge of travel and tourism is extremely important to the use of less structured methodologies.

The results also indicate that all of the instructional methodologies are effective or have been effective at some time during the individual's high school or college career. This also supports the hypothesis of Skipper Charles because the individuals develop from structured to unstructured methods and it is appropriate to apply the appropriate instructional technique to the student during their evolutionary development.

Foundational nature of the experiential education is directly dependent upon not only foundational knowledge, but the ability to be able to use this methodology. It is also very important that the individual has an ability to use higher cognitive skills such as problem solving and strategic planning. The results indicate that the comfort zone of the student needs to be reinforced with at least four to six practice cases before they feel comfortable using the experiential education methodology in extensive group work. This method has an extremely high motivational value that stimulates student involvement, especially if performed in groups and if the student is part of the formulating processes of courses and cases. Student involvement is extremely high because of the freedom to synthesize and gather information on the data that has a meaningful base to them.

It was also important to provide the student the necessary methodology and structure so that they can work through the problems to a successful conclusion. An open-ended format without structure may not allow the individual to have the necessary comfort level to complete the task. Structure seems to be an important element to the success of the use of the experiential techniques. Another aspect of the outcomes associated with this type of technique involves the ability of the individual to develop team working and problem solving skills as a direct result of group dynamics.

This study supports the general hypothesis of Skipper Charles that high cognitive development is directly associated with the freedom of instructional techniques. It has also been shown by this study that motivation is an extremely important aspect to this instructional method. It also points out that this particular study was short-term and the long-term effects are not directly known but begs the point that longitudinal studies need to be conducted with this instructional methodology.

POSTCARDS AND THE FRAMING OF INTERSPECIES ENCOUNTERS

The following essay considers the role of animal imagery on postcards marketed in Canada's Rocky Mountain Parks. These popular souvenir items have helped shape dominant systems of environmental knowledge. Because of this, postcards should be considered in discussions regarding the ecological health of the region.

The Canadian Rocky Mountain Parks have always been one of my favourite vacation destinations. Snapshots and nostalgic memories abound of holidays passed in this particular part of Canada. Each one of these holidays included a trip to the local post office to mail postcards to friends and family back home. Until recently I gave little thought to the dozens of postcards purchased and sent on these annual vacations. My current research, however, has me wondering about the broader environmental and cultural implications of this ritualistic holiday act. A large number of these souvenir items feature images of bears: bears that have become a commodity of "the wild." The following discussion considers this commodification as it relates to current environmental and interspecific concerns facing Canada's Rocky Mountain Parks.

The study of postcards is, by necessity, an interdisciplinary venture, one that raises questions about the role of images and icons in the production of discursive systems (Nancy), as well as relationships between written and visual texts (Mitchell).

These inexpensive, popular souvenir items have historically been neglected in the realm of academic inquiry, and it is only in recent years that scholars have considered how these cultural texts can have meaning beyond the realm of personal correspondence; as Annette Pritchard and Nigel Morgan argue, "picture postcards are a rich cultural reservoir of popular perceptions of people and places". My own critical interest in postcards centres on the relationship of image and text; I ask, in particular, how these elements work to shape dominant cultural understandings of nature and the nonhuman world.

In recent years, many environmental historians have argued that a perceptual division between ideals of "nature" and ideals of "culture" is at the root of many current environmental problems. The notion that "nature" exists outside of and stands separate from human society and technology presents a challenge for addressing ecological problems in the twenty-first century. Not only does this dominant way of thinking mask many environmental tensions, but also it creates a sense of separation between most people's lived experiences and the environmental impact of their day-to-day activities. To conceive of "nature" as existing separately from "culture" is to deny the sense of interconnectedness that affects all forms of life on Earth. As Neil Evernden argues, "Nature is [...] nowhere near as independent or as 'given' as we like to suppose". For those concerned with addressing twenty-first century environmental issues, a critical re-thinking of what "nature" is and means is necessary.

In spaces designated as National Parks, there exists a specific way of viewing the nonhuman world. This particular way of framing and engaging with the nonhuman world—what I refer to as "National Park Nature"—is thoroughly mediated by the tourism industry. National Park Nature frames the landscapes of Jasper and Banff National Parks as "unspoiled" and "pristine" "wilderness playgrounds" to which one can "escape" in order to engage in healthy recreational pursuits, gaze upon "exotic" scenery, and live in harmony (even if only for a few days) with the animals who are "protected" by Park borders. The repetition of visual and textual codes reinforces this position, and goes a long way toward masking very real environmental tensions in these landscapes.

Canadian National Parks face many of the same stresses as other regions of the Canadian landscape, stresses that are masked through the rhetoric of "pristine" wilderness so dominant in National Park Nature. Philip Dearden points out, for instance, that "samples taken of the snow pack in the Rocky Mountain parks—sites that we think of as being among the most pristine on earth—show higher concentrations of many pesticides than near-urban and agricultural sites".

Acid rain, pollution, habitat fragmentation, and competition among native and introduced species of plants and animals affect the parks as much as they do areas that lie outside park boundaries and, as such, representations of these landscapes as uninfluenced by human activity, "wild," and environmentally pristine are, at best, well-intentioned myths. Moreover, as John Urry has argued, preserving a particular area for its "special environmental quality" often has the effect of drawing large crowds to the region, a process that creates a new set of environmental concerns. As Urry writes, "to designate somewhere as a national park is to generate a kind of magnet, sucking in potential visitors who otherwise might visit many different places". The concentration of thousands of visitors each year to Canada's national parks virtually ensures that the "pristine" and "untouched" qualities for which they are so often celebrated will not be found.

Visual technologies have set up very specific ideas of what nature means in a Canadian context; as Timothy Luke argues, the "green gaze" of landscape photography "becomes the normalizing framework for imagining what Nature really is". This has had the result of masking human impact upon the nonhuman world and it does not address fundamental questions regarding consumption and human activity outside national park borders. Moreover, this point of view does not easily accommodate introspective questioning regarding the status quo values that have created the social need for National Parks.

Cultural production has long dictated the ways in which animals are conceived of and, ultimately, treated in Western society. From novels and fairy-tales to paintings, films, advertisements, and postcards, representations of nonhuman species continually shape the dynamics of interspecies interactions.

These representations have firmly solidified the perceptual gap that exists between "nature" and "culture" in North America. In the realm of nature, such animals as bears, deer, and bighorn sheep are conceived of as "wild" and "untamed," while nonhuman animals encountered in spaces characterized by notions of "civilization" fit into very different systems of representation. In urban centres, for instance, nonhuman animals tend to be grouped into categories that label them as either "pets" or "pests," both commonly recognized as resulting from human desires, behaviours, and habits.

Images of nonhuman animals have been part of the visual identity of Banff and Jasper National Parks for decades, and certain animal species have come to be synonymous with the wilderness experience of the region. However, as recent studies have indicated, populations of animals we tend to associate with Canada's Rocky Mountain Parks have, in fact, been a little less "natural" than current tourist promotions would have us believe. As Dick Dekker has argued, populations of animals we currently associate with Canada's Rocky Mountains have fluctuated over time due to human activities, among them hunting and, more recently, Parks management policies (26-29).

In spite of this, the current rhetoric of tourism promotion in Canadian Rocky Mountain Parks focuses on the "wildness" of faunal species in this region. A recent Parks Canada brochure, for instance, discusses the difference between animals in Park spaces and animals in urban zoos, a difference that, in this context, is being attributed to the relative "tameness" of zoo animals in comparison to the animals one might encounter while on holidays in Banff or Jasper. "Is there a difference," the brochure asks, "between a wild bear and one in a zoo?

We can only guess what the bear might think. But from our perspective, isn't the very thing that makes wild animals so attractive to us the fact that they are indeed wild? Unfortunately, when animals become used to being around people, they are in danger of losing that very thing that makes them special, their wildness". This sense of "wildness" leads readers of this pamphlet to believe that their experiences in the Canadian Rockies will be more authentic than their encounters with animals at a zoo or a theme park.

Even though such publications rely on promoting a sense of "wildness" with regard to the nonhuman animals living in the Canadian Rockies, the history of visual representations of these animals tells a different story. In postcard imagery, familiar pictorial codes are adopted and, as such, have the effect of "taming" these animals according to dominant cultural expectations. Only selected species of animals are represented, and they tend to be represented in ways that are both aesthetically-pleasing and non-threatening to human consumers of these objects. These popular images decontextualize the subject of the photograph from the lived actualities of the individual animal's day-to-day existence.

As Christopher Steiner argues, in the context of tourism, a sense of authenticity is created through repetition—as he writes, "tourists are not looking for the new but for the obvious and the familiar". The postcard is one of the most common means by which this "iconographic redundancy" is perpetuated and, as such, it plays a key role in defining what constitutes an authentic wilderness experience for the thousands of people who visit the region each year. Lucy Lippard describes postcards as "photographic cliches" and argues that they are "at best [...] a consensus of what viewers hope to see". In many ways this is true, as postcard imagery draws upon iconic imagery and shapes what is seen and experienced during these sorts of wilderness vacations in very powerful ways.

However, there also exists an element of individuality operating within the consumption of postcard imagery. The purchasing and sending of postcards, Peter Osborne explains, also situates tourists as "subjects of their own performance" of travel. By participating in the cyclical process of postcard consumption, tourists visiting the Canadian Rocky Mountain Parks not only claim a piece of the mountain landscape for a handful of pocket change, but also use these popular souvenir items as a means to stake their presence in this culturally-privileged landscape.

The images and textual messages on these cards combined with the means of consumption—either mailing them to family and friends as "evidence" of individual presence in this space, or the addition of these cards to photographic albums upon the visitor's return home—personalize the tourist experience through a mass-marketed vehicle.

Postcards, then, mediate between the individualized experience and the mass-produced vacation adventure that defines the wilderness industry in such places as Jasper and Banff National Parks. These spaces are the geographic "Other" to the day-to-day urban existence of most people living in North America, and this designation is reinforced through the textual and visual language consumed through the exchange and consumption of souvenir postcards. In particular, postcards featuring images of "wild" animals go a long way toward creating a geography of environmental difference in the Rocky Mountain Parks.

Among other things, the animals featured on these popular souvenir items signify a space that is markedly different from most people's day-to-day existence. In this context, images of bears found on picture postcards do not depict individual animals but, rather, come to stand as iconic symbols of what is expected in a commodified tourist encounter in such spaces as Banff and Jasper National Parks.

A large part of tourist expectations in the Canadian Rockies has historically focused on the presence of animal species that have come to be collectively termed "wildlife." Postcards and other such souvenir items featuring photographs of animals help to construct and sustain what sociologist Adrian Franklin terms the "zoological gaze," or "the manner in which viewing animals has been organized socially over time". In the context of Rocky Mountain tourism, there exists an expectation when one travels to these locations that one may have an encounter (albeit, it is hoped, a safe and mediated one) with such species as bears and mountain sheep—species that tend to be featured on picture postcards sent from the park.

The promise of encounters with animals has been a significant tourist draw to destinations such as Banff and Jasper National Parks, and this is something that tourism promoters have continually emphasized in promotional materials. For instance, a 1934 brochure on Jasper National Park claims that: one of the great charms of the park is the abundance and fearlessness of its wild life.

To wake in the morning and see a deer below one's window, a black bear ambling off into the forest, or, on the trail, to be able to come close to the shyest creatures of the wild, the mountain sheep and goat; to watch the beaver at his busy engineering or the lordly elk, moose and caribou making their stately way through the woods, is a pleasure which makes every walk or ride a possible adventure.

The expectations of interspecies relations deriving from

these touristic promotions frames dominant understandings of what constitutes acceptable behaviour toward nonhuman species both within and beyond National Park borders. In this example, the nonhuman animals who inhabit the Park are presented as part of the scenery, existing entirely to be gazed upon and enjoyed by those who take their vacations in Jasper National Park. This hierarchy of species is replicated through the production of picture postcards, which serve as a lasting reminder of the vacation experience.

Both the touristic encounter and the material object of remembrance normalize the implicit power dynamic that exists between human and nonhuman species in this context. As my own personal postcard collection attests, certain animals have become standard symbols of the Canadian Rockies and have been featured prominently in tourist photography consumed in Jasper and Banff National Parks. While I have not conducted a scientific sampling of all the postcards ever sold in the Rocky Mountain Parks, it is safe to say that bears have featured prominently in postcard imagery for several decades.

Much tourist photography in the region plays upon the sense of fascination Western society has traditionally had with bears (Shepard and Sanders). Many postcards sent from the Canadian Rockies repeat this theme: scenes of bears on golf courses, bears on hotel properties, small children feeding bears, bears approaching cars on the highway, and, my favourite, a bear sitting in the driver's seat of a car. According to these examples, it would seem that the Canadian National Railway's claim that "comical bears are always on hand to greet visitors and pose for pictures" is indeed the case in the Canadian Rockies. Postcard images depict bears as non-threatening and seemingly existing entirely for human enjoyment and entertainment.

G. Morris Taylor's photograph, entitled "Four of a Kind, Jasper Park", demonstrates a very important link between imagery and industry in the construction of National Park Nature. This photograph shows five black bears—a mother and four cubs—crossing the railroad tracks in Jasper National

Park. It is significant that the corporate logo of the rail company is visible on the train cars behind the bears.

Whether this compositional element was added by accident or on purpose, one is reminded of the economic interests both the CPR and the CNR have historically had in the Rocky Mountain Parks. These companies have continually relied on images of National Park Nature (of which ursine iconography is a significant part) to attract tourists to the region.

As many postcards attest, the juxtaposition of so-called "wild" animals with evidence of human activity and technological innovation has been an especially popular component of Rocky Mountain tourism. The anthropomorphism evident in many postcard images trivializes these animals at the same time as it underscores the difference thought to exist between human and nonhuman species.

A postcard featuring a photograph of a bear in the driver's seat of a car, for instance, appears humorous because automobiles exist outside the realm in which we have been socially conditioned to expect to encounter such animals. Ideals of nature and culture remain distinct in these photographs; it is obvious which of these pictorial subjects is to be read as "wild" and which is to be understood as evidence of humankind's "taming" of the nonhuman world, even though the divisions between these two realms are not as clear-cut as they may first appear. The comparison between nature and culture (or "wild" and "tame") within the same pictorial frame strengthens dominant cultural understandings of both, in that each serves as a counterpoint to the other.

Bears may not drive automobiles, but their habits and habitats are necessarily intertwined with human activity. For instance, highways cut through ursine habitats and the continual development of human infrastructure continues to put humans and bears in close proximity to one another, often with adverse results. These examples demonstrate the blurring of the boundaries separating ideals of "nature" from those thought to define the realm of "culture." As William Cronon argues, "to protect the nature that is all around us, we must think long and hard about the nature we carry inside our heads" ("Foreword" 22).

In many instances, the animals on the picture postcard come to stand for the interspecific encounter itself. This phenomenon is often emphasized through the handwritten messages inscribed on the back of the card. This relationship between the mass-produced and the individualized is an especially interesting aspect of W.J.T. Mitchell's "image/text problematic" in the context of postcard studies. Simply put, postcards are a mass-produced item sold in large quantities to the thousands of visitors who flock to Banff and Jasper Parks each year.

Many people inevitably end up with the same postcard; however, both the message on the back and the personal connotations deriving from encounters with animal imagery (i.e., a nostalgic memory of one's own glimpse of a bear in the park or, conversely, pangs of regret at not experiencing the expected encounter) add an individualized element to these popular souvenir items.

Illustration 3 is a good example of this process as it plays out on both sides of the picture postcard. This card, sent to a Miss Heather Peden in Minburn, Alberta in August 1951, was postmarked in Banff and features a photograph taken by Byron Harmon of a mother bear and three cubs. Harmon is one of the best known photographers in the history of the Rocky Mountain Parks, and his images continue to visually define this region.

This card is a good example of Harmon's animal imagery. The message on the back of this card reads: "Dear Heather, Here is a picture of the bears we keep watching for but haven't seen yet. We'll be at Banff tonight so I'm sure we will see some there. We've had a fine time. Love, Auntie." At the top of the card is an additional message that was scrawled some time afterwards—it reads: "Later—we saw a bear and two cubs, a coyote, and some moose." Without a glimpse of the creatures depicted on the front of the card, it is implied, the wilderness experience would not have been complete. If imagery exoticizes the mountain landscape by replicating views of the non-urban, wilderness experience, the text used in conjunction with this imagery often serves to familiarize these spaces. It is this dichotomy between the seemingly exotic and the familiar that makes the study of postcards a particularly rich area for framing human relationships with the nonhuman world.

The role of text in the process of familiarization becomes especially evident when we consider the role of pre-printed text on postcards—that is text that is part of the card's design as opposed to the personal, individualized notes scrawled on the back of the cards.

In the context of animal imagery found on postcards, the addition of text serves to reframe human relationships with nonhuman animals. Illustration 4 is a good example of this, and is one of many photographic postcards that features people happily engaging with bears in the Canadian Rockies. This postcard is entitled "Hello You" and shows a small child posed next to a bear cub in Jasper National Park. The photograph used in the card was taken by Joe Weiss, a Jasper-based photographer who operated a photographic studio in the Park during the early decades of the twentieth century (Collinson).

The words "Hello You" on the front of the card serve as a functionalized transcript of the exchange taking place between the two central figures in this photograph. We are to read this as a friendly encounter, and the juxtaposition of a human baby with an animal "baby" would no doubt have made this a popular postcard image.

The position of the two figures within the photographic frame is also significant. The child, dressed in white, stands on the walkway that runs alongside the cottage behind the two figures. Both the path and the cottage can be read as evidence of human domestication of this space. Conversely, the black bear stands on the edge of the nonhuman world. Despite the physical closeness of these two figures, the mythical divide that separates nature from culture is played out in this postcard.

Postcards featuring text that recasts the behaviour of

nonhuman animals in terms of human habits and customs have been especially popular over the course of the history of Banff and Jasper National Parks. Dietary habits, in particular, have provided much material for popular postcard designs in recent decades. One postcard, for instance, features a photograph of three bears (a mother and two cubs) foraging for food around a garbage can.

This, as visitors to the Rocky Mountain Parks are warned, becomes a common and dangerous occurrence when food (or waste containing human food) is left in the open. Open garbage bins attract bears into spaces claimed by humans (i.e., campgrounds, picnic sites, and hiking trails). This often leads to encounters that pose a threat to both species, however, the seriousness of a potential human-ursine encounter is negated by the caption on this card: "Ugh, peanut butter and jelly again!"

It features a colour photograph of three bears gathered around an elegantly set outdoor dining table. The front of the card describes the scene as a "coffee break," and the pre-printed text on the back reads: "Afternoon refreshments are enjoyed on the lawns of a Canadian Rockies resort, with much gusto and noise, by three self-invited bears."

Cards like this have historically been very popular—they are considered humorous because they show something unexpected. In these examples, the anthropomorphic qualities ascribed to the bears—complaining about their sandwich fillings or getting a caffeine fix—makes them seem somehow easier to relate to, and therefore, frames the potentially dangerous, wild, and unknown as something familiar. This framing, of course, provides little comfort to either species when human-ursine encounters end in interspecies violence and bloodshed.

The study of the tourist imagery of the Canadian Rockies can be used to trace shifting attitudes and regulations governing human encounters with nonhuman species. There exist countless examples of both picture postcards and tourist snapshots showing people posing with and feeding bears in Banff and Jasper National Parks. Illustration 6 reproduces a photograph taken approximately sixty years ago, and shows a group of young tourists enjoying the company of three young bear cubs.

This image, taken from my own family history (the woman in the white skirt and dark sweater is my grandmother), is not an isolated example. In this photograph, and in many others like it, excited visitors to Banff National Park cluster around these "wild" animals as a species that would rarely be seen in one's home landscape. My grandmother and her two girlfriends hold out tasty-looking morsels for the cubs, while two younger boys in the foreground convey, respectively, a sense of sheer fascination with the cubs (the boy on the right can barely tear his eyes away from the scene) and the need to record one's experience with wildlife in a visual format (the boy on the left is self-consciously looking back at the unidentified photographer of this scene).

As this image demonstrates, human interaction with bears in Park spaces has not been limited to souvenir postcards. In the first few decades after Jasper was established as a national park, tourists were encouraged to actively engage with the ursine citizens of the region. Newspaper advertisements appearing in the Edmonton Journal during the 1920s, for instance, encouraged people to ride the train from Edmonton to Jasper to see and feed the bears in the Park. The Canadian National Railway (CNR) actively promoted this type of "wilderness encounter" and facilitated means for Park visitors to interact with these animals.

A promotional pamphlet produced by the CNR during the 1930s gives information about a special taxi service for tourists staying at the Jasper Park Lodge; for fifty cents guests could take a taxi from the front door of the Lodge to "see the bears". The visual and textual messages reproduced in pamphlets and on postcards created a sense of excitement around these excursions; "seeing the bears" became a standard part of the tourist itinerary in the Canadian Rockies.

As ecological sensibilities towards nonhuman species have shifted, the framing of interspecies encounters also underwent a transformation. The front of one postcard features a photographic image to which colour has been added for visual effect.

The image shows a mother bear, with her cubs, leaning into the passenger side window of an automobile parked along the side of the road. I have found other examples of this photograph used on postcards, and the repetition of the image certainly seems to validate earlier touristic encounters such as those offered by the CNR and experienced first-hand by my grandmother.

The pre-printed text on the back of the card, however, tells a different story: "First lesson in panhandling. Feeding bears is strictly against Park regulations, for the protection of both parties but Mama can't read." This text makes reference to park policy, which forbids feeding the bears, however, the image on the front of the card suggests that this is still something that one might experience on their vacation to the Park (although the vintage of the car in the photograph could also be read as suggesting a more nostalgic look back at a seemingly simpler and, perhaps, less regulated time).

Further, this postcard clearly reinforces a human-nonhuman power dynamic; the text refers to the mother bear as an illiterate pan-handler, and the photograph depicts the bears in a "cute" and "entertaining" manner and, as such, reinforces the notion that nonhuman animals are disempowered creatures existing for the exclusive enjoyment of visitors to the Parks.

In recent years, activist and educational campaigns have begun to incorporate familiar postcard imagery in unexpected ways. For instance, in 1993, the Canadian Parks and Wilderness Society (CPAWS) launched a postcard campaign aimed at halting development in Banff National Park. Subscribers to Borealis, CPAWS's official publication, were given postcards featuring photographs of recent construction projects in Banff bearing captions such as "Banff: Is this a National Park?" and "Not all Postcards from Banff are Pretty," and information about the rate of commercial development in the Park (Locke 3). Visual campaign material, such as the imagery used by CPAWS in this instance, relies on the well-known format of the picture postcard, but disrupts visual codes typically associated with the popular souvenir item. The blend of the familiar and the unexpected have made this an effective tool for environmental activism.

In the early 1990s, Parks Canada and photo-finishing labs in Banff, Jasper, Lake Louise, and Waterton parks teamed up to create a postcard bearing the caption, "A Fed Animal is a Dead Animal," in four different languages in an attempt to discourage tourists from engaging in the common, yet highly dangerous, practice of feeding wildlife. It is significant that a campaign aimed at disrupting the wilderness ideal would adopt the postcard format in an attempt to educate tourists about the problems associated with this behaviour.

Most of the images used on this card were actual examples of tourist snapshots culled from the rolls of film dropped off for developing at the participating photography businesses, and the similarity between these "snapshot" images and the popular postcard images speak to how widely accepted certain ways of visually framing these landscapes has become.

For instance, the photograph in the bottom left-hand corner has striking similarities to the photograph discussed in the previous example. Both images feature a mother bear and her cubs approaching humans in the relative comfort of their automobiles. The inclusion of the words "A Fed Animal is a Dead Animal" on this example, however, shifts the currency of these photographs from tourist souvenirs to material objects of environmental education.

This is one of the few photographic postcards from the Canadian Rocky Mountain Parks that breaks with traditional ways of representing nonhuman species. While these cards are consumed and distributed in a different manner than traditional postcards—the "A Fed Animal is a Dead Animal" card is distributed free of charge by photo-finishing businesses—the fact that such a familiar format is being used in this manner speaks volumes about the power of these "ideal souvenirs" (Geary and Webb 3-4) to shape attitudes and behaviours.

Index

S

T

Z